THE FORGÈD FEATURE

THE FORGÈD FEATURE
Toward a Poetics of Uncertainty
New and Selected Essays

by

BEN BELITT

*It is the forgèd feature finds me—the rehearsal
of own, of abrupt self, there.*
—GERARD MANLEY HOPKINS

*What the hammer? What the chain?
In what furnace was thy brain?*
—WILLIAM BLAKE

FORDHAM UNIVERSITY PRESS
New York
1995

© Copyright 1995 by FORDHAM UNIVERSITY PRESS
All rights reserved.
LC 94-45816
ISBN 0-8232-1603-9 (*hardcover*)
ISBN 0-8232-1604-7 (*paperback*)

Library of Congress Cataloging-in-Publication Data

Belitt, Ben, 1911–
  The forgèd feature : toward a poetics of uncertainty : new and selected essays / Ben Belitt.
   p.   cm.
  Includes bibliographical references.
  ISBN 0-8232-1603-9 (hardcover) : $30.00. — ISBN 0-8232-1604-7 (paperback) : $17.95
  1. Ben, Belitt, 1911– Aesthetics. 2. Literature, Modern—20th century—History and criticism—Theory, etc. 3. Poetry—Translating. 4. Poetics. I. Title.
PS3503.E39F67   1995
809—dc20
                                                                          94-45816
                                                                              CIP

CONTENTS

Acknowledgments	ix
Foreword	xi

I · The Forgèd Feature:
Pursuits and Predicaments

A. Pursuits

1. Literature and Belief: Three "Spiritual Exercises"	5
2. Meaning and the Sonal Imagination	21
3. In Search of the American Scene: "Demographic Vistas"	29

B. Predicaments

4. The Enigmatic Predicament: Some Parables of Kafka and Borges	41
5. The Heraldry of Accommodation: A House for Mr. Naipaul	66
6. The Depth Factor: Saul Bellow	87
7. Memoir as Myth: The Odysseys of Pablo Neruda	97

C. Translation: Grammars and Consciences

8. The Translator as Nobody in Particular: Faiths and Fidelities	119
9. Lowell's *Imitations*: Translation as Personal Mode	128
10. The Vanishing Original: Transvaluations	142
The Laughing Neruda	142
A House of Fourteen Planks	148
The Mourning Neruda	153
The Burning Sarcophagus	162

II · Toward a Poetics of Uncertainty:
Trial Balances

Preface	177
11. Toward a Poetics of Uncertainty	179

i. "What Porridge Had John Keats?"	179
ii. Between the Dice-Cup and the Urn	181
iii. "The Journey Itself": Coleridge, Baudelaire, Rimbaud	182
iv. Coleridge—Metaphors of Voyage: The Serpent and the Path of Sound	185
v. Coleridge and Blake: The Contrariety Principle	189
vi. Coleridge's Water Spider	190
vii. The Postponements of Wallace Stevens: What Poetry Does	192
viii. Machado and Blake: The Egg and the Eye	195
ix. Blake: The Eye and the Lie	197
x. Blake: The Bird and the Airy Way	200
xi. Hopkins's Windhover	203
xii. Blake and the "Holy-Holy-Holy" Sun	205
xiii. The Bell and the Artichoke: Coleridge and Neruda	208
12. Sight: Second or Sudden—Versions of Witness	211
i. Jean Cocteau: A Dog, a Cab, a House	211
ii. "What They Looked Likest"	213
iii. Keats: Surprise and Excess	215
iv. "A Clean, Well-Lighted Place"	218
v. Three Displacements by Light: Sacred and Profane	219
vi. William Carlos Williams: The Glass Pitcher and the Nightingales	222
13. Hopkins Observing: "Rehearsals"	229
i. "These Things, These Things Were Here and but the Beholder Wanting"	229
ii. Hopkins Observing: Looking at High Waves; Water Coming Through a Lock	232
iii. Hopkins Observing: Evaporation, Precipitation, Crystallization	235
iv. Hopkins Observing: Celestial Mechanics	239
v. Hopkins Observing: The Bafflements of the Bluebell	244
vi. Hopkins Observing: A Trial Balance	249

14. Hopkins Transforming: "It Changed Beautiful Changes"   258
       i. Hopkins Transforming: The Observer as Celebrant   259
       ii. Hopkins Transforming: The Observer as Artificer   263
       iii. Hopkins Transforming: The Observer as Victim   266
       iv. Hopkins Transforming: The Observer as Comforter   273

ACKNOWLEDGMENTS

My thanks are due the editors of *Salmagundi, Review '74, The Bennington Review, The Southern Review, Triquarterly, Voyages, Mundus Artium, Razon y Fábula* (Bogotà), *Parnassus, The Southwest Review, Mundo Nuevo* (Paris), and *Poets on Poetry* for permission to reprint many of the essays appearing in this volume.

B. B.

FOREWORD

A word is due the reader regarding the range and purpose of the essays that follow. My intent has been twofold: to bring together a representative selection of critical essays bearing on my interests as poet, critic, teacher, and translator; and to furnish an ongoing review of my concern with the encoding of languages and the exigencies of their imaginative retrieval. Beginning with a triad of pieces on (A) the uses of belief, linguistics, and *place* as shaping forces in the concretizing of the literary occasion, it moves on to (B) an examination of the fictive medium in terms of a number of "predicaments"—"enigmatic," "heraldic," mythopoeic (Neruda as "latter-day Homer"), political, taxonomic (modes of the penetrability and impenetrability of contexts, depth strategies in the creation and construing of meanings). The texts are the opportune ones that happen to have come my way as observer-reporter of twentieth-century prose—parables, novels, autobiographical memoirs—and cover a broad range of multinational talents: Kafka, Borges, V. S. Naipaul, Saul Bellow, Pablo Neruda.

A third section (C) is devoted to the theory and practice of translation and embraces a personal repertory of risks, choices, and problematics encountered during my labors as translator of poetry and prose over the last thirty years or more. The endless debate over the "liberal" and the "literal," the private and the public, the "faithful" and the willful modes of mediating between grammars and consciences in behalf of the "one true translation" is rehearsed in terms of the texts and controversies that produced them. A concluding piece attempts a "revaluation" of the Neruda canon apart from the rigors of translation, as a prolegomenon for the posthumous appraisal of a master and a palimpsest of legends for the reader.

Finally, there is a more recent sequence of four essays occasioned by my growing interest in the uses of the "new physics" of quantum mechanics and its uncanny relevance to the accountability of poetry. Here, my emphasis is on the *reading* of poetry rather than the writing or historicity of the textual artifact—the lexical use of the multiple way as a mode of engaging the interaction of *meanings* and *things* in their shaping of a vision that acknowledges the "uncertainties" of language and reality. Needless to say, the "forgèd feature"—Hopkins's phrase—also involves a revaluation of Gerard Manley Hopkins as "scientific" rather than priestly worker in the smithy of the senses; but I hope that a pun on the operative word is also permissible—"forgèd" in the double sense of the crafting and tempering of the steely life of things; and a counterfeiter's signature of the human venture on the currency of the cosmos. The touchstones applied deliberately mingle traditions and individual talents—Keats, Blake, Stevens, Bishop, Yeats, Baudelaire, Rimbaud, W. C. Williams, Machado, Rilke, Cocteau, Wordsworth, Coleridge—to intimate the timeless applicability of the hermeneutics of incertitude.

The result, I would hope, is no mere miscellany of disjunct pieces to be viewed in isolation as a retrospective chronicle of Things Past and anomalous occasions. They also comprise a continuum to be read backward and forward like a palindrome of persisting preoccupations that embody a single, haunting intuition: that in all transactions involving the reciprocity of landscapes and languages there is an element of incertitude that measures the parameters of human reflection on the phenomenal life of things.

To this end I have enlisted a variety of nomenclatural ploys to follow the guises of Uncertainty to their sources in literature and quantum mechanics: "eidolons," "predicaments," "enigmas," "parables," "fictions," "fables," "myths," "translations," "equations," "postulates," "theories," "laws," "lies." The unexpected bonding of imaginative discourse with twentieth-century physics, to which I have devoted the concluding essays, is the cumulative outcome of my continuing search for an iconographic life that combines the scribal and phenomenal worlds in a precarious equation for "reality." It may well be that the parting gift of our dwindling millennium for scientist and poet alike is the riddle of an ineffable Remainder.

BEN BELITT

Bennington College
Bennington, Vermont

I
The Forgèd Feature: Pursuits and Predicaments

A. Pursuits

1
Literature and Belief: Three "Spiritual Exercises"

I

THOSE WHO HAVE HIS *Note-Books* to hand will be aware that I have taken the second half of my title from Gerard Manley Hopkins, who had it from Saint Ignatius Loyola, who had it from the Abbot Garcías de Cisneros. For Hopkins, the novice, preparing for the Olympiad of his induction into the Society of Jesus, the *Exercises* served the calisthenic purpose of grooming the incumbent priest for a crisis of commitment that led to the higher mysteries of his calling. For my own purposes, the choice of three devotional texts is neither worshipful nor canonical; what I would hope to do is suggest the co-existence of a sacred with a secular subtext for individual talents committed to the creation of a literature for laymen, and its imaginative encompassment in language. My concern is not with a City of God, but with a poetics for men of letters generally.

We can begin with a poor man's version of Pascal's Wager—that confidence game for pietists of little faith who prefer the fatalism of the gaming wheel to the prayer wheels of the East. You may recall its street-smart inelegance, its bow to the baize of the croupier's table:

> He who calls heads and he who calls tails are guilty of the same mistake; they both are wrong: the right course is not to wager. "Yes, but we have to wager. You are not a free agent; you are committed. Which will you have, then?" . . . "Heads: God exists!" If you win, you win everything; if you lose, you lose nothing. . . . Bet he exists!

We can begin our little foray into literature and belief by putting both chips on the gaming table: we can begin by assuming we believe in Bibles. "Bet the Bible exists!" The wager, at the very least, is eschatologically advantageous. For the Laodicaeans among us, it provides a kind of spiritual insurance which turns gambling into a species of cautionary divination. And let us, at some midpoint between idolatry and condescension, choose from the artifacts of Christian-Hebraic discourse three texts for examination without regard for the protocol of worship, in the spirit of that wager. And, as a third condition, let us be somber.

Here, whatever our stock of operative beliefs, is an avowedly devotional anthology of belief which has penetrated into every aspect of humane activity in the last 4,000 years of Western European history—which is inseparable from our literature, from our ethics, from our certainties, from our anxieties, and from all the objects of our violence and tenderness equally: a believer's canon of private and public worship for those delivered from conditional modes of assumption to absolute commitments that transcend history and touch the very plasm of reality. In applying to these texts, after all, we apply to 4,000 years of our contemporaneity, as well as to the old codices of our Jewishness and our Christianity. Here are the persuaded, the assured, the convinced, the obsessed, the inspired—the saints, the heroes, the defaulters and the "fools" (Saint Paul's word) of belief; and here is the testimony of their eloquence and their dedication. I am proposing that we forfeit all definition, appeal to the textual witness of their experience, and move blindly and without baggage into the literature of their belief.

"To ask with infinite interest," said Kierkegaard, "about a reality which is not one's own, is faith."

II

Praise ye the Lord. Praise ye the Lord from the heavens: praise him in the heights. Praise ye him, all his angels: praise ye him, all his hosts. Praise ye him, sun and moon: praise him, all ye stars of light. Praise him, ye heavens of heavens, and ye waters that be above the heavens. Let them praise the name of the Lord: for he commanded, and they were created. He hath also stablished them for ever and ever; he hath made a decree which shall not pass. Praise the Lord from the earth, ye dragons, and all deeps: fire, and hail, snow, and vapours, stormy wind, fulfilling his word: mountains and all hills; fruitful trees, and all cedars: beasts and all cattle; creeping things, and flying fowl: kings of the earth, and all people; princes, and all judges of the earth; both young men, and maidens; old men, and children: let them praise the name of the Lord: for his name alone is excellent: his glory is above the earth and heaven. He also exalteth the horn of his people, the praise of all his saints; even of the children of Israel, a people near unto him. Praise ye the Lord.

—Psalm 148

If the whole duty of the believer is to affirm the object of his belief, the above passage is certainly an exemplary one. Here, one feels, is the way all belief *ought* to sound: jubilant, resolute, inexhaustible, hyperbolical. The text is, of course, from Psalms, which in the Greek is a word deriving from *psalmos*, or a song sung to the plucking of a stringed instrument; and in the Hebrew from *tehillim*, meaning "praises." Apparently, the praiser has applied himself to his theme—the creativity of his Creator—in both senses of the word, for the passage is at once songlike and eulogistic. He begins by praising the universe in terms of its creative energies—the phenomena of light and warmth like the sun, moon, and stars; the phenomena of order, like height, matter, and heaven; the phenomena of power, like the angels—and exhorting them in turn to praise. He celebrates all that is unknowable to him "above the heavens" and then passes on to a category of mysteries "from the earth" interpretable to him only in part: dragons and deeps, fire, hail, snow, wind, and mountains. He concludes with the theme of God's differentiated creativity—of the transformations of matter which epitomize the life-process and serve the needs of man: fruitful trees, cedars, beasts, cattle, creeping things, flying fowl, human life in its princely and rational aspects, childhood, youth, and old age; and, finally, the tribal history of Israel itself.

The data of the psalm, however, are only a secondary aspect of its content; what remains primary is the *psalmos*, or the *song*—the affirmation of a productive God, which needs but a single word to sustain it: *Gloria!*: "*Praise! Praise! Praise!*" It is the recurrence of this word, in all the changing urgencies of its rhythm, which gives the text its extraordinary mood of elation and certainty. The psalm, if it is "believable" to outsiders at all, is believable, not because it recommends itself to the intelligence as a statement of demonstrable doctrine, but because it exists as an immediate datum of sensibility. The inflection is doxological rather than logical, infectious rather than reflective. Like Saint Paul, who was "determined not to know anything among you, save Jesus Christ and him crucified," the Psalmist has concentrated all knowledge into a single commitment: that of giving praise. He has, in other words, equated reality with adoration. To believe rightly is to affirm joyously; and he stands ready to say *Yes* to the mystery of creation and his own destiny because it is an article of his belief that the Creator is an aspect of his collective and individual destiny and endows it with His divine imprimatur: that Jehovah "exalteth the horn of his people . . . even . . . the children of Israel."

Here let us digress for a moment. Let us concede with the Psalmist that praise is an inalienable mandate of all genuinely operative religions. Let us define praise in its broadest devotional sense as the will or the wish or the need to affirm a numinous entirety of belief. Let us oppose to the idea of *praise* the idea of *appraisal*— the will or the wish or the need to *verify*, where a fundamental skepticism and self-sufficiency are implied. Let us agree that the praiser represents a mode of liturgical assent, and the appraiser a mode of provisional corroboration: that one lies within the domain of spirit as a non-negotiable absolute, and the other in the domain of suasion and the usable world; that one worships while the other questions, one unifies and the other atomizes, one turns to song and symbol, and the other to dialectic.

Does it follow, however, that praise must *always* exist in the believer as an irreducible intensity—that belief must always be undivided and single-hearted, like the Psalmist's, in order to be "true"? Can there be such a thing as *praiseless* belief where human worth and the viability of an ongoing cosmos are in doubt? If not, how is praise possible for the modern spirit, in a time of techniques. methodologies, and sciences which invite the skeptical manipulation of all the categories of thought and matter, and substitute cunning for awe? How can we ever hope for the joy of the Psalmist in a world that is knowable and unhaunted, if his single-mindedness rests upon the *haunting* of a cosmos and the celebration of *mystery*. If Prospero has served as the tutelary spirit for the re-haunting of a world plunging toward Renaissance omniscience, is not Hamlet the spokesman for joyless, aweless, distracted, fragmentary, postulating man?

> I have of late—but wherefore I know not—lost all my mirth, forgone all custom of exercises; and indeed, it goes so heavily with my disposition that this goodly frame, the earth, seems to me a sterile promontory, this most excellent canopy, the air, look you, this brave, o'erhanging firmament, this majestical roof fretted with golden fire, why it appears no other thing to me than a foul and pestilent congregation of vapors. What a piece of work is man! how noble in reason! how infinite in faculty! in form and moving, how express and admirable! in action, how like an angel! in apprehension how like a god! the beauty of the world! the paragon of animals! And yet, to me, what is this quintessence of dust? man delights not me: no, nor woman either, though by your smiling you seem to say so.
>
> —Act II, scene ii

Here, certainly, we have the obverse of the praise-bearing Psalmist and the "hero of faith"—we have, instead, the divided sensibility of the appraiser, whose melancholy and mistrust alienate him from the universe at the moment of highest consent. Reversing the fable of Balaam, who was sent to curse the tents of Jacob and remained to bless them, Hamlet, it would seem, invokes the blessing as though it were a curse. Yet, for the contemporary mind, is it not also a fact that the blessing is *there*, in the only way, perhaps, that we can invoke it? And discounting the melancholia and estrangement of the speaker, are we not right in asking, after all: But isn't this a *kind* of joy? Isn't Hamlet's place with the praisers?

I think it is; and the assumption that praise implies a *joyful* vocation, or that joy, in its devotional sense, must be present in the praiser as a state of manifest sensibility, is a delusion. On the contrary, praise does not imply an *occasion* of joy, but a *premise* of joy—the belief in joy, or the creation of it out of the demand that joy *be*. For the artist, joy may even be *imagined* into existence; indeed, one of the profoundest achievements of the Romantic poets was their rediscovery of the tragic, the "strenuous" character of joy, and its affinity with despair, in their search for a principle of belief. For Keats, it was "in the very temple of delight" that "veil'd melancholy" had her "sovran shrine," and only he "whose strenuous tongue can burst Joy's grape against his palate fine" could enter. All of Michelangelo's sibyls, prophets, martyrs, warriors, diviners, lean from their niches with their chins on the flat of their palms and their weight on their forearms and knucklebones, brooding on the melancholy of a scrutable universe, as though they awaited a second coming of the Sphinx, rather than Einstein's equation for energy. Out of joy, also, John Donne concludes his suite of Holy Sonnets with the cry: "Those are my best days when I shake with fear," Kierkegaard bases his psychology of religious experience on a condition of "fear and trembling," Gerard Manley Hopkins declares that his heart "lo, lapped strength, stole joy" in the hours of "now done darkness" when he lay wrestling with his God. It is in the pursuit of joy that, according to Pascal, man "makes for himself an object of passion, and excites over it his desire, his anger, his fear, to obtain his imagined end, as children are frightened by the face they have blackened." And in our own time, Auden has spoken to our joy with the proposal—certainly as old as Saint Paul—that love "needs death, death of the grain, our death, / Death of the old gang."

Similarly, we can account for much of the anguish and the obdurateness of Job as his sheer insistence upon joy and the will to praise, in a situation ghoulishly designed to give him no cause for either. The two themes "Let the day perish wherein I was born!" and "I know that my Redeemer liveth!" are not two, but one, and are equally a medium of praise. Only when this is borne in mind can we account for the existence of one psalm beginning, "Make a joyful noise unto the Lord," and another beginning, "My God, my God, why hast thou forsaken me?" in a "book of praises." For further light on this paradox, we can hardly do better than appeal to the example of Job himself—the praiseless hero of faith—and to his crucial lamentation in Chapter 19.

III

Know that God hath overthrown me, and hath compassed me with his net. Behold, I cry out of wrong, but I am not heard: I cry aloud but there is no judgment. He hath fenced up my way that

I cannot pass and he hath set darkness in my paths. He hath stripped me of my glory and taken the crown from my head. He hath destroyed me on every side, and I am gone: and mine hope hath he broken like a tree. . . . Have pity upon me, have pity upon me, O ye my friends; for the hand of God hath touched me. . . . Oh that my words were now written! Oh that they were printed in a book! That they were graven with an iron pen and lead in the rock for ever! For I know that my redeemer liveth, and that he shall stand at the latter day upon the earth: And though after my skin worms destroy this body, yet in my flesh shall I see God: whom I shall see for myself and mine eyes shall behold, and not another, though my reins be consumed within me.

—Job 19:6–10, 21, 23–27

Note that the passage begins in blasphemy and ends in adoration. Job, in effect, appeals from the wisdom of God to the wisdom of man, calling the whole world to bear witness to the criminality of his Creator. God has inexplicably "overthrown" him, "compassed" him, "fenced" him, trapped him, "stripped" him, dishonored him, "destroyed" him, "broken" him. The tone is one of outraged betrayal: a loveless despot has struck at the sources of good will and an anarchy of the spirit is at hand:

> I cry out of wrong, but I am not heard: I cry aloud, but there is no judgment.

Job implies that belief is no longer possible in a world where a cynical and destructive God has run amok—a malevolent misanthropist against whom there is neither redress nor judgment. Seemingly, the passage is moving toward a statement of man's tragic dependency upon man: henceforth, man must make his love and his belief out of his own pitiableness. Job's abandonment is all mankind's: tenderness, if it is to come at all, must be found in the circumstance of man's common vulnerability. Despair must call helplessly to despair, indignation to indignation, pity to pity:

> Have pity upon me, have pity upon me, O ye my friends!

To all intents and purposes, Job is prepared to formalize his position for all time "with iron pen and lead forever" as the new humanism of the future. Yet, precisely at the point when his denunciation of Jehovah has been accomplished without possibility of compromise, when hope itself has been "broken like a tree," the adoration of Job blazes out in a passage which, for *entirety* of belief, is unmatched in the Bible:

> I know that my redeemer liveth, and that he shall stand at the latter day upon the earth: and though after my skin worms destroy this body, yet in my flesh shall I see God: whom I shall see for myself, and mine eyes shall behold and not another, though my reins be consumed with me."

Let us examine the passage more closely. Note, in the first place, that the outcry completely reverses the logic of the preceding sentences, which have emphasized only the bewilderment and demoralization of Job and implied the unknowability of God. Yet Job's word in the new context is absolute, unqualified, buoyant: "I *know*"—not "I pray that," or "I hope that," "I guess that," "I believe that," or any of the available synonyms which indicate a *partial* awareness *on its way* to certainty. "*Know*" carries with it the full assault of consummated belief: in the grammar of consent, it stands for a commitment graven into the tables of reality to which nothing can be added or from which nothing can be taken away. In the same way, the substitution of *redeemer* for the earlier *God* suggests that an irresistible element of doctrine has forced its way forward, "against all common sense," and transformed chaos into commitment, rebellion into adoration. Where the context would seem to invite despair—or, at best, a plea to an unknown God of redemption—God is already addressed in His role of Redeemer and invested with His properties. Job's "knowledge" has already achieved the object of prayer by that "leap of faith" which renders prayer and proof equally unnecessary. God and Redeemer have become interchangeable words: nothing is conceivable in the unspeakable abandonment of Job except redemption.

Similarly, the force of the word *liveth* in the new context remains to be noted. Its juxtaposition with *know* and *redeemer* is one of those triumphs of intoxicated certainty which turn belief into a species of magic; for its effect is to overturn chapters of lamentation and argument, reverse the direction of the meaning, and transform the sensibility of the speaker. Where an alternative word—*reigneth*, for example—would have produced nothing more than a pietistic formula of submission:

> I know that my redeemer reigneth

the effect of *liveth*:

> I know that my redeemer liveth

is to personalize the experience of belief itself and enact the excitement of God's nearness. For despite the chapters of complaint and inquisition, the debates and rebuttals of his "comforters," the immediate evidence of his own ill usage, the issue for Job has remained not whether his God was a *just* one, requiring the forensic mediation of experts and the skills of midrashic debate, but whether he was a *living* God, close at hand, available, and his own. The word, then, is climactic, as well as poignant: for it brings to light the psychic truth that underlies the apparent or polemical truths of Job's endless denunciations. It is the nearness of a *living* God which renders further argument idle, in the end, volatilizes all issues, and proves irrefutable. Job's wrangling and his logic and his evidence count for nothing. His comforters repeat a rubric for preachers and pedants, to no purpose. The phenomenon of life has only to insist on itself as a *fait accompli* to which the whole soul of Job bears witness, to supplant them all with a passionate image of God's manifest availability:

> Though after my skin worms destroy this body, yet in my flesh shall I see God; whom I shall see for myself and mine eyes shall behold and not another though my reins be consumed within me.

The living God moves in the body of a malcontent. The premise of the Book of Job is essentially a *comic* one, as it was for that other agonist of self-loss, Dante Alighieri. For though the apostate "from the land of Uz" was capable of every heresy, he was incapable of disbelief.

IV

> If God be for us, who can be against us? . . . Who shall separate us from the love of Christ? shall tribulation, or distress, or persecution, or famine, or nakedness, or peril, or sword? As it is written, For thy sake we are killed all the day long; we are accounted as sheep for the slaughter. Nay, in all these things we are more than

conquerors through him that loved us. For I am persuaded, that neither death, nor life, nor angels, nor principalities, nor powers, nor things present, nor things to come, nor height nor depth nor any other creature shall be able to separate us from the love of God, which is in Christ Jesus our Lord.
—Romans 8:31, 35–39

Here, as in Job, the believer's task is a strenuous one, in that it calls for affirmation in circumstances that in themselves furnish no basis for belief: he must reconcile the apparent contradiction between a calamitous turn of events—tribulation, distress, persecution, famine, nakedness, the sword—and the absence of an intervening God. All evidence points toward the removal of God from the riotous world of His creation. The hostility of the universe extends from the very first things—life, angels, principalities, height, depth—to things present, to the very last things: martyrdom and God's love. The situation is thus an absolute test of conviction: with no help whatever from the objects of the material universe, with the circumstance of God's actual removal from events apparent to all, he must affirm the ridiculous. He must celebrate the beneficence and the actuality of his God at a time when he himself is "killed all the day long" and "accounted as sheep for the slaughter."

Obviously, the predicament is not a promising one for empirical demonstration: it cannot be accommodated to the processes of the laboratory or the inductive fantasies of the geometer. Even the speaker's passion is, in the long run, a disservice, since it renders him blind to the manifest absurdity of his position and denies him the tactical advantages of cunning. It is possible that, with caution and ingenuity, a case might be made for the satisfactions which are always present for the man of true faith and blameless conscience—yet the assertion that "in all these things we are more than conquerors" is a piece of inflamed bravado for which there is no evidence whatever. In the same way, the image of "sheep for the slaughter" is almost cynical in its insensitivity: it leaves no room for heroic elaboration and equates his martyrdom with the mindless butchery of the slaughterhouse.

How, then, are we to account for the thrilling plausibility of the passage and the optimism of a speaker who must make his certainty out of nothing at all: out of nonsense, paradox, and impossibility? For despite all the arguments that good sense can furnish to discredit the strategy of the speaker, the fact remains that he has established exciting contact with his hearers: he has "made his point" even if his thinking has been preposterous. Not only does his certitude strike with the immediacy of a physical sensation—as an impulse to action rather than an idea to hold in reserve—but it pursues its initiative boldly to the very end, in a masterstroke of hyperbolical absurdity:

> I am persuaded, that neither death, nor life, nor angels, nor principalities, nor powers, nor things present, nor things to come, nor height, nor depth, nor any other creature, shall be able to separate us from the love of God, which is in Christ Jesus our Lord.

The crucial word here, of course, is "persuaded"; but surely it is absurd in a context which has heaped persuasion in the opposite pan of the scale and stressed only the persecution of the believer. Persuaded by whom and by what? We are compelled to answer that the "persuasion" relates to none of these things: it refers to nothing whatever in the outside world, but is entirely a persuasion from within. Unlike the suasion of logic, it is not a process or a Socratic exercise in *elenchus*, but an entirety—a state of awareness, of inwardness, which cannot be altered from lesser to greater by a more or less fortunate realignment of circumstances. It can merely exist—or it can not exist: but if it does exist, it is the factor underlying all others—the enabling premise out of which consciousness itself creates its first cause.

Given such a state of awareness in the believer, even his *incredulity* is put to creative use and made to serve belief instead of discrediting it. Instead of freeing the skeptical process to deploy and combine and eliminate inductively, it looks *away* from the event and puts the question a second time at a higher level of intensity: "Who shall separate us from the love of Christ?" By this time, however, the question has lost its interrogative character entirely—it is no longer a call to speculation, but a mounting crescendo of conviction: "Shall tribulation, or distress, or persecution, or famine, or nakedness, or peril, or sword?" The speaker has discovered that his question is literally inconceivable to thought: to put the question is to impel the certainty; and gazing directly into his certainty, he turns knowledge into ecstasy: "I am persuaded, that neither death, nor life," etc., etc.

V

What can we learn about belief in its devotional sense from this triad of believers? In the first place, that belief is not an appendage, or an accessory, or an apparatus, like a Diesel engine, which exists to ensure the satisfactory operation of a second effect outside of itself. Though it is famous for moving mountains, it was not devised with this in mind. Indeed, belief is often not *devised* at all. It is not the product, in Job, of a plausible solution to conflicts and alternatives which present themselves to the intelligence for appraisal and are thereafter fitted to a doctrine. It does not, in the Psalmist, exist to construct systems with the mathematician's pursuit of one proposition to the next, to the limit of the exploitability of the logic. It does not, in Saint Paul, submit to the correctives by which we ordinarily test perception before bringing it to bear upon reality: evidence, plausibility, experiment. It subserves nothing, confirms nothing, mediates nothing. It is neither tidy nor homogeneous nor auxiliary. It is not even very dignified. It does not ask of logic: Am I congruous and consistent? of experiment: Am I demonstrable? of ethics: Am I desirable? of history: Am I real—and straightway collapse when its concongruity or its fantasy have been established.

I do not mean to say that beliefs are not *interpretable* on occasion in all these terms, or that the believer's passion has not been made to drive engines, detonate explosives, drag crosses, heap arguments, write epics, and contemplate values. On the contrary, it would be my contention that belief is the enabling genius of history that accomplishes both the work and the destiny of the world. There is nothing that belief in its sacred and secular guises cannot *do*, even, as with Job, to disavowing itself to reappropriate the full force of its passion. Our problem up to this point, however, has not been to suggest the *uses* of belief, but how belief, as a mode of being or an act of imagination, *inhabits* its subject and encompasses his reality.

But let us now put the question a second time. This time, let us engage belief as an activity, as *praxis*, rather than a *condition* of awareness. Let us ask: What can belief *do* for the sensibility of the believer? Taking our examples in turn again, we would have to say that the effect is the same in each case, though it may vary in the density and pressure of the outer event. Belief discovers the point at which will and assent are made one, casts out instinctual and intellectual fear, and then gives praise. In one case, the event will warrant the believer's praise and appear inevitable; in another, it will render praise unthinkable; in the third, it will render it absurd. In every case, however, belief will appropriate its object with the entirety of its passion and *remove it from the event*. Even where the event offers plausible occasion for praise, as with the Psalmist, belief will straightway seek out the implausible remainder and convert itself into awe. If the event itself resists thanksgiving, as with Job, belief will overturn history, suspend logic, undo doctrine, in order to achieve praise. It will build on contradiction, in the center of cleavage, imbalance, illogic; it will be "all things to all men," like Saint Paul; it will turn itself into imagination and fulfill itself at all costs to the limit of its creative entirety.

But is not belief then a mixed blessing? What of bias, fanaticism, prejudice, the furors of the fundamentalist? Are they not also modes of belief? How is one to distinguish between the "creative entirety" of the believer—that yea-saying monolith—and the monomania of the bigot? Is it not possible that the praiser, moving away from the event without the correctives of reality, logic, and consensual appraisal, may end up in fanaticism? Is it not possible that a belief which suspends thought, overturns history, and divinizes the ridiculous denies the dignity of the human condition?

Yes, it is possible. The axiom that must accompany our examination from the outset is: that beliefs, like radium and x-ray, disintegrate as well as penetrate. Concepts may lie still—but beliefs must keep operative; and, as William James has pointed out, belief—to which he gave the name of *option*—has a right to be called genuine only when it is "forced, living, and momentous." It is precisely on the word *living* again that I would like to rest the distinction that must be drawn between belief and bias, fanaticism and worship. It is the crucial word in James, as in Job, because *living* implies action which, whatever its inwardness, is explicitly productive and, in the deepest sense, contemporaneous. It is the *living* option which experiences, transforms, reimagines; which "beareth all things, believeth all things, hopeth all things, endureth all things." On the other hand, the option of the bigot is a dead option. In the "many mansions" of the Father, it is incapable of confronting either its own existence, or any existence outside itself. It is nerveless, unimpressionable, stopped.

VI

It is time to ask a final question two ways: What is the importance of literature for belief? and of belief for literature? Let us consider the second half of the question first, and return a simple-minded answer: beliefs are important to literature because they create the occasion for the practice of literature and minister to its momentum. They inhabit its subject matter. For example, it is Milton's belief that the time has come to "justify" the ways of God to man in terms that will give stature and passion to the rational genius of his century and hasten a Reformation of the spirit: he "therefore" proceeds to set down twelve cantos of *Paradise Lost*. "Because" he is a convinced Christian, he chooses from the many conceivable projects competing for priority the story of our first parents from the Book of Genesis, and peoples his tale with the dizzying hierarchies of the Old and the New Testaments. "Because" he is a Puritan, he stresses the redemptive power of individual labor in the sad finale of his fable and intimates that though Christ mediates and Grace is abundant, man must sue for it "running." His Eve, one may conjecture, is a consequence of his many public avowals on the subject of divorce. education, and marriage; and his Satan brings the well-known Miltonic passion for civil liberty—with the aid of seventeenth-century gunpowder—to the throne of Jehovah Himself. There is, moreover, a whole repertory of inherited "beliefs" which Milton, as a cultivated European, brought to bear on his theme from a lifetime of reading in Greek and Latin authors: ideas, techniques, myths, place-names, allusions, allegiances. Doubtless, Milton "believed" that poetry was "simple, sensuous and passionate"; he "believed" in blank verse, free will, landscape gardening, heroic similes, the Reformation, twelve cantos, the deposition of kings and the abolition of prelates. And *Paradise Lost* is, from one point of view—admittedly a simplistic one—the result of belief operating on beliefs to induce belief.

However, as we have already noted, the believer's way is often an intractable and disorderly way. How can it be related to literature in this sense? How can we reconcile the selective processes of literature with the inspired muddle which the believer is pleased to invoke as his intuition? Here it is possible to make capital of all that is actually untidy, divided, and contradictory in the creative process of the artist and bring it to bear on the experience of the believer. For the creative act, despite its symmetrical façade, not only is characterized by conflicts and ambiguities, labyrinthine blockages and collapses which open the way to the inchoate, but exists to provoke them. It is an inalienable function of the artist, we learn from Keats, to heap doubt upon doubt, cleavage upon cleavage, to keep them in contradiction, and survive in the ensuing pandemonium; in this respect, the artist's way and the believer's way are one. It was to this faculty that Keats—somewhat misleadingly—gave the name of "Negative Capability," which he defined as a state in which "a man is capable of being in uncertainties, mysteries, doubts, without any irritable reaching after fact and reason"; and he went on to observe that it was, above all other things, "this quality which went to form a Man of Achievement, especially in literature, and which Shakespeare possessed enormously." For Blake, the equation could be expressed even more succinctly: "Without Contraries, is no Progression."

What, then, is the importance of literature for belief? In the first place, literature offers the believer a medium to which he can retire with all his doubts and contradictions intact, and bring them into expressive play. He can come to his art "ready like a strong man, to run a race"; or he can come to it rocking, retching, and wrestling. In either case his medium will accept him without the forfeit of a single anxiety or certainty. Like Praise, of which it is certainly a form, literature will insist on itself against all logic and complete its entirety at all costs. If it is important that two alternatives be kept in contradiction, to the immediate dismay of the intelligence, literature will keep them at bay while life rages for solutions. If the artist is beguiled to compromise with events, while his real misgivings lie sealed away in abandoned areas of his sensibility, his art will pursue him there and wait for an answer. If his mind is seemingly ready with all the wit of the ages while his consent delays and denies, the resources of literature are there to disclose his confusions and give the lie to his bravado. In short, it is possible through the medium of literature for the artist to function with maximum fullness at two levels of awareness, as the vessel of a double disclosure: the beliefs which his will imposes on the appearance of things through the semiotic fiction of his medium, and the unruly intuitions which explode out of his psychic life.

For each of these needs, literature has its stock of expressive materials and precision tools: symbols and images, to build in darkness and transmit the divided commitment of the writer in metaphorical guise, unmediated by concession or the entrapments of consistency; drama, to find the moment of "option" when conflict is "forced, living, and momentous"; fable, to bring it to rational sequence in time; statement, to ply back and forth between the abstract and the reifications of the particular; music, to measure and order; rhetoric, to define, condense, insinuate, exaggerate, hallucinate, unite, assert, and disturb. Thus, literature can keep exact pace with the truth of the believer in both its singleness and its heterogeneity. It can bring belief to order, not by reducing life, but by exceeding it, so that it contains both the contradiction which logic rejects and the uncertainties of which the artist himself may remain unaware—the illumined half of cognition by whose light the artist brings his language to order, and the darkened half, in whose shadow the unconscious life constantly beckons to its encompassing eidolons.

2
Meaning and the Sonal Imagination

THERE IS A SPECIAL KIND of acoustics which attaches itself to meetings of this sort[1] in which the poet presents his credentials to the uneasy reader: there is an echo—an overpowering echo—of the past; and what echoes is the whole history of man's assault upon the Unknown. I do not mean by this the "problem of communication" as such—though that also keeps one's ears ringing—but the extent to which we are ready to confront the unknown and dispel the convenient and habitual. Somewhat grimly Eliot has likened the meaning of a poem to the "piece of meat which the old-fashioned burglar brought to keep the dog quiet." Coleridge, a great connoisseur in the Unknown, shocked the positivists of his day with the unnerving contention that "the immediate object of Poetry is pleasure, not truth."

I should insist, if pressed, that every poem of merit must have a truth of a sort. But I should like to suggest that there are other kinds of meaning, other modes of communication, than those which may be advantageously decanted into prose "truths"; and that, in many cases, to seek to do so is to misappropriate not only the poem, but the very intention for which it was written.

A poet is a Voice, and not a Meaning.

Meaning is concerned with a premise of the *known*; poetry is concerned with a premise of the unknown—the resolute unknowability of the world. All that is known by the poet is provisionally known: the little time and language he appropriates in the lonely act of turning life into poetry, the steady or unsteady beating of his own pulses, the felt similitude of things to other things. The finished poem returns the poet to the Unknown; but it leaves a poem which may be known in as many guises as there are readers and critics. There is no assurance that, as in Adam's dream, the reader will "wake and find it truth." All that can be finally known by poet and reader together is the rightness with which all has been brought to order in the poem. The name by which we call that order is "meaning." Meaning, in the words of Cocteau, is a *"rappel à l'ordre"*—a call to order—a form of silence in the aftermath of the speaking voice and the spoken thing.

Too often, meaning is reduced to a feat of amateur detection which assumes that a poem is a kind of murder or a jewel theft, with a corpse, a hidden weapon, and a blueprint of the plumbing, all of which can be logically deduced by any Englishman with a large magnifying glass and credentials from Scotland Yard. Poe is a notable offender in this respect: his "Philosophy of Composition or How I Wrote *The Raven*" is a work of science fiction rather than an account of the imaginative process—the hoax of an experienced criminal with a perfect plan for tunneling under Lloyd's of London while the customers are laying bets at the tables: "It is my design to render it manifest that no one point in its composition is referable either to accident or intuition—that the word proceeded, step by step, to its completion with the precision and rigid consequence of a mathematical problem." But poems are not perfect crimes, for all their apparatus of passion, intention, and obsessive ingenuity in transforming fantasy into experience and experience into fantasy. Their procedure is also visceral or vascular or sonal, rather than rational. They move like snails under a shell, carrying the coiled weight of their language over a sensitive paraphernalia of sticky horns and protoplasm in little bursts and thrusts, leaving the glistening accident of their chemistry behind them. Meaning is the trail of the snail. To talk about the final "meaning" of such a journey is to invent the geography of a spherical world after sailing a square one, like Columbus's, with sheer chaos dropping away from each of the four edges.

What one can talk about is *composition*, just as one would have to talk about the behavior of the ocean, rather than maps and compasses, to account for Columbus's "discovery" of a New World. By "composition" I would understand a *medium* which supports and sustains the psyche on its way to organic destinations: a matrix of language like a sea, with tides, densities, depths, pulling at both ships and swimmers with an underwater gravity of its own. It is in this sense that one must talk about composition—the *co-positioning* of words—rather than compasses, destinations, dictionaries, certainties, in accounting for the *behavior* (Hopkins's favorite word!) of poems. For the containing medium of all poetic activity is words. Without words, nothing; failing the next word, the poem itself fails; finding the next word, the poem has been moved; voicing the last word, the poem has been disclosed.

And so the poem moves, banging its nucleoles and its proteins like an amoeba, extending its skin and then streaming into it, making aural sense and holding that sense to its function, as though the ear were not one sense out of five but a kind of *brain* with a commitment to continuity as substantive and comprehensible as that which governs the operation of syllogisms and inductive thought. The poem makes *noises* rather than sense, noises called words, and the imminence of the next exactly appropriate word is contained in the texture and momentum of the noises—not the ideas—that precede it.

At this point—as Eliot said on another occasion—I should like to stop, short of metaphysics or mysticism. I do not know whether words create concepts or concepts create words. Only God knows—and He says that in the Beginning was the Word and the word was God—which is too circular a ploy to assist our mystification. Some people closer to God than I can claim to be—Blake, for one, and then the more denominational prophets of both the Old and the New Testaments—have associated the faculty of *knowing* with *hearing*. Paradoxically enough, the Visionary has been a Hearer rather than a Seer. If Saint Paul and Saint Peter are acceptable witnesses to the disclosure of knowledge, the first thing that generally happens to the Visionary is that he is blinded by an excess of light, like halation in overexposed film. According to one account, Paul remained so for three years. Joan of Arc heard voices before she saw visions, and understood neither.

Blake is positively pontifical on the score: "*Hear* the Voice of the Bard / Who Present, Past, and Future *sees*": not "see what I see," but "*Hear* what I see." His Piper, whom I take to be an embodiment of the Poet himself, is a sonal phenomenon many times over—a "Voice"—before he is a written one.

> Piping down the valleys wild,
> Piping songs of pleasant glee,

> On a cloud I saw a child,
> And he laughing said to me:

He is notable not because he sits on a cloud—which is a sumptuously visual posture—but because he forces his breath through a hollow reed, thereafter to be known as a woodwind, and discovers the principle of audible song, and the song demands a context:

> 'Pipe a song about a Lamb!'
> So I piped with merry cheer.
> 'Piper, pipe that song again';
> So I piped: he wept to hear.

He is then instructed to serve as his own instrument: to choose a public occasion and to *voice* the melody without the aid of the reed, as the embodiment of a *context*.

> 'Drop thy pipe, thy happy pipe,
> 'Sing thy songs of happy cheer.'
> So I sung the same again,
> While he wept with joy to hear.

He voices the song by *making words for it*, as though the sonal imagination, as the source of all meaning, precedes the verbal one. Only then are the words put "in a book that all may *read*"; a pun—*reed/read*—is allowable here:

> 'Piper, sit thee down and write
> In a book that all may *read*.'

This is ingeniously accomplished in Blake's poem by sharpening to a point the very reed that gave the Piper his function and ushered him into the world as *gleoman* piping a song *about nothing at all*: i.e., by turning the reed into a *pen* that "stains the water clear" and preserves the word in scribal form:

> So he vanish'd from my sight,
> And I pluck'd a hollow reed,

And I made a rural pen,
And I stained the water clear.

Finally it is Blake's overmastering irony that the Word has been preserved in its visual form for the sole purpose of rendering it *audible* again, at a later time, by all latecomers to the feast of the world's knowledge:

And I wrote my happy songs
Every child may joy to *hear*.

This, I take it, is a parable of the poet's vocation and the mysterious pre-eminence of the Sound as the source of the Sense. We are too likely to forget that words, as a medium of organized sound, a kind of *musique concrète*, have an independent existence, as the color red in the tube or on the canvas exists independently of the poppy; that they may function merely as incantation, or a species of hypnotic musicalization; as striking or stupefying noises; as arrangements for trapping or immobilizing time, like senatorial filibusters; as units of association or triggers of memory which have the power to evoke the past as directly as certain smells or the celebrated cookie of Proust; that the artist in words is as interested in the pleasure words give as he is in their "truth"; in the mystery of the word as well as its meaning; that it is the function of words to invite the enigmatic as well as dispel it; that words are non-representational, and have depths and trajectories as well as sequences; that they can be filled, half-filled, shallow, idle, or empty; that, in the words of Coleridge, the poet should "endeavor to destroy the old antithesis of Words and Things: elevating as it were words into things and living things, too."

On the other hand, the fact that poets, who ought to be making their own sounds, are already committed to a prepared score for the weighting and voicing of all the sounds for all the words they will utter does not seem a promising one for poetry. It suggests that the poet is defeated even before he is started, that the medium of language itself is constitutionally unimaginative. Instead of the eight musical tones and the five ruled lines of musician's notepaper for the matching of sound to the heart's immediacies, Poetry offers him an apparatus of built-in accents called Language, with all the labials, sibilants, and plosives already blackening the paper of his dictionary. To the French he gives the French language, to the Italians, Italian, to the Urdu, Urdu. The translator, caught in the crossfire, is the first to learn the sad and irreversible fact that it is the nature of all language to be chauvinistic, patriotic, and adamant—as, let us say, the diatonic scale of the musician is not. What to do, then, about the total tyranny of language which compels exact correspondences with a whole manual of "found sound" if English poets are to write intelligibly in English, Urdu poets in Urdu, and Omar Khayyám in his native Persian?

One of the answers, of course, is the far-fetched and aggressive phenomenon of *meter*: the jamming of language with the sonal and accentual program *of the poet*. Coleridge has traced the origin of meter to the "balance in the mind effected by that spontaneous effort which strives to hold in check the workings of passion." More annihilation! I would trace it to the poet's determination to be heard in his *own* time—the time, let us say, of iambic pentameter or trochaic trimeters, or whatever system of stresses and silences corresponds to his own heartbeat—rather than a time prefabricated for him by the Dictionary. Hold a poem to your ear and you will hear a battle of timetables: the metronome of correct and literate discourse dictated by the language into which poets are born—and the beat of a *prosody* which carries with it the intimate breathing of the poet.

Even if one concedes the poet's license to make new words out of old, like Joyce, or create noises which never existed before, like the scientists who teach us how to say *nylon, quasar, xerox, homomenthyl salicytate*, the Dictionary will insist that the accent *always* fall on the syllable prepared for it by the gods; and that in the interests of good sense, the poet had better comply. If he rebels, he is likely to produce a national anthem that reads (or sings): "And the rocket's red glare / THE bombs bursting in air," which is not a true rendering of sonal reality, or write footnotes, like Yeats, saying that he happens to prefer "my FANatic heart," to my faNATical, or even my faNATic heart.

Another device of the poet to force his way past all that is ready-made in language is the phenomenon of *inflection*. Unfortunately, it is easier to get readers of poetry to agree that it is *there* than to capture for non-poets the subtleties and indirections of its actual behavior. One can begin by saying that inflection is the result of the poet's attitude toward the statement he is making—a saturative coloring of the total force of the poet's intention and the changing urgencies with which it is being uttered, felt, organized, understood. It measures the pressure under which a statement is being made and the human intonation of the context in which it is intended to function: the means by which the conventional signs and noises of language have touched the personal life of the poet and taken on his expressive identity. In this sense, a poem is never totally known until its inflection is known; and failures of understanding are immediately apparent as failures or falsifications of inflection. The poems of Hopkins and Donne are often unreadable unless the inflection, often monaural in their "scoring," has been penetrated from beginning to end and flawlessly rendered. Inflection is as personal as a fingerprint, and continuous as one's skin; or, to put it a little superstitiously, it is the spirit giving life to the letter and holding all meaning to the drama of the poet's experience.

Finally, there is metaphor. Poetry has often been defined as an art of metaphor—by which is meant, doubtless, that a poem is essentially a system of emblems, ludic rather than cognitive in character, a blazon of symbols and sounds with which the poet, like the Knight in Wordsworth's *Prelude*, goes forth to encounter reality "as if conscious of the blazoning [his] shield bore." "*As if*": that is the provenance of metaphor. As if the true content of a poem were not a fact or a fiction, but a state of being. a condition of awareness, a pleasurable sense of similitude. . . . Like the novelist, the philosopher, or the scientist, the poet may *begin* with a truth of experience or an idea about it. But he places emphasis not on unyielding fidelity to the source of the truth in the data of the originating experience or its termination as an idea, but on the imaginative extension of the truth beyond the real or the rational, or the knowledgeable, into the immediate, the symbolic, the analogical, where reason often surrenders its initiative. Truth is a point of departure rather than a destination or the itinerary for a journey. To this end he turns all into metaphor—because he wishes to make magical what was only actual: to render time-*less* and place-*less* the experience which emerged at a particular time and in a particular place, and was not "magical" but actual. Only by so doing can he be really free to complete and intensify the truths of human life in a way that experience alone cannot do, or the philosophical contemplation of experience. His aim, in short, is one of transformation, rather than observation or information, and his quest is for an imaginative unit which can release the largest amount of energy in the most haunting and renewable form over the broadest perspective of human destiny: the metaphor.

Somewhere in our time, I suspect, a revolution not Russia's or China's has literally razed the old boundaries and compelled a new realignment of all the elements that bring the mind of man to bear on the arts with which they envision reality. At some point in our century, if not long before, a nucleating bomb with the literal power to atomize sensibility, language, and knowledge as we formerly conceived it has fallen on all the arts alike. Its charge is compounded in part of all the modes by which we seek to empower and manipulate the magnet of our universe—our "knowledge": the startling acceleration in our time of a "science" of psychology, a "science" of semantics, a "science" of anthropology, a "science" of cybernetics, etc.—and the increasing literacy of the artist regarding such assumptions. In other part, it reflects the avid empiricism of an era in which paint, stone, language, the physics of sound, and the physiology of human perception have all been increasingly bombarded, displaced, opened, pierced, like the solids of Henry Moore or the planes of Picasso—*estranged* by the artist to explore new visions of time, space, logic, number, chance, and the psyche, and the processes appropriate to it, at the expense of the old meanings.

In short, the persistence of Uncertainty may be an indispensable measure of the enlargement, or the anguish, of the creative spirit in the presence of contemporary possibility—"as if," says Eliot, "a magic lantern threw our nerves in patterns on a screen." It helps us to measure the task of collective enlightenment that still confronts us, like an enormous metaphor for how the world might be, if our consciousness could be enlarged to contain it.

Note

1. An earlier version of this essay was presented at a symposium on "Poetry and Meaning" (Howard Nemerov, Stanley Kunitz, Ben Belitt), at Skidmore College, April 12, 1973.

3

In Search of the American Scene: "Demographic Vistas"

> I hear America singing
>
> —Walt Whitman

AMERICAN POETS SINCE Whitman have reason to wonder what Whitman heard when he "heard America singing." Presumably, they were singing on key and in perfect American, and left their mark on both the language and prosody of the poet and his vision of a national scene. In the poem named, Whitman, as it happens, is concerned more with the proletarian diversity of the singers—carpenters, masons, shoemakers, plowboys—than with the American matrix of their song. Significantly, he omits the poets; but elsewhere he singles out "poets to come" with benevolent pugnacity as a "new brood, native, athletic, continental," answerable for "the substance of an artist's mood" and the "singing that belongs to him." He then withdraws, with the tact of a favorite uncle schooled in the self-help of an enlightened psychology:

> I am a man who, sauntering along without fully stopping, turns a
>   casual look upon you, and then averts his face,
> Leaving it to you to prove and define it,
> Expecting the main things from you.

As a "native" American singer who feels neither "new" nor "athletic" nor "continental"—and would rather choose the adjectives for himself—I admit to some uneasiness. If "poets of the Modern" have had to "prove and define," rather than to postulate, their claim to the "ensemble" of American song since *Leaves* of *Grass*, it is due largely to the aggressive cast of Whitman's evangelism. Countercharges of chauvinism do scant justice to the depth and perspective of Whitman's genius and blink aside an incorrigible hunch that America, after all, *ought* to be there. "Agents" must have their "scenes," as Kenneth Burke would say; and though Dante was not preoccupied with the specifically Italian inflection of his *Divine Comedy*, or Milton with a premise of British supremacy in Eden, or Homer with a prosody for militant Greeks, Italy. England, and Ilium are there, with their gods and cosmologies.

The "vista" for American poets, then, is a "democratic" one, but the "politics of vision" has proved more mischievous than Whitman imagined. It was possible in 1959 for a major American talent of the 1940s to repudiate the manifest diversity of two decades—Eliot, Stevens, Marianne Moore, Ezra Pound, among others—as a "diseased" and "academic" art, and proscribe T. E. Hulme's *Speculations* (1924) as "the *Mein Kampf* of modern criticism."[1] The mischief touched chaos a year later when a slate of forty-four "new American poets"[2] with "their own tradition, their own press, and their public" was thrown up like a barricade between 1945 and the present to ensure the purity of poetry in our time. Thus it is that the bucket of William Carlos Williams goes down into the American Dream and the bucket of T. S. Eliot comes up; and "the abounding, glittering jet" of Yeats's vision is nowhere in sight. The vista is no longer "democratic" but oligarchic; and the poets are the orphans of Whitman rather than his "*élèves*."

Let us grant, nevertheless, that we would all like to be as American as Coca-Cola or pumpkin pie. We would like to enlist among Whitman's "indigenous rhapsodes" "native authors and literatuses" flooding themselves "with the immediate age as with vast oceanic tides"—with "spinal, modern, germinal subjects," "tonic and alfresco physiology," "rude, rasping, taunting, contradictory tones," "vista, music, half-tints," "a new literature, a new metaphysics, a new poetry." We would like, in short—the language is still Whitman's—to negotiate for "the Yankee swap." Others will claim, as their American due, total access to "the free channel of ourselves"—Whitman's word—"significant only because of the Me in the center," and defend their option with peyote and lysergic acid. Most plaintively of all, they would like, in this nineteen-hundred-and-sixty-fourth year of our neo-Faustian era, to have a real, right, disestablished, demoniacal, intuitional experience.

Obviously, all these satisfactions are not forthcoming as inalienable aspects of the American scene, and must eventually be appraised in terms of what they displace in the economy of American letters. In my own case, I prefer to dwell on the poet's traditional commitment to his conscience and his medium as "the main thing" rather than bow to the avuncular ultimatums of a giant. I prefer to dwell, not on a platform for hearty Americans, nor on an American esthetic emergency, but on the facts of an imaginative venture as reflected in a first volume of poems published in 1938—in itself no monument of contemporary letters, but symptomatic, I think, of the poet's quest for the American scene in that decade. I choose a tone of wonder, because I find myself genuinely curious, dubious, and ungainly in the public scrutiny of processes and motivations which I have habitually resolved as *poems* rather than as tactics for poets or patriots.

Prefaces to first volumes are rare since the hortatory days of the founding Romantics, but are occasionally infiltrated in the guise of copyright acknowledgments. My first volume, published in 1938 under the title of *The Five-Fold Mesh*, carried a prefatory note which I now read with some puzzlement:

> In making this selection of poems written over a period of eight years, it has been my hope to suggest a discipline of integration, rather than a series of isolated poetic comments . . . to state a problem in orientation . . . in an expanding record of change. What has been sought, in a word, is an effect of sequence—a sequence which, beginning with simple responses to the natural world, moves on to an awareness of the personal identity, and attempts finally to establish usable relationships between the personal and contemporary world.

In comparison with Whitman's bristling resolution to "cheer up slaves and horrify despots," the language seems subdued; indeed, there were many to remind me that the program had long served first volumes from the time of the Psalmist to the present, and need hardly be made a matter of public record. The concern with contemporaneity, however, with poetry as a "discipline of integration," an "expanding record of change" with "usable relationships," a "problem in orientation," may help to suggest the predicament of the poet who, engaging his "scene" for the first time, discovers that *place* is not given him ready-made as a datum of "the American imagination," and that the American identity is the most elusive chimera of them all.

Rereading the earlier lyrics of *The Five-Fold Mesh*, I find all the categories and permutations of Polonius—lyrics tragical, tragical-comical, tragical-comical-pastoral, tragical-comical-pastoral-historical—but little that shows the cut and thrust of the American scene. The tragical-pastoral predominates, in the guise of poems that seek enigmatically to blend some undivulged personal quarrel with suitable staples of landscape: fields cloven and left fallow, fountainheads, March cardinals, primroses, woodbine, laurel, hawks, berries, violets. The tone is one of stoical and sententious ambiguity, with ominous allusions to the majesty and the ironies of unreflective self-denial: "Lay not your shoulder to this rock / The bridegroom bends to bitter water"; "Never mind, never mind / The uncloven field, the unheaped rafter"; "No hand in the indignant hour / May move to comfort or to curb: / The strength shall vanish from the flower / The healing wither in the herb"; and (I thought climactically): "Now it were valor to unbend the flesh / Burst the bright harness of dissembling sense, / The fine and five-fold mesh, / And loose the inward wound to bleed afresh." A single example will suggest the outcome of this vague and hermetic strategy for eluding two landscapes, one inner and the other outer, and erecting in their place the literary pathos of the *Minnesinger*:

From Towers of Grass

Long enmity of part and part,
Of strict mind, mutinous under steel,
Has leaned this spear upon my heart
And clapped this armor at my heel—
Some difference, wanting not for fuel
Of trickster blood and warlike bone,
Nursing a sword's point, blue and cruel,
On some primordial whetting-stone.

> Useless to cry the shape of laurel,
> The lilac star and June cockade:
> Grow strong against this mortal quarrel
> And heap a summer palisade—
> Seal, seal the green, ephemeral tower
> That keeps me hostage here, who know
> How I am succored with a flower,
> How done to death with snow.[3]

The result here is not a scene, or an identity, but a pastoral compromise. The "place" is nowhere, or inside the compounding defenses of the quatrain or the sonnet, like a maze without a minotaur; and the hoped-for "record of change" is not yet apparent.

Yet "agent" and "scene," I would contend, are *there* as shaping forces in a drama of conscience; and one need not labor the patriotic casuistries of Whitman to assume that they are American rather than Roman or Alexandrian. What bemuses me now, and was not apparent to me in 1938 as a poet preoccupied with his craft, is the total absence of place-names—the direct confrontation of geographical fact as a cartographer or a naturalist might view it—in all but a handful of the poems. Whitman, on the contrary, creates the American opportunity at once by "Starting from Paumanok" (the red man's word for Long Island), which he sees like the mapmaker, from above, as a "fish-shape" island, and then appropriates the whole of Mannahatta (talking Indian). He finds nothing antipoetic in a place-name like Brooklyn (talking Danish)—now a formula of condescension among fastidious Americans; and he has "endless announcements" for Ontario, Erie, Huron, Connecticut, Massachusetts, Chicago, and points east, west, north, and south, which he transforms into a kind of Pindaric formula for exultation. Similarly, Emily Dickinson, in her own view of things, was seeing "New Englandly" behind the hedgerows and sherry glasses of Amherst, and was avidly geographical; William Carlos Williams sought to "induce his bones to rise into a scene" of Paterson, New Jersey, whose squalors and incongruities rival Brooklyn's; Hart Crane waited under the shadows of the Brooklyn Bridge and toiled toward redemption in Key West, "drinking Bacardi and talking U.S.A." Robert

Frost mended wall north of Boston and hunted witches in New Hampshire and Vermont; Wallace Stevens looked away from the marzipan world of Oxidia, "banal suburb," to "An Ordinary Evening in New Haven."

I do not propose to suggest by this that the American scene is a kind of gerrymander—a good American word for the unnatural division of place for political advantage—in which the poet stakes out his "territory" and sings out his stations like a portable loudspeaker. Indeed, I assume that the dangers of this point of view are already apparent to all; that the poet aggressively committed to the American inflection of his "scene" and his language may reveal nothing but the persistence of the colonial mentality. He may exchange the historical sanity of Whitman's contention that "the English language befriends the grand American expression" for the idiocy of William Carlos Williams's "We poets have to talk a language which is not English." In his programmatic rejection of the feudal, he may invite the platitudes of the capitalist, and in his rejection of the European, he may entrench himself like a troll or a tick in the "folklore" of a region.

The American perspective, then, is not the province (I use the word narrowly) of the tactical ethnologist, the historian, the patriot, or the visiting Frenchman; but the "poetry of place" does offer clues to the quality and depth of the poet's engrossment in the American scene. If we are to talk about creation at all, we must talk about names, habitations, worlds, uncertainties—usually those we are born into; and it is significant that Book III of William Carlos Williams's *Paterson* bears the epigraph of a citizen of the world who liked to regard himself as "The Last Puritan":

> Cities are a second body for the human mind, a second organism, more rational, permanent, and decorative than the animal organism of flesh and bone: a work of natural yet moral art, where the soul sets up her trophies of action and instruments of pleasure.
> —George Santayana

I find this combination of geography and "psychology" a promising one; and I therefore reread with pleasure two poems from *The Five-Fold Mesh* which name names and appoint hours, as if for a duel or an assignation. One, a poem about a charwoman who regularly appeared with mop, pail, and goiter in the corridors of 20 Vesey Street, where I worked for some months as editorial assistant on *The Nation*, bears the signature of a time and a place as indispensable facts of the imaginative occasion. It is, without seeking to be so, an "American" poem. Let me cite it in its entirety:

Charwoman

(Lower Manhattan: 6:00 P.M.)

Clapping the door to, in the little light,
In the stair-fall's deepening plunge,
I see, in the slate dark, the lumped form, like a sponge,
Striking a rote erasure in the night—

And keep that figure; while a watery arc
Trembles and wanes in wetted tile, as if
It wrote all darkness down in hieroglyph
And spoke vendetta with a watermark.

That shadowy flare shall presently define
A scuffed and hazardous wrist, a ruined jaw
Packed into goiter like a pigeon's craw,
A bitten elbow webbed with a naphtha line;

While light shall lessen, blunting, by brute degrees,
The world's waste scanted to a personal sin,
Till all is darkness where her brush has been
And blinds the blackening marble by her knees,

★ ★ ★

I mark what way the dropping shaft-light went;
It flung the day's drowned faces out, and fell
Hasped like a coffin, down a darkening well:

And poise on the shaftway for my own descent.[4]

The other, by far the most ambitious piece in *The Five-Fold Mesh*, is in three parts and bears the name of "Battery Park: High Noon"—again a symptomatic, and perhaps an "American" commitment to punctuality and place. The poem is too long to be presented in its entirety; but, like "Charwoman," it is bounded by the geography of lower New York and the schedule of *The Nation* magazine: in this case, the lunch hour, when it was possible on fine afternoons to walk toward the geographical spur of Whitman's Mannahatta, through the Wall Street crevasses, to the Old Trinity Churchyard, the Aquarium, the Park which gives the poem its name, and, finally, the pleasure-boats leaving for the Statue of Liberty and the brilliant expanse of the harbor. The opening section should suggest both the style and the psychological occasion of the poem—which is a curious transposition of two places, in which, by a trick of vision, an afterimage of my Virginian childhood was superimposed for a moment on the fact of my residence in New York City.

> *Battery Park: High Noon*
> *Suddenly, the old fancy has me!*
>   Suddenly,
> Between flint and glitter, the leant leaf,
> The formal blueness blooming over slate,
> Struck into glass and plate,
> The public tulips treading meridian glare
> In bronze and whalebone by the statue-bases—
> Elude the Battery Square,
> Turn, with a southern gesture, in remembered air
> And claim a loved identity, like faces. . . .[5]

Two matters concern me in each of the two poems named: one, the startling increase in specificity and power which flows from the *total* commitment to "place"—specificity of rhythm, form, language, and self-knowledge, as well as particulars of the American scene; and the other, the deepening of the imaginative occasion by a contradictory shift from the theme of place to the theme of *dis*placement. In the "Charwoman," for example, the poet's quarrel with himself, vaguely disposed of in an earlier poem as "some difference, wanting not for fuel / Of trickster blood and warlike bone" is given a protagonist—the charwoman—and explores a cause: the haunting complicity that the young and the sound may feel in the presence of the maimed and the aging, the political and moral enigma of "the world's waste scanted to a personal sin" for which nothing stands ready to atone.

I note also that, with the increasing proximities of the scene, the imaginative particulars of the poem have been brought optically and intellectually into closer range of both the poet and his reader. The fact of goiter is confronted with pity and terror in the "ruined jaw / Packed into goiter like a pigeon's craw"; the occupational marks of the charwoman are clinically incised in a manner that one critic has called Flemish: by a composite of highlight and chiaroscuro which focuses painfully on "A bitten elbow, webbed with a naphtha line," like a cartoon etched in detergents. Similarly, in "Battery Park" the metropolitan landscape and statuary are ironically and substantively seen, as the Virginia landscapes were not: "The public tulips treading meridian glare / In bronze and whalebone by the statue-bases" are both actual and submerged. They stand memorially against their mid-city background of "flint and glitter," "glass and plate," "pigeons and peanut shells" and reject all pastoral compromise. To the extent that they do so, the poem, the lighting, and the scene are not "Flemish," or impressionistic, actually, but "American."

It is this engagement of uncertainty with the actual—to the point at which, in Hopkins's words, "what you look hard at, seems to look hard at you"—that I find crucial to the poetry of place and the criteria of "American" song. With more time, I might go on to illustrate how in the two collections that have followed—*Wilderness Star* (1955) and *The Enemy Joy* (1964)—the geographical fact has constantly enlarged itself to toughen my idiom and refine my sense of "vista" as a poet writing democratically in "American." I would dwell on the circumstance by which the theme of place and displacement leads the poet by inevitable stages to the timeless themes of reality and appearance, permanence and change, being and nonbeing, as they led Whitman: to the *myth*, as well as the fact, of departure, and the possibility that all places are actually one place and all poetries one poetry, and that one travels, as the dancer moves, in order to "reach the still point where the dance is."

It is the same point that Whitman sought on the furthest perspectives of his art when in "Passage to India" he invoked the "aged, fierce enigmas" "below the Sanskrit and the Vedas." It was the vision that was uppermost in my own mind when I concluded a section of "Battery Park" with an exhortation which has since carried me into many Americas, inner, outer, and continental, and led to new scenes and displacements:

> Bend then to seaward. The element you ask
> Rarer than sea is, wantoner than time:
> You bear it on you, strangely, like a mask,
> And dream the sailing in a pantomime.
>
> *The element is blood.* Tired voyager, turn:
> The reckoning you take is yet to learn.
> Somber, at fullest flood, the continents ride
> And break their beaches in a sleeper's side.

Notes

1. Karl Shapiro, "What's the Matter with Poetry?" *The New York Times Book Review*, December 13, 1959.
2. *The New American Poetry, 1945–1960*, ed. Donald M. Allen (New York: Grove Press, 1960).
3. From Ben Belitt, *The Five-Fold Mesh* (New York: Alfred A. Knopf, 1938). "From Towers of Grass" © 1933 by Ben Belitt; reprinted by permission of Alfred A. Knopf, Inc.
4. From Belitt, *Five-Fold Mesh*. "Charwoman" © 1938 by Ben Belitt; reprinted by permission of Alfred A. Knopf, Inc.
5. From Belitt, *Five-Fold Mesh*. "Battery Park: High Noon" © by Ben Belitt; reprinted by permission of Alfred A. Knopf, Inc.

B. Predicaments

4

The Enigmatic Predicament: Some Parables of Kafka and Borges

I

1

To "MAKE UP STORIES," rather than to "tell the truth," is presumably to dissimulate, and all dissimulation, rationally viewed, confounds, rather than assists, reality. In this sense, fiction adds to the riddlesomeness of things; or it elects to make up stories about riddles—stories of gods, demons, causality, destiny, "life." From this point of view, Oedipus is our exemplary hero of the antifiction. His confrontation with the Theban Sphinx not only destroyed the sanctity of the enigmatic way, but constituted a revolution in the criteria of knowledge itself. Until the advent of Oedipus, to tell a story of men or gods, to be "true to life," was to engage the enigmatic with a fiction. All storytelling was a venture into the Inscrutable, in which the storyteller said, with Saint Paul: "Behold, I will show you a mystery." After Thebes, the great custodians of the Mysteries—oracles, libation-bearers, sibyls—gave way to the Answerer and the defeat of enigma. Presumably, the era of dialectic was at hand.

The fictive art I am concerned with here is specifically literary. It pertains to those artifacts of narrative prose subsumed under the function of storytelling, as long or short as you please—that self-extending "tapeworm" (of which Forster has written[1] with such amused tolerance) which exacerbates and gratifies the "primeval curiosity" of the reader; asks "*What next?*" through a thousand and one nights; saves the life of Scheherazade; and transforms us "from readers into listeners, to whom 'a' voice speaks, the voice of the tribal narrator squatting in the middle of the cave, and saying one thing after another until the audience falls asleep among their offal and bones."

Hans Vaihinger learnedly reminds us[2] that the artificial character of these verbal ventures is already implicit in the Latin of "*fictio*, as an activity of *fingere*, that is to say, of constructing, forming, giving shape, elaborating, presenting, artistically fashioning; conceiving, thinking, imagining, assuming, planning, devising, inventing." The movement toward the *enigmatic* is similarly suggested by the Latin *aenigma*: "conceits, figments of the brain, phantasies, phantastic ideas, imagination, imaginary ideas . . . counterfeit ideas, stratagems, dodges . . . chimaeras." It is precisely this relationship between fiction and enigma, the contrived and chimerical thing, that I wish to examine in the work of two contemporary masters whose express intent seems to have been to compel a simultaneous awareness of both: to bombard fiction with enigma and enigma with the fictive in the service of some insight which needs to be better understood. For this purpose I have chosen the parables of Kafka and Borges—because, supposedly, their explanations are offered in the guise of enigmas, and their insights are enacted in the form of miniature fictions.

2

First, a word regarding the rhetoric and strategy of parable. Parable, we can say academically, is a fiction implying a comparison, a similitude in the guise of a fable, a plot permeated with symbolic meaning. In a time of little faith, it is a means of addressing, "in code," as it were, a message to men of perfect faith and of screening out the skeptic, the hypocrite, the informer, and those not "in the know." For example, in a time of Soviet repression of public criticism of the status quo, on the part of a regime demanding the conformity of the artist, *The Cancer Ward* of Solzhenitsyn is a mode of parabolizing the sickness of the time under the guise of a story about cancer. It provides a means of public double-talk in which a dissenter and teacher in constant peril of his life can communicate with other dissenters on a closed circuit, "in code," on the Christian principle that "to whosoever hath, to him it shall be given" and that pearls are not to be cast before swine. The parable, then, is a hermetic directive to the "elect" through which action is turned into fable.

The parables of Jesus—flung, as it were, in handfuls, as if the Sower took no account of where they fell—show us fable at all stages of completion, incompletion, compression, and suspension. At times the "plots" that we have come to expect of fable have been so compacted or abbreviated that there is little likelihood of putting them to edifying use. Even a full-dress parable, like the parable of the Sower (Matt. 13:3–23)—which takes its time and proceeds by stages so explicit in their imagery that they may be construed dialectically—aroused the instant consternation of the Disciples, to whom, said Christ, it was "given to know," and required the detailed exposition of the teller. Without the glosses of the master, the purport of Christ's parables apparently remained inaccessible. The hoped-for transformation of perception did not occur.

Or, as Kafka remarked, "In parable, you have lost." In fiction, however, the confusion is fruitful. In fiction, the problem is increasingly polarized as fable turns into "story" and parable into enigma. Fiction asks: How much *plot* is needed for the mind to manipulate if we are not to revert to the riddling hallucinations of the Sphinx? How are we to cover chaos with a plot, to deliver us from the inscrutable? Where does the enigmatic factor of an *unknown intent*, on the way to making itself known, set in? Are we all agreed about the common "meaning" that a "right" reading of the fiction should produce? Or is enigma forced upon us because we find ourselves in essential disagreement and all the disagreements are true?

At this point I should like to allow Kafka to raise and resolve contingent issues in his own way in his parable on parable. The essential concern of "On Parables" is epistemological. That is to say, it asks, with Saint Paul, "whether there be knowledge," and if there be knowledge, what it is good for—whether it is tentative, terminal, or illusory. Presumably, if it is illusory, it would constitute an order of *fiction*, and fiction might then claim for itself a *fait accompli*: that it is "true" in the sense that it constitutes a mode of *surrogate* or fictive knowing or, at the very least, illusory knowing.

In all fiction, as in all assumptions of knowledge, there would remain for both the philosopher and the writer of fiction the problem explored in such depth by Nietzsche in his "will to illusion,"[3] as to whether in myth, art, and metaphor there is always a kind of "lying, in the extra-moral sense"; whether such "delusional conceptions [are] necessary and salutary provisions of the instinct"; whether all life and all knowing "*needs* illusions, i.e., untruths regarded as truths"; whether we habitually "operate with things that do not exist, with lines, surfaces, bodies, atoms, divisible time, divisible space"; whether "error might [not] be one of the conditions of life"; whether "the recognition of delusion and error as conditions of knowing and feeling" would be "endurable" without art.

Nietzsche goes on to observe that "we must love and cultivate error: it is the mother of knowledge"; and doubtless the novelist would similarly concede that the cultivation of error (or "illusion") is the mother of fiction, however "realistic" its pretensions. "Without the assumption of a kind of being which we could oppose to actual reality, we should have nothing by which we could measure, compare, or picture it; error is the presupposition of knowledge." For Nietzsche, thinking was moreover contingent upon language:

> We are continually seduced by words and concepts, into imagining things as simpler than they really are. . . . A philosophical mythology lies hidden in language which breaks through at every moment, no matter how careful we may be. . . . Indeed, the most erroneous assumptions are precisely the most indispensable for us. . . . Without granting the validity of the logical *fiction*, man could not live. . . . A negation of fiction . . . is equivalent to a negation of life itself. . . . There is nothing but a moral prejudice that regards truth as of more value than illusion. . . . There would be no life at all were it not on the basis of perspective valuations and semblances. . . . the perspective is the basic condition of all life.

Thus, supposedly, the philosopher—and it may be, the inducer of esthetic fictions, the novelist so-called—places himself not only beyond "good and evil" but beyond "truth and falsehood" as well. If this seems too shocking a heresy for esthetic idealists, or too willfully symptomatic of modern relativism, it is worth remembering that 2,500 years ago Aristotle placed tragedy above epic precisely for the reason that its "imitation" was *fictive* and, as such, constituted a more universal, more *plausible* mode of the truth than "history."

But why talk in parables at all? It is the essence of parable to avoid showdowns of this nature, and leave the issues suspended. But certain implications of Kafka's little parable should be paraphrased for what they are worth. In the first place, its effect is to suggest that parables are a species of nonfunctional "wisdom"—that is to say, one does not acquire the wisdom of parable in order to deplete or discredit it. Parables are *fabulous* ("he means some fabulous yonder"[4]), *unknown* ("something unknown to us"), *imprecise* ("something that he cannot designate more precisely"), and *useless* ("merely parables and of no use in daily life"). Parables are *exceptional* rather than daily, in the sense that a work of literature is less daily than an empirical act of thought. Conversely, parables are *truisms* already deeply known to us all ("We *know* that already"). All they "really set out to say" is "merely that the incomprehensible is incomprehensible." Parables, moreover, appear to have a way of rendering the knower himself *unreal*: "If you only followed the parables you yourselves would become parables," and all existence would be *parabolized*. Finally, as insights, parables serve what might be called an epistemology of *loss*. Their value, as knowledge, is to enhance our "consciousness of ignorance"—but that is the beginning of philosophy. The vocation of Socrates began with a visit to the Oracle at Delphi and a "parable," and ended with a philosopher's conviction that "I know that I do not know."

3

A sequence of corollaries can be traced to make clearer the parabolic stance of Kafka as a whole—what, in his preface to larger fictions to come, he is saying about fiction as a mode of knowledge. In "An Imperial Message," for example, Kafka's premise is that there is an unimpeachable Source to whom all is known: an "Emperor," removed, remote, infallible, mortal, in whom all data originate. From Him proceeds all knowledge; and all knowledge leads to messages. The known thing not only is communicable, but exists to be communicated. Messages, in turn, lead to messagebearers, and this in its turn leads to "journeys"—a search for those for whom the known thing was intended.

The parable makes it clear that the message is also momentous, and must be exactly imparted to the message-bearer. That it is "whispered" on a deathbed suggests that there is something profoundly confidential about all knowledge; and that it must be confirmed suggests that the datum is profoundly misinterpretable. Kafka goes on to say that though the messenger is "powerful," "indefatigable," "cleaving a way through the throng" to the "chambers of the innermost palace," he will "never get to the end of them," for the resistance of circumstances and things would be infinitely multiplied: more courts, more stairs, more palaces, more years, more gates, more cities, "to the center" of the imperial capital and a "world crammed to bursting with its own refuse."

Two questions are relevant to the parable in hand: (1) For whom was the knowledge intended? and (2) If knowledge is not communicated, does it really exist? Kafka gives them both short shrift; indeed, it may appear to some that he begs questions rather than confronts them. His answer is that the journey, the datum at its mysterious point of origin, and its communication by the messenger were all unnecessary. Anyone can "dream it to himself" by his window. Thus, all apparent knowledge is a dream, by the self, in the self, to the self—what Nietzsche called "mythological dreaming," the "invented world of the unconditioned, the self-identical man," "the will to deception," which is indeed "the soul of art." "It is our laws and our conformity to the laws that we read into the world of phenomena—however much the contrary seems true." There is no Emperor, no messenger, no single mind for whom the message was intended. "The 'agent' has merely been read into the action—the action is all there is. . . . There is only a naive, human manner of arranging things."

In "The News of the Building of the Wall" we have another "epistemological" parable regarding messages, "news," knowledge. Here the effect of "The Imperial Message" is, as it were, reversed, as Kafka reflects on an alternate possibility: "What if the message *had* been delivered?" In the present case, the message arrives "late, some thirty years after its announcement." It is received, not by the storyteller himself (who is barely ten at the time), but by his father. The child, however, is witness to the event, of which he "remembers the smallest circumstances"; and the circumstances are almost conspiratorial in their secrecy. A boatman approaches and beckons, messenger and father meet in the middle of a slope, and, once again, the message is whispered "into my father's ear."

The results of the messenger's mission, however, are ambiguous and unexpected. The son himself "did not understand what was said," the father "did not seem to believe the news," the messenger "tried to convince him that it was the truth, but Father still could not believe it," even though the message-bearer "almost tore open his clothes . . . in order to convince him that it was so." The problem for parable, then, is altered. Has the messenger communicated at all, and is his mission accomplished? If he has indeed communicated, why was he not believed? And if the father believed, what was his knowledge "good for"? Was it truth or illusion?

Characteristically, the issues are left suspended. The fiction moves steadily toward the enigmatic, to which it apparently surrenders, even though its content is supposedly knowable, positive, terminal. The father remains "meditative," the boatman sails away, the recipient of the message returns home and straightway "reports from the threshold what he had heard." The child, as bystander, has "no exact recollection of his words," but "because of the extraordinary circumstances . . . their meaning sank into me so deeply that I still feel able to give a kind of verbatim version of them." He proceeds to do so, and his words pass into the stream of "popular interpretation." The message proves to be little more than a rumor, at once threatening and reassuring. The Emperor, in whom all knowledge is vested, is being threatened by "infidel nations with demons among them" who "shoot their black arrows at the Emperor." It is rumored that "a great wall is going to be built to protect" him. That constitutes the whole of knowledge.

In a further parable on "Couriers," Kafka continues to speculate on the discomfort of messengers, deputies, couriers—that is, on the sources and the terminal aspects of knowing. His misgivings at this stage appear desperate, as well as implacable. Is *anything* known at all? Are there even directions, journeys, goals? The effect of his answer is to turn fiction into phantasmagoria. We all wish to be message-bearers of the King, he argues, rather than kings. "Like children," we wish to receive, disseminate, and communicate knowledge rather than create it. But there are no kings from whom true knowledge may be said to derive; our messages are "meaningless" and invalid. All that really exists is an enigmatic "oath of service," a commitment to "shout the King's messages" to one another and thereby incur the "misery" of things. Human knowledge is nothing more than the compulsive "shouting" of unauthorized "messages."

4

A final cluster of parables will, I think, help to consolidate the nature of Kafka's commitment to enigmatic fictions. The first, "The Invention of the Devil," is essentially a parable on the anguish of the enigmatic predicament as such, the "misery" of things already imputed to the delusory mission of the "courier." The "Devil" of the title is clearly the demon of the ambiguous, the multiple, the contradictory—of the heterogeneity and pluralism of the world in the presence of a mind that longs for homogeneity, for unity. Here, knowledge is viewed as "possession" in the demonic sense of the word. To "know" is to be appropriated by the irreconcilable pluralism of things, to be dis-possessed of one's own identity—or of the unifying delusion of the rational process—and to be made legion. In this sense, Kafka repeats the formula for demoniacal possession or, if you wish, for schizophrenia—to which Luke refers in 8:30: "And Jesus asked him, saying, What is thy name? And he said, Legion: because many devils were entered into him." In the same way, Kierkegaard was led to wonder: "Can you think of anything more frightful than that it might end with your nature being resolved into a multiplicity, that you really might become many, become, like those unhappy demoniacs, a legion, and you thus would have lost the inmost and holiest thing of all in a man, the unifying power of personality?"[5]

In "The Invention of the Devil," such a state has actually come to pass: a sense of possession, deprivation, alienation; a sense of the "diabolic" character of this intrusion; of "earthly misfortune" incurred by an act of knowing that leaves the knower without choice, conviction, or the rational subordination of expendable or contingent things to what is irreducibly constant—hence, "deceived." The deception would seem to lie not in the *data* by which the knower is "possessed," but in the temptation to know, *itself*—the trustful and "scrupulous attention" with which the knower has opened himself to the appropriation of data, in which nothing "exterminates" anything else or "subordinates" itself to the coexisting multipleness of things, as would be the case in syllogistic or dialectical thinking. It is in this sense that one has "become legion," and perhaps it is also in this sense that the enigmatic factor in all art partakes of the "diabolic." The enigmatic works in *multiples*: it aims at the "suspension of disbelief" or the "possession" of the reader; and it goes on multiplying its multiples. It not only retains all that it evokes, but resists every effort on the part of the knower to dispose of the content of knowledge in such a way that one thing "exterminates . . . another until only a single one is left . . . or they subordinate themselves to one great devil."

The second parable is devoted to yet another fictive variation, the *legendary*, and may serve to mitigate somewhat the despairing pluralism of "The Invention of the Devil." Here it is the nature of a God, rather than the devil, that demands to be known, and the parable's medium is Prometheus, a defier of "emperors" and absolutes, whom legend assumes to be the tutelary spirit of the whole human condition. The properties of Prometheus, however, are of less concern to Kafka than the mode by which his story has passed into common knowledge. And in the beginning we are told that "there are four legends concerning Prometheus," just as, presumably, there are four gospels concerning Jesus which must be put "in accord with" their tellers or messengers: the "gospel *according to* Matthew, Mark, Luke, and John."

The implications are again multiple. There is a pluralism of knowledge; but there is also a hope that the truth of the God may be arrived at "orchestrally," by a synoptic reading of all four—arranged in parallel columns, as it were, like the synoptic reading of the gospels. Kafka proceeds to so arrange them, as four variations on a single message. The question in all this, of course, is whether four legends constitute one truth. If not, how many legends are needed? Or is this another parable about the essential unknowability of Prometheus and the defeat of knowledge?

We have only the final paragraph to guide us. Here we meet, in another guise, the essential *paradox of parable*: that legend, like parable, tries to "explain the inexplicable." The fact is well known to all mythologists and historians of religion; all gods have their "aetiological" or explanatory myths, which generally constitute the service of the god. It has always been the task of religious ritual to explain the inexplicable, and, in more secular terms, it may also be the function of all fiction and all knowledge. The reader can only set down faithfully the contradictory import of Kafka's parable: (1) that all legend contains a "substratum of truth" (and all truth a substratum of legend?); (2) that all truth is inexplicable; (3) that therefore all legend which turns into apparent truth turns itself into the "inexplicable"; and (4) that therefore truth and legend are equally fictive and enigmatic. The "inexplicable mass of rock"—the brute substantiality of things untouched by the operations of thought, belief, fiction, delusion, truth—*remains*.

Finally, "The Problem of Our Laws." There may be some question as to whether this is a parable at all, since the speculative cast of the piece outweighs—or outpaces—the parabolic. Nevertheless, it synthesizes many of the concerns that have already furnished Kafka with occasions for parable: messages; messengers; mysteries; wisdom; truth; fiction; interpretation; presumption; traditions; an "elite" from whom all knowledge derives, who originate, administer, and "rule"; and the "ruled," who "live on a razor's edge" of incertitude, and submit.

One must first opt for a meaning, or a complex of meanings, within which one is content to see the key word—LAW—operate. Perhaps the most obvious and convenient meaning should be the first to go: "law" in its literal sense as *legislation* or *litigation*. Juristic procedure for the purpose of defining rectitude and judging deviations from it—the tactic "of bringing a single case under some law in order to apply its theory of rewards and punishments" (Vaihinger)—is merely one permutation of the intended meaning. As the parable makes clear, Kafka has in mind all movements of the reason and the psyche which (according to Vaihinger) "deliberately substitute a fraction of reality for the complete range of causes and facts": abstractive fictions, practical fictions, mathematical fictions, heuristic fictions, scientific fictions," as well as "legal fictions" as such.

In this vein, Kafka goes on to remark that we are all "ruled by laws that [we] do not know"; that "only a few and not the whole people are allowed to have a say in their interpretation"; that "their interpretation has been the work of centuries" and has now "acquired the status of law"; and that "the very existence of these laws . . . is at most a matter of presumption." As usual, Kafka postulates an elite of the intellect—"a small group of nobles who rule us"—philosopher-kings; princes of the intellect and administrators of syllogistic propriety; benevolent despots and guardians of the "law and order" of logic, who preside over a "mystery confided to the nobility." He then goes on to question, heretically, whether "when in accordance with these scrupulously tested and logically ordered conclusions, we seek to orient ourselves somewhat toward the present or future, everything" is not "only an intellectual game"—in other words, a system of *fictions*, delusions, arrangements of convenience. Perhaps "these laws that we are trying to unravel"—the right action of the human reason which is compatible with reality and should legitimize all truths—"do not exist at all."

It is here that Kafka gives fullest play to his discomfiture and skepticism. After all, he remarks, "The Law is whatever the nobles do"—i.e., whatever Socrates and Aristotle "did" with their reasoning faculties are the "laws" of right reasoning because they did it. He makes mention of a "party" of dissenters or anarchs of the reason who "see everywhere only the *arbitrary* acts of the nobility." These anti-intellectuals, or antinomians, duly warn their fellow plebeians against a "false, deceptive, and over-confident security." They remind the gullible that "the tradition is far from complete"—as, indeed, sophisticated scientific thought today constantly cautions the vulgar. The nature of inductive scientific procedure as such is inherently fragmentary, nonterminable: a work-in-progress that, like Zeno's arrow, mathematically shortens the distance between itself and the target toward which it travels but, by the same mathematical logic, can never reach it. They challenge that "preponderance of evidence" by which science, at a given point of its trajectory, regards its case as "demonstrated" or "proven," announces a terminal datum—or "law"—and functions in relation to it as one would to a "truth." They even go an irrational step further to envision a time when the "law" will "belong to the people and the nobility will vanish."

Here Kafka recoils. He reminds us that the "party which believes that there is no law"—the anarchs and the heresiarchs—

has, after all, "remained small." It is small because of a universal craving for the postulate that Knowledge Does Indeed Really Exist Somewhere—even if it must do so enigmatically, with the "nobility." We would all rather have enigma—the enigma of the law—than anarchy or nullity. Therefore, "nobody would dare to repudiate the nobility" that rules, pontificates, governs, coordinates, orders, and consoles with a "fiction" of orientation and knowledge, and renders the world bearable. The essential "divinity that doth hedge a King" hedges all knowledge; it is *all* divine. No knowledge is secular. Knowledge is innately mysterious, arcane, privileged, arbitrary, unknowable, and the conviction of knowledge must therefore remain a fiction to all except the nobility, who will never divulge the "mystery" over which they preside during their lifetimes and which they take with them into their death.

II

1

The case for Kafka as "precursor" to Jorge Luis Borges would be apparent to those familiar with the enigmatic fictions of both, even without Borges's little essay on "Kafka and His Precursors." In that knowledgeable and crotchety piece, Borges admits to a long predilection for the art of Franz Kafka, which has left him with a dowser's instinct for "his voice, or his practices in texts from diverse literatures and periods."[6] He goes on to cite six such texts, with a preciosity which will surprise no one familiar with the encyclopedic habits of the Director of the Argentine National Library and laureate of the chair of English and North American Literature at the University of Buenos Aires.

Similarly, the reader of Borges is constantly aware of the "voice, or . . . practices" of Kafka in that labyrinthine world over which Borges presides as presumptive heir and successor. The scope of this essay permits only the most cursory look at the continuities of Kafka and Borges, but even a cursory look will serve. For one thing, to supplement, or to polarize, the import of his longer fictions, Borges, like Kafka, has often chosen to write in "parables." That his parables concern *himself*—are, in effect, "explanatory myths" of his double stance as artist in fiction and the "other Borges," now legendary for his taste for "hourglasses, maps, eighteenth-century typography, the taste of coffee and the prose of Stevenson" (L 246) and the language of Anglo-Saxon epics—is clear from the title of his parable "Borges and I."

In a sense, "Borges and I" continues Kafka's long meditation on the theme of knowledge and enigma—this time with a shift of emphasis to the artist as knower. Borges surmises, as Kafka foresaw, that the artist in parable must reckon with two consequences he is destined to invite: (1) "If you follow parable, you yourself become parable"; and (2) "In parable, you have lost." Similarly, the "daily" Borges speaks to the Borges whose "perverse custom" it is to "falsify" and "magnify" things, to conjure up "games with time and infinity" which volatilize or liquidate the identity. "I am giving over everything to him," he confesses. "I live, let myself go on living, so that Borges may contrive his literature. . . ." And his conclusion is literally Kafkaesque: "I lose everything," including the conviction of knowledge itself. "I do not know which of us has written this page" (L 247).

It should not escape us that Borges was content to call his most celebrated collection of stories and parables simply *Ficciones*, as if he wished to ally himself generically with the world of illusion rather than a premise of truth or reality. His point, in this shadow play, is that fiction makes the maker of fictions fictitious—just as, in another parable entitled "Everything and Nothing," he contends that drama, as another mode of fiction, rendered Shakespeare "fictitious" to himself. The paradox in each case is the same: in fiction (Kafka would say in parable) one "has everything and nothing." On the one hand, fiction liquidates the identity of the teller and invests him with identities not his own; and, on the other, it induces an omniscience which is no longer partial or adventitious, but totally known to the teller of fictions. For the duration of the fiction—as in Kafka's "Invention of the Devil"—he is a congeries of *personae*, an "invention," a *fait accompli* of fictive clairvoyance. The devil of the ambiguous, the multiple, and the heterogeneous has pre-empted the consciousness of the storyteller and reduced him to "nothing"; but it has also endowed him with the infallibility and entirety of his fiction: "everything."

In "Everything and Nothing" Borges goes a step further and

identifies the artist's faculty for self-surrender as histrionic. "At the age of twenty-odd years," he writes, Shakespeare

> had already become proficient in the habit of simulating that he was someone, so that others would not discover his condition as no one; . . . but once the last verse had been acclaimed and the last dead man withdrawn from the stage, the hated flavor of unreality returned to him. . . . Thus hounded, he took to imagining other heroes and other tragic fables. . . . At times he would leave a confession hidden away in some corner of his work, certain that it would not be deciphered; Richard affirms that in his person he plays the part of many and Iago claims with curious words, "I am not what l am" [L 248–49].

Thus, the fictions of drama, like the fictions of the novelist, are viewed as "controlled hallucinations" leading to the old terror of the loss of self, of which both Kafka and Kierkegaard spoke—the pandemoniac state of "being so many," of being "legion," of being "possessed." The implications are that the fictive way—if not the function of fiction itself—is essentially enigmatic: that only fiction, as a mode of knowledge, leaves us with the *certainty* that, for the duration of the fiction or the play or the parable, illusion is totally ours. "We are not what we were," says reader to writer with a shock of unprecedented recognition; "we are many. Reality is not our concern." Theirs is the enigmatic predicament in which they have "everything and nothing."

The enigmatic predicament of all things—actor, action, scene, purpose, cognition—the *enigmatizing* of existence—is the supporting vision of the "*ficciones*" of Jorge Luis Borges. Compared with the radical bleakness of Kafka's characteristic manner, however, his approach is baroque, subliminal, "poetic." Whatever his debts to Kafka, and they are considerable, the mode of Borges is Spanish rather than Gothic; that is to say, his precursors are Calderón, Góngora, Quevedo, Cervantes, Unamuno, even Maimonides—that confluence of erudition, dandyism, the balladic, the gauchoesque, and the *mozárabe*, shifting its densities and surfaces as the need requires, but supporting the skipped heartbeat that sustains the Spaniard's sense of reality: *La vida es sueño*.

In his parable on "Inferno I, 32," Borges will invoke Dante, as he did Shakespeare in "Everything and Nothing," only to say of the dying Dante that "In a dream, God declared to him the secret purpose of his life and work; Dante, in wonderment, knew at last who and what he was and blessed the bitterness of his life. Tradition relates that, upon waking, he felt he had "received and lost an infinite thing . . ." (L 237). He will exhume the "story of a broken and scattered God" of Diodorus Siculus, only to add that "something infinite had been lost. . . . Men have lost a face, an irrecoverable face. . . . Who knows whether tonight we shall not see it in the labyrinths of our dreams and not even know it tomorrow?" (L 238–39). He will paraphrase Coleridge: "In our dreams . . . images represent the sensations we think they cause; . . . we dream of a sphinx in order to explain the horror we feel" (L 240). In his "Parable of Cervantes and the *Quixote*" he will conclude, "For in the beginning of literature is the myth, and in the end as well" (L 242) (thereby implying the pluralism of Kafka's Prometheus, who steadfastly rejects the expectation of terminal outcomes and opts for the multiplicity of the mythic way). He will insist, in his parable of "The Witness," that "one thing, or an infinite number of things, dies in every final agony . . ." (L 243). In another parable on Cervantes he will say that "Don Quixote . . . senses, standing before the dead body of his enemy, that killing and engendering are divine or magical acts. . . . He knows that the dead man is illusory, the same as the bloody sword weighing in his hand and himself and all his past life and the vast gods and the universe" (L 245). He will remind us, in "The Zahir," that "the words 'live' and 'dream' are rigorously synonymous" (L 164). The fictions of Borges multiply their permutations tirelessly—"enigmatic circumlocutions, or 'kennings'" in which one hears the tumblers of dream and reality shifting in their great locks and engaging their secret components as if to spring open to the keys of the Borgesian mystique. In this sense, the bedeviled protagonist of "The Waiting" has written the epitaph for all artists in fiction: "He was in this act of magic when the blast obliterated him" (L 168).

2

In an essay on "The Mirror of Enigmas," Borges handily furnishes the critic with an apparatus of metaphor, precedent, and learned example worthy of Maimonides the Cordovan's *Guide for the Perplexed*, playing the critic's advocate to an undertaking that he knows to be impervious to elucidation. Beginning in his accustomed manner with "the thought that the history of the universe—and in it our lives and the most tenuous detail of our lives—has an incalculable, symbolical value" (L 209), he invokes the anguish of Kafka's plebeians in "The Problem of Our Laws," or the dilemma of the child in his "The Imperial Message." The anguish of both writers is clearly epistemological, hinting darkly at some scale which weighs all actions by balances unknowable to us, and at messages whose pathos is mysteriously heightened by the impossibility of our ever receiving them. Thus, Borges catches a plane of light from Arthur Machen ("the outer world . . . is a language we humans have forgotten or which we can scarcely distinguish"); flashes it scarily on a surface of De Quincey ("'The least things in the universe must be secret mirrors to the greatest'"); and then concentrates its total glare on the celebrated passage from 1 Corinthians 13:12, which he fussily renders in two limping translations, as though he himself could not produce the Elizabethan touchstone in 1611 English: "Now we see through a glass, darkly; but then, face to face: now I know in part; but then shall I know even as also I am known."

Borges then moves on to a parabolic tactic learned from Kafka and Kierkegaard—the synoptic multiplication of alternatives, the building of a labyrinth of instances. Rabbinically, pedantically, ironically, he combs the indices of Léon Bloy for six "different versions or facets" of the *speculum in aenigmate* (the "mirrors and enigmas" of Saint Paul), which he arranges in parallel columns, as it were, like a kind of Midrash. In the first, dated June 1894, the mirror is seen as a "'skylight through which one might submerge himself in the true Abyss, which is the soul of man. The terrifying immensity of the firmament's abysses is an illusion, an external reflection of *our own* abysses, perceived "in a mirror"'" (L 210). The second, from November of the same year, apparently concerns a fanciful meditation on the Czar as "'the leader and spiritual father of a hundred fifty million men. . . . In the mysterious dispositions of the Profundity, who is really Czar, who is king, who can boast of being a mere servant?'" (L 210). The third, from a letter written in December, returns to Paul's "'enigma by means of a mirror'" and maintains that "'Everything is a symbol, even the most piercing pain. We are dreamers who shout in our sleep.'" The fourth is from May 1904. "'*Per speculum in aenigmate,* says St. Paul. We see everything backwards'" (L 210–11). The fifth is from May 1908. "'A terrifying idea of Jeanne's, about the text *Per speculum.* The pleasures of this world would be the torments of Hell, seen backwards, in a mirror'" (L 211).

The sixth is dated 1912; apparently concerned with "*L'Ame de Napoléon,*" the passage is made to illuminate another of the recurring preoccupations of Borges, the theme of "precursors": "another hero—man and symbol as well—who is hidden in the future." Borges quotes two passages from Bloy: (1) "'Every man is on earth to symbolize something he is ignorant of and to realize a particle or a mountain of the invisible . . . '"; and (2) "'There is no human being on earth capable of declaring with certitude who he is. No one knows what he has come into this world to do, . . . his sentiments, his ideas, or what his real name is. . . . History is an immense liturgical text where the iotas and the dots are worth no less than the entire verses or chapters, but the importance of one and the other is indeterminable and profoundly hidden'" (L 211).

The upshot of this tactic and these examples vindicates all those convinced that Borges is writing synoptically rather than "serially": the *simultaneity* of his six contexts not only constitutes a mode of knowledge but confirms the strategy of its magic. The insight they serve, however baffling their reversals and multiplications, composes like a mosaic in the "mirror" of the intended "enigma." In his own words, the six contexts taken together constitute an "angelic cryptography" for a "hieroglyphical world," and support a conviction which profoundly concerns the nature of all fictions, whether of art or of reality. They align Borges among the "heresiarchs" who "permute" words, "add up the numerical value of letters, consider their form, observe the small letters and capitals, seek acrostics and anagrams and perform other exegetical rigors . . ." (L 212).

In this respect, at least, Borges's position differs markedly from the enigmatic pluralism of Kafka's "Prometheus." It is as though, committed to the premise—impenetrable to Kafka—that all legend contains a "substratum of truth" and therefore must founder on the "inexplicable mass of rock," Borges has found a magical way out that turns him into an exegete of the inexplicable. With an incandescence unthinkable to Kafka's

Prometheans, he passes on to that "substratum" of numbers, letters, astrological and orthographical "rigors" where the "truths" of myth may be engaged as cryptograms interpretable by the elite, to whom it is given to crack codes without ever disclosing their "message" and to triumph over the "rock" by becoming custodians of the priestly tablets.

The effect is to deny the relevance of manifest meanings to the world: "It is doubtful that the world has a meaning. . . . *No man knows who he is.*" According to Borges, it is the purpose of fiction to render that ignorance *intimate*; to hold the mirror up, not to nature, but to the dream of the heart's conjunction with the world; to compel the heart to take up the "burden of the Mystery," each out of his own dream, and imagine the common dream of the world's knowledge. Like Kafka's questioner in "The Imperial Message," each may "sit at [his] window when evening falls and dream it to [himself]." Knowledge is a multiplication of instances, images, illusions (Blake's "minute particulars of mankind" or Yeats's "Path of the Chameleon"). Its tension lies in their coexistence, its insight in their contradictions. Only in a fictive complex of this nature can any "man know who he is"; and only by these signs can his "character" be absorbed into his collective humanity. Literature is greatest, "truest," most archetypal, when it is most enigmatic.

3

In this sense, the total canon of Jorge Luis Borges constitutes a "synopticon" of parables, a Kabbalah or *Book of Splendor* which repeats the lineaments of that Cosmological Man in whose limbs, says the *Zohar*, are incorporated all the attributes that pertain to being a man at large in an inscrutable cosmos. One is tempted to say of it, as Rabbi Simeon ben Yohai says of the hidden meaning of the Torah, "How precisely balanced are the upper and lower worlds!" and then add, "The garment is made up of tales and stones; but we are bound to penetrate beyond."[7] Touched at any point, Borges's work gives back the same geometrical pathos, "vertiginous symmetries," the same content of knowledge, the same dynamic of contradiction and diversity, the same secret, as though a single enigma were central to all, and all lines intersected at the center. It is as though Borges wrote of "forking paths," "circular ruins," lotteries, libraries, compasses, searches, miracles, spheres, avatars, mirrors, selves—gave us "everything and nothing"—in order to maximize the Unknown and confront it as we cannot in reality.

One case in point must suffice: for this purpose I have chosen the fable of "The God's Script." The prevailing image of "The God's Script" is *scribal*, if not actually orthographic. Its concern is with the *written* rather than the "whispered" word of Kafka's "The News of the Building of the Wall," and the writing is literally "hieroglyphical"—a "god's script," or a priest's. In this sense, it recapitulates the themes of "Tlön, Uqbar, Orbis Tertius," and "The Library of Babel"—the search for an "Ursprache," or absolute of gnomic discourse, which would contain in its very orthography the signature of the Unknown, which is also the signature of Borges himself.

It is significant that the place and the circumstance chosen for "The God's Script" is a prison—a circle divided by a wall, on one side of which sits, ponders, "perishes," a captive "magician of the pyramid," and on the other side of which a caged jaguar paces. Both are reiterated motifs of Borges's "destiny" as poet and artificer of the Labyrinth; but the conjunction of jaguar and magician is the uniquely mystifying economy of the present tale. Readers of Borges have long been familiar with the omnipresence of the feline principle—in its savage state—in the fictions and poems of his *oeuvre*. If writers can be assigned to tutelary animals, as totems of the scribal mysteries, the jaguar or tiger[8] is the sign of Jorge Luis Borges, as unmistakably as the burro presides over the fictions of Juan Ramon Jiménez and the bull over the domain of Greek tragedy, or, for that matter, Blake's "Tyger" over the prophecies of Golgonooza. Nor will readers of Kafka have to be reminded of the curious coincidence of three different parables that similarly unleash the "animal in the synagogue," the "leopards in the temple," and the tiger in the "training cage" of Burson, to stalk the unknown in feral ambiguity. All are heraldic beasts of the pre-verbal, guarding the fictive way.

The track of the tiger is seen again and again in the fictions of Borges. It is written into the total fable of Borges by Borges the poet, in the "three tigers" of "The Other Tiger," where it would appear that the "third tiger" is specifically enlisted for the fictive mysteries of "The God's Script":

> We'll hunt for a third tiger now, but like
> The others this one too will be a form
> Of what I dream, a structure of words, and not
> The flesh and bone tiger that beyond all myths
> Paces the earth.[9]

It is seen again in the conclusion of Borges's "New Refutation of Time": "Time is the substance I am made of. . . . it is a tiger which destroys me, but I am the tiger . . ." (L 234). It recurs in the guise of the "infinite Tiger" of the Muslim Fakir of "The Zahir": "This tiger was composed of many tigers in the most vertiginous fashion: it was traversed by tigers, scored by tigers, and it contained seas and Himalayas and armies which seemed to reveal still other tigers" (L 162). It stalks through the memory of Otto Dietrich zur Linde of the "Deutsches Requiem": "I can still repeat from memory many hexameters from that superb poem, *Tse Yang, Painter of Tigers*, which is, as it were, streaked with tigers, overburdened and crisscrossed with transversal and silent tigers" (L 144).

The jaguar of "The God's Script" belongs among the "silent tigers"; indeed, its posture seems heraldic, as well as hermetic, as if to give a certain opulence of design to an otherwise abstract and vortical composition. For Tzinacán, the magician of the pyramid of Qaholom, it seems to constitute no threat as, say, does the double door of Frank R. Stockton's " The Lady or the Tiger?" Indeed, Tzinacán comes to dwell on the presence of the jaguar last of all, among the many "anxieties" that "consume" him; and when he does so, he remembers him piously and "with pity" as "one of the attributes of the god." For a fleeting moment, one remembers the avidity of the leopards in Kafka's parable who "break into the temple and drink to the dregs what is in the sacrificial pitchers"; but these leopards also "become part of the ceremony" in a sacramental act of compassion.

The attention of Tzinacán, however, is fixed on other matters—terminal and eschatological matters, ultimately to be polarized, as the title suggests, in the calligraphy of a "single magical sentence," a "formula of fourteen words," "a single word," a "script" or alphabet of letters, or in a "single sound." All are recognizable permutations of the writer's predicament in the presence of the closure of *language*—a *written* language whose relation to knowledge as such still eludes the understanding—hence, a "prison."

Borges quickly dispenses with the "lateral" exigencies of his story. Time is at once excised from his fiction ("I have lost count of the years") and the antecedent circumstances, or what remains of them as "history," speedily dwindle to a point: "On the eve of the burning of the pyramid," the magician was tortured, his god was overturned, and he "awoke in this prison from which I shall not emerge in mortal life" (L 170). The remainder of the tale, vortical as Poe's "Descent into the Maelstrom," concerns the speculative anguish of the protagonist—the attempt on the part of Tzinacán to arrive at some terminal datum of knowledge by the magic of intellect. Its development would have to be called labyrinthine, for unlike Poe's rider of the Maelstrom, pitting his powers of ratiocination against a spatio-temporal deadline which steadily narrows the cycles of his descent by discernible laws of momentum, the predicament of Tzinacán is timeless, directionless, *stilled*. The mathematics of centripetality, so intriguing to Poe, accomplish nothing for the magician. His thinking is neither syllogistic nor serial; it is not even circular. It is, like the thought process in a Borges parable, synoptic and adventitious. It can be said to proceed in phases, bursts, ricochets; or else it spreads, like ink in blotting paper, and is suddenly folded over to reveal the enigmatic symmetry of the psyche.

The phases of Tzinacán's thinking, tangential and helic by turns, can be retraced as a kind of diagram of the enigmatic process. The first impulse of "the architect of the pyramid" is, understandably, a search for order and number; "the order and the number of stone-carved serpents or the precise form of a medicinal tree." Hours later, however, he senses that he is "approaching the threshold of an intimate recollection" as a "traveller feels a quickening in the blood." Instead of pressing for an order already present in art and nature, he "begins to perceive," in the free-flowing proliferations of his own psyche, "the outline of a recollection. It was the tradition of the god"—a god who "wrote on the first day of Creation a magical sentence" with the power to ward off all evil. As Borges goes on to explain, the god's sentence is secretive, infallible, and terminal—one of those "messages" Kafka ascribes to the Emperor of his parable, irresistibly intended for a single, elect listener, the destined vessel of the god's enigma. Of it, Tzinacán can say only, "No one knows where it was written nor with what characters, but it is certain that it exists, secretly, and that a chosen one shall read it." And he grasps at once that his own "destiny as the last priest of the god" is the "privilege of intuiting the script."

There follows what is described (characteristically) as "a kind of vertigo." Its appropriateness is at once apparent from the spiraling movement of his thought—the vatic "spreading of the inks" of sensibility and the intuitional thrust of his "magic." For a moment, he feels lost in the enormity of the Unknowable: "the generations of cereals, of grasses, of birds, of men." He remembers ancient forms, "any one [of which w]ould be the speech of the god"—mountains, rivers, empires, stars, "mutations and havoc." At the conclusion of the cycle, however, he is ready to predicate a "magic . . . written on my face, perhaps I myself was the end of my search" (L 170).

And then he remembers the jaguar.

4

Here we have what Borges might have called a "compass point" in the labyrinth, in which excitement spreads rapidly to all sides, and all composes itself with a kind of zodiacal fatality in the "sign of the jaguar." The intricacies of Borges's speculations need not be pursued in detail. What is important is the passion with which an image, ingenious and reckless in its conjunction of the visceral and the metaphysical, is pursued to its last shock of revelation. The image is that of a jaguar as cosmos—an enormous palimpsest into whose "living skin," as into a hieratic parchment, has been inscribed the design of the god. A host of possibilities is vertiginously suggested in the paragraphs that follow: that there is a secret "order and . . . configuration of the spots"; that the "black forms running through the yellow fur" constitute a single word, or even a single sound, a text to be deciphered, "a generic enigma," an "infinite concatenation of facts," a "divine sentence," "shadows or simulacra" of *all, world, universe*" (L 171).

At this point, parable, in its usual sense of enigmatic preachment, might be assumed to have accomplished its objectives. The remaining half of the story, however, seems bent on subverting its own closure, dislodging the structures of metaphor and allegory which are the triumph of its rational magic, magnifying chaos. The story swirls with contradictory and disjunct sensations: dream, nightmare, sleep, "indifference," suffocation, "loss," panic, death—the pathos and the dismemberment of the "heresiarch," the compulsive keeper of the heresies. The discharge is wildly visionary. One thinks of the recondite terrors of another voyeur of the hermetic way, William Butler Yeats, who under the "frenzy of the fourteenth moon" in his castle at Lough Key, became "lost in that region a cabalistic manuscript had warned me of," in which "image called up image in an endless procession and I could not choose among them with any confidence"; Yeats said he had strayed "upon the Path of the Chameleon, upon Hodos Chameliontos."[10]

Near the end of "The God's Script," Tzinacán wakes to a realization that might be called terminal if it were not so impenetrably ambivalent. On the one hand, he is aware that "More than a decipherer or an avenger, more than a priest of the god, I was one imprisoned. From the tireless labyrinth of dreams I returned as if to my home to the harsh prison. . . ." On the other hand, he is aware he has not "*awakened to wakefulness, but to a previous dream. This dream is enclosed within another, and so on to infinity . . .*" (L 172). He blesses the jaguar, blesses his "old, suffering body," blesses all the modes of closure that he had previously sought to transcend or transpose. He is content to "let the days obliterate" him in his prison, with its incomprehensible duality of jaguar and magician.

Here again, Borges might have settled for the pittance of an edifying conclusion. What actually follows is a shaking of the total fabric of the meaning—a "union with deity," an "ecstasy," a rending of the veils, a kind of doxology of visionary assertions. The language and the imagery are conventionally apocalyptical: blazing lights, wheels, roses, circles, fires—a lyric improvisation on the mystery of "origins," causes, and effects. But the effect is oddly conclusive. It is as though, having submitted to all closures, all modes of incarnate humanity, all incarcerations, all "prisons," the wall that divided the magician from the jaguar has been dissolved. Only then does the import of Borges's conjunction of jaguar and magician become clear, and the enigma of his prison surrender its secret. The "prison" is the *prison of language*, which divides magician and jaguar as language itself divides the artist from the fictions he would create or the message he would whisper. With the dissolution of the wall, language and fiction are made one. They join in an animal mystery and embody the god's enigma as a truth of immediate knowledge.

Borges's trope for the enigma is, of course, the "sign of the tiger." His secret purpose, inscribed into a corner of his composition, like a mandala or a watermark, promised the reader, midway in his story: "In the next cell there was a jaguar; in his vicinity I perceived a confirmation of my conjecture and a secret favor." At the conclusion of the story, the "favor" is apparent. It grips the reader like an intuition that illuminates the whole character of fictive writing. It suggests that all Borges's fictions are "tigers," and all literature a "teeming labyrinth of jaguars," repeating "the generic enigma of a sentence written by the gods," each in his own spots, "the black forms running through the yellow fur," to the cursive vanishing point of man's dream of knowledge.

It is this exuberance of *unknowing*, the almost predatory gusto of his conjunction with the Beast of Enigma, which distinguishes the fictions of Borges from the fictions of Kafka. Presumably, both enact the anguish of ungratified ignorance and the malaise of the anomalous predicament. In the case of Borges, it is a vertigo whose circuitions lead to magical breakthroughs of the psyche; with Kafka, it is a *nausée*, with no exit from the windowless room or the carapace of the cockroach. Both enter a labyrinth and toil toward some act of epistemological violence which leads to a prison, a circular ruin, a bestiary, a cathedral, a lumber room, a stone quarry. Both whisper messages out of range of our hearing—with a difference, however. One feels it first as a phenomenon of *tone*, or what Herbert Tauber calls the "atmosphere of silence and taciturnity" that haunts the desolation of Kafka: the despairing cold of cathedrals, courtrooms, corridors, attics, unpeopled streets lit only by a single, enigmatic window. By contrast, the world of Jorge Luis Borges, for all its patina of Anglo-European erudition, is Byzantine in its passion for arabesque and metaphysical mosaic. As Lorca would put it, his is the provenance of the Duende ("daemon") rather than the Angel or the Muse. For one, the sacred books remain sealed, the door of the Law slams shut, and the burrowing beast accomplishes marvels of self-entrenching panic. For the other, the Duende of the ambiguous points the way out toward those wheels of water and fire, the "faceless god concealed behind the other gods," and the "infinite processes that formed one single felicity," whereby Tzinacán, the magician of the pyramid, having understood all, can now understand the jaguar's inscription.

NOTES

1. E. M. Forster, *Aspects of the Novel* (New York: Harcourt, Brace, 1927).
2. Hans Vaihinger, *The Philosophy of "As If"* (New York: Barnes & Noble, 1966).
3. The extrapolations from the Collected Works of Nietzsche are from Hans Vaihinger's discussion of *The Will to Illusion*, in ibid., Part III, Section D, pp. 341–62.
4. All quotations from the parables of Kafka are from Franz Kafka, *Parables* (New York: Schocken Books, 1946), with translations by various hands.
5. Søren Kierkegaard, *Either/Or* (Princeton, N.J.: Princeton University Press, 1944), II, 135.
6. Jorge Luis Borges, *Labyrinths: Selected Stories and Other Writings*, ed. Donald A. Yates and James E. Irby (New York: New Directions, 1962), p. 199; hereafter, references to this volume will be indicated by the letter L and included inside parentheses in the text.
7. *Zohar: The Book of Splendor*, ed. Gershom Scholem (New York: Schocken Books, 1963), pp. 121–22.
8. *Tigre* is also the local Argentine word for jaguar.
9. Jorge Luis Borges, *Selected Poems, 1923–1967*, ed. Norman Thomas di Giovanni (New York: Delacorte, 1972), p. 131.
10. W. B. Yeats, *Autobiographies* (New York: Macmillan, 1927).

5

The Heraldry of Accommodation: A House for Mr. Naipaul

> Are we, perhaps, here just for saying: House . . . but for saying, remember, oh, for such saying as never the things themselves hoped so intensely to be?
>
> —Rainer Maria Rilke

THE HOUSE ON SIKKIM STREET

ONE IS TEMPTED, in reading V. S. Naipaul's *A House for Mr. Biswas*, to transform the routine mission of a realtor with more lucrative claims on his time and custom into the heraldic rhetoric of an older dispensation: "The House of Biswas." For realists schooled, like Naipaul, in the tactical trivialities of the quotidian, the move will doubtless seem ill-advised, grandiose. Not for nothing does his protagonist, halfway into a novel conspicuous for its total recall, invoke the name of Tom Sawyer and Huckleberry Finn and dwell on the "solace of Dickens" as a talisman for "everything he feared and suffered" in experience. The "good old-fashioned" commitment to "history"—the history of foundlings and hard knocks which characterize the rise of the English novel—the whole ontology of the autobiographical chronicler-scribe—is apparent in the scale and dawdle of Naipaul's conception. It is significant that the protagonist for whom a house must be found is, like David Copperfield, Ernest Pontifex, and Stephen Dedalus, a journalist of mediocre talents committed to a gospel of "REPORT NOT DISTORT!" and assigned to the "investigation of Deserving Destitution." His beat is the Neediest

Causes Fund; his chore, to "read the applications from Destitutes, reject the undeserving, visit the others to see how deserving or desperate they were," and grind out "harrowing accounts of their plight." His formula for testing a new typewriter is the failed first sentence: "At the age of thirty-three, when he was already the father of four children . . ." and his journalistic lead as drudge for "The Trinidad Sentinel" the melodramatic ploy: "Amazing scenes were witnessed yesterday when . . . Passersby stopped and stared yesterday when . . ."

Stylistically, Mr. Naipaul's novel similarly resists inflationary reading in the epic or mock-epic vein. Those familiar with the repertory of an *oeuvre* dazzling for its verbal sophistication and perfection of pace and pitch—*In A Free State, The Mimic Men, Guerrillas*—will read *A House for Mr. Biswas* as a tour-de-force of simulated *ordinariness* in which dialogue and narrative conspire to defeat the high style of heraldic discourse—all that jargon about "houses," "gules," heroic epithets, and sumptuous fatalities. Naipaul seems content with the barest necessities of narrative—a kind of fictive doggerel pluckily unpretentious and lackadaisical in its penchant for the simple declarative sentence and the substitution of quantitative detail for linguistic nuance. To all intents and purposes, the bread and bran of factual anecdote—durable, homespun, pedestrian—will do. The address is not Homeric or Tolstoyan or Dickensian: indeed, the casual reader might be ready to dismiss it as Brahminized Arnold Bennett, with a hearty mix of storytelling staples aimed at survival over the long haul. The same holds true for the dialogue. Behind the basic Trinidadian which furnishes the patois of the Port-of-Spaniard may be heard a Hindi transcription of Huckleberry Finn, wise in the ways of the street and the anglified colonial, slurring in syntax, *echt pidgin*, colloquial:

> "Afternoon, boss."
> "Haul your tail. Who the hell tell you you could lay your hand on my son?"
> "Son, boss?"
> "He try to thief my money," Anand said.
> "Was a game," the fat man said.
> "Haul off!" Mr. Biswas said. "Job! You not looking for any job."
> "You not getting any, either."

"But boss," the younger man said. "Mr. Seth say he did tell you."
"Didn't tell me nothing."
"But Mr. Seth say—" the fat man said.
"Leave them alone, Dinnoo," the younger man said.
"Father and blasted son."
"Is in the blood," the fat man said.
"You mind your mouth," Mr. Biswas shouted.
"Tscha!"

Then why talk of "heraldic" equivalents at all in such an embarrassment of paucity? Why try to retrieve for *A House for Mr. Biswas* the high style of anagogical myth if Naipaul's intent is to avoid the aggrandizement of persons, places, and things as implacably as Joyce sought to enlist them? Why not stick to the vulgate of a modest and dreary undertaking, since Naipaul himself, with a whole palette of European colors and the knowledgeability of a curator, was content with the monochromatic? The most plaintive of all possible answers would be the dogged insistence: "Because it is there!" It is there in the cumulative subtlety and curettage of Naipaul's skills as a connoisseur in narration, a hewer of character, and a shaper of actions. In Naipaul's hands, tact, fact, bulk, transparency, patience, are not only equal to themselves but equal to something more massive; and the bounding coordinates of compassion and irony, scaled low to fit the rhetoric, kindle the whole of a filial vision, pointing the gaze outward, like vibration in painting. There is no doubting the depth of Naipaul's intention in the curiously ebullient tale of the housing and unhousing of an ancestor: all roads lead to an Ithaca of sorts, as in Joyce, and the augmenting tensions of the chapters are doxological as well as elegiac. Though he writes without program and does not wait for epiphanies along the way, like Joyce, "amazing scenes have been witnessed." The passerby has "stopped and stared." Between jest and earnest, pathos and the saturnine, a house has been established which already guarantees the successions of its present chronicler; and Biswas, at length on his Slumberking mattress, between the Colonial Hospital and a "dangerous" staircase in Port of Spain, with only ten weeks to live, has had his vision:

> Bigger than them all was the house, his house. How terrible it would have been, at this time, to be without it; to have died

among the Tulsis, amid the squalor of that large, disintegrating, and indifferent family; to have left Shama and the children among them, in one room; worse, to have lived without even attempting to lay claim to one's portion of the earth; to have lived and died as one had been born, *unnecessary and unaccommodated.*

The culminating words of Naipaul's "Prologue" carry the shock of unexpected eloquence. They not only break out of the "low style" to more complex considerations of "necessity" and "accommodation," but compel closer scrutiny of the Prologue as a whole. "Accommodation," as Lear was to learn, is a corollary of the motif of Status writ large; and it is hardly likely that Naipaul has missed any of the vagaries and innuendoes which cling to the heraldry of "housing." Politics gives us Houses of Representatives and Bishops; theology gives us houses of bread (Bethlehem) and Pauline metaphors of somatic sanctity; astrology gives us zodiacal houses; books bring us to publishing houses, fornication to brothels, theaters to audiences, literature to a House of Atreus or a *House of Fame*, or a poet's parlance for prayer ("For we unhouse and house the Lord"); and nautical usage to lighthouses or to concepts of anchorage in secure places. All are strategies of "necessity and accommodation"; all postulate scale, breadth, status, shelter, encompassment. closure.

Thus, the whole of Naipaul's novel, "housed" between its Prologue and Epilogue, may be viewed anagogically as Naipaul views its division into parts and subtitles: "Pastoral," "The Chase," "Green Vale," "'Amazing Scenes,'" "Among the Readers and Learners," "The Void," "The Revolution," and, finally, "The House." Page by page, the house for Mr. Biswas casts a longer and longer shadow. Colors and ironies multiply rapidly in the nondescript grays of the narrative matrix, take on the sweep of a Proustian *ouverture* or the "skeleton key" to a personal mythology as full of perils and enchantments as the *Odyssey* or *Don Quixote*. In the House of Biswas one sees, or thinks one sees, caverns and windmills, Telemachan quests for a father-figure, heraldic houses in search of their spiritual franchise. One remembers the cleansings of The House of Dedalus and Atreus, the fantasies of the bat-winged Thoth, god of writing, the *History of Tom Jones, Foundling*, and *The Adventures of Huckleberry Finn*, the bohemian rebellions of Tonio Kroger, the magical buffooneries of the crafty ("He is a real smart man. You better keep an eye on him, Bhandat!") Odysseus.

Yet returning to Naipaul's Prologue to *A House for Mr. Biswas*, one finds that it is everything that Forster's mythopoeic prologue to *Passage to India* is *not*: unlapidary, unmysterious, toneless, *interior*. It is not concerned with aggrandizing landscapes—or houses—for the reincarnation of a god. It fixes on the locative case reduced to a point of maximum closure: a "portion of the earth" vaguely felt to be a "claim," lebensraum for a failed and fantastical nonentity—a "house for Mr. Biswas." Beginning with an architect's scrawl for the house on Sikkim Street, it turns the last "portion of the earth" left the sacked and convalescent Biswas—all that he once deemed "wondrous," "audacious," "stupendous"—into a travesty of hapless improvisation. From the outset, Naipaul's touch is ruthless in its conversion of pharaonic innuendo into a "squat sentry box, tall, square, two-storeyed, with a pyramidal roof of corrugated iron . . . assembled mainly from frames from the dismantled American Army camps at Docksite, Pompeii Savannahs, and Fort Read." Into that pleasaunce of pyramids, savannahs, volcanic fallout, and colonial rubble, the satirist's crayon slashes a doorway without a door, a concrete shower-room "perpetually wet," western exposures with "no protection from the sun," thresholds "punched into the eastern wall," a stairway of heavy planks "hung precariously at the back of the house" in lieu of a forgotten "staircase to link both floors," four years of unpaid mortgages, and an exorbitant asking price of $5,300.

Naipaul then passes from functional aspects of shelter—rooms, staircases, verandas, kitchens, furniture—to a history of houses, a heraldry of orphanage and deracination in the purest sense of the word: the rootings and uprootings of a *fliegender Indianer* "condemned," with a wife and a family of four, to a single cell of the familial ziggurat "crowded with Shama's sisters, their husbands, their children." "As a boy," we read, "he had moved from one house of strangers to another; and since his marriage [to Shama] he felt he had lived nowhere but in the houses of the Tulsis, at Hanuman House in Arwacas, in the decaying wooden house at Shorthills, in the clumsy concrete house in Port of Spain." Pasha-like, in "pants and vest on the Slumberking bed in the room which contained most of the possessions he had gathered after forty-one years," reading the *Meditations* of Marcus Aurelius, Biswas luxuriates in the laral magic of his transformation of status, like a proper bourgeois:

> What a change from those backyards, overrun with chickens and children, to a drawing room made . . . as cozy and rich as something in an advertisement! What a change from the Tulsi's house!

Yet his dream of a "readymade world" in which "every relationship, every possession" is dedicated to the rediscovery of "pleasure, surprise, disbelief" is already caught in the trivial wear and tear of things:

> The very day the house was bought they began to see the flaws in it. The staircase was dangerous; the upper floors sagged; there was no back door; most of the windows didn't close; one door could not open; the colotex panels under the eaves had fallen out and left gaps between which bats could enter the attic . . . the sawdust stuck to your hand when you passed it along the shelves.

To say that Mr. Biswas is assailed by classical postulates of thermodynamics is precisely what the low threshold of Naipaul's rhetoric does not permit. Time does not pass in the house of Mr. Biswas as it does in Bergson or in the hourglass section of Virginia Woolf's *To the Lighthouse*; its touch does not appear "unimaginable," as in Wordsworth. On the contrary, the emphasis of Naipaul's very plain prose is on second- and third-hand tackiness, mediocrity, the conspicuous expendability of the jerrybuilt. ("'Jerrybuilder!'" Biswas is to cry on the first afternoon of his occupancy of the house on Sikkim Street: "'Tout! Crook! Nazi and blasted Communist!'") For all its "solid, respectable, modern front," the house of Biswas offers only the most perishable of façades, a cut above the "crude wooden things in the country not much better than huts," but already cursed with pillars that "rested on no foundation," and marked for obsolescence in the catabolism of the slum. "Sewer pipes had not been laid down in this part of the city. . . . the septic tank became choked. . . . The lavatory bowl filled and bubbled." The universal corrosion of iron and cement which epitomizes the colonial way in all the fictions of Naipaul—Jimmy Ahmed's Caribbean Commune for "guerrillas," the Collectorate of Ogguna Wanga Butere in the "free state" of South Africa, the cocoa plantations of Ralph

Singh, the "mimic man" of the New World, "pretending to be real," the "Domain" of the poor man's Brazilia in *A Bend in the River*—threaten the house on Sikkim Street with similar desuetude and "disorder."

But Mr. Biswas, in the end, does not see himself as either threatened or deluded. In his fond, backward look, the levées of the Slumberking persist, as the fantasy of knightly encounter with giants persists in the mind of the ailing Quixote. "It was astonishing," we read,

> how quickly [his] disappointment faded, how quickly *they had accommodated themselves* to every peculiarity and awkwardness of the house. And once that had happened, their eyes ceased to be critical, and the house became simply their house. . . . Now, at the end he found himself in his own house, on his own half lot, his own portion of the earth. That he should have been responsible for this seemed to him, in these last months, stupendous.

Even in Naipaul's unsparing Epilogue, where the sum of negations is tallied with an assessor's eye for deteriorative havoc, and decorum demands the pre-emption of all sentiment, there is no hint of a Fall of the House of Biswas. The debt remains, $4,000, "like a buffer at the end of a track"; the zest goes out of his hackwork for "The Trinidad Sentinel"; he is forbidden to climb staircases in the aftermath of a heart attack; he is put on half-pay and then terminally sacked. He grows puffy, lethargic, distempered: but we read, in so many words, "the doors at the house were open"—in invitation rather than default—"everything seemed to grow bright," "the house did not fall."

The Houses of the Tulsis

The point in these circuitous declensions is that the house on Sikkim Street marks the beginning of a dynasty, and, with a pinch of the satirist's salt, merits the epithet of "heraldic." Behind the dynastic myth lies a long legend of houses, jostling one another and subdividing like ice fields, which are viewed collectively by both Naipaul and Mr. Biswas as "houses of the Tulsis." They exist in a curious aura of *simultaneity*, as the Sphinx and the pyramids of Gizeh may seem to be simultaneous when viewed in a single *coup d'oeil* in the total ambiance of a desert. Actually, the movement of the narrative is labyrinthine: from Hanuman House, to the "decaying wooden houses in Shorthills," to the "clumsy concrete house in Port of Spain," with deflections into the "barrack-like" compounds of Green Vale and the mud huts of The Chase—all "houses of the Tulsis": a series of hegiras, expulsions, repatriations, which cast Mr. Biswas out upon the world and draw him back into the tribal maw with a dreamlike vagrancy.

At the center of Naipaul's fiction lies Hanuman House itself, intact over its hoard of familial "accommodations," like a dragon on a magical treasure, alternately expelling and reassembling the unplaceable Mr. Biswas. It must matter to satirists that the House is named after "the benevolent monkey-god, Hanuman," whose concrete statue drolly crowns its balustrade; that its ground floor contains the unlikely Hanuman Store which replenishes the dragon-hoard of the Tulsis; that its founder was the Pundit Tulsi, whose family once flourished in India, but whom local legend has reduced to "an irreverent and extremely popular song" and "a creature of fiction"; that it is now ruled jointly by an avuncular mother-in-law and a tribal entrepreneur "dressed more like a plantation overseer than a store manager." For the casual reader, the effect will be oneiric, Protean, contradictory. For Mr. Biswas himself, its "splendours," recalled by his over-awed mother in the first days of his courtship, are literally illusory:

> She described a house he hardly knew. She spoke of a drawing-room with two tall thronelike mahogany chairs, potted palms and ferns in huge brass vases on marble-topped tables, religious paintings, and many pieces of Hindi sculpture. She spoke of a prayer-room above that, which, with its slender columns, was like a temple.

For Naipaul, opening his chapter on "The Tulsis," it is:

> an alien white fortress. The concrete walls looked as thick as they were, and when the narrow doors of the Tulsi Store on the ground floor were closed, the House became bulky, impregnable, and blank. The side walls were windowless, and on the upper two floors the windows were mere slits in the facade.

From here on, the ambiguities multiply rapidly in the nap of the narrative. We learn that within the troglodytic compounding of caverns and middens, there are areas "reserved for the visitors," verandahs that enclose or encircle or expand dreamily on a universe of orphans, an innermost recess, like the harems of the Alhambra, inhabited by the male heirs of Mrs. Tulsi, presiding over the morning *puja* in *dhoti* and miniature caste marks but destined for European colleges, contemptuously invoked by the unregenerate Biswas as "the gods." When Mrs. Tulsi, whose lot it is to "faint often" and unpredictably, is stricken with her mysterious indisposition, a "Rose Room" full of "basins and quaint jugs and tubes and smells" opens up to receive her and a cadre of daughters soak her in bay rum" from the soles of her feet to her shoulders," like attendant houris. There is a prayer room, a drawing room, a Book Room including a copy of *Collins Clear-Type Shakespeare* and a shelfful of Mr. Biswas's consolatory library of mentors, a "Blue Room," where he is conveyed in the aftermath of a nervous breakdown and plied with spoonfuls of Ferrol and Ovaltine; and an unfathomable system of single cells as random as a termite's trail, where whole configurations of the Tulsis pullulate covertly like larvae. Biswas himself, condemned "to be a wanderer with no place he could call his own, with no family except that which he was to attempt to create out of the engulfing world of the Tulsis," is assigned to "the long room," where, together with his bride, "the thorough Tulsi, the antagonist the family had assigned him," he lives "beseiged by sleepers" in a wilderness of bedrooms, plotting "revenge."

The ambivalence of Biswas as a latecomer to the karma of the Tulsis is perhaps Naipaul's most whimsical evocation in the long comedy of dispossession. There is something phantasmagoric about his characteristic mix of skepticism, rebellion, and fantasy, something that alternately dilates and contracts like a cat's eye, as "necessity" and "accommodation" compete in the swirling fiction for the "peaceful persuasion" of a heresiarch. The effect is Kafka-like: one remembers the claustrophobic rebellions of Joseph K in the lumber-room of the Whippers, the capsized cockroach in "The Metamorphosis," the tunneling mole, "besieged" by sinister scufflings in "The Burrow." Burrowing in the Hanuman subsoil, in his first spelunkal phase, Biswas glimpses order in chaos:

> Though Hanuman House had at first seemed chaotic, it was not long before Mr. Biswas had seen that in reality it was ordered,

with degrees of precedence all the way down, with Chinta below Padma, Shama below Chinta, Savi below Shama, and himself far below Savi. . . . He saw that in this communal organization children were regarded as assets, a source of future wealth and influence.

When he is cast out into "The Void" to "paddle his own canoe" as journeyman "sign-writer" and painter of hummingbirds, petty shopkeeper, sub-overseer for the Tulsi estates, and, finally, feature-writer for "The Trinidad Sentinel," he returns to the honeycomb with disaffected changes of heart. In his truces with the Tulsis, Hanuman House becomes a "world more real than The Chase, and less exposed; everything beyond its gates was foreign and unimportant, and could be ignored. He needed a sanctuary. . . . He could go to Hanuman House whenever he wished and become lost in the crowd." With the passage of further time, indifference turns into acceptance and he is "pleased and surprised to find that he . . . had a certain license." Meanwhile, the fortunes of Hanuman House decline dizzyingly. Marriage takes away one wave of the children; the elder "god" is absorbed into a "laxly Presbyterian family with one filling station, two lorries, a cinema, and some land." Mrs. Tulsi disappears into the Rose Room, "devising economies and issuing directives about food," a "cantankerous invalid." There is talk of abandoning the House for a new estate at Shorthills in the mountains northeast of Port of Spain. The marble-topped tables are overturned. The brass vases are dented. Tenements and stores are sublet to a changing order of overseers, and the exodus of the Tulsis is accomplished.

Naipaul's unfailing inflection in all this remains curiously high-spirited, feisty rather than lachrymose. It is obvious that he has taken his tone from the antic Biswas himself—the "paddling-addling" buffoon for whom, whatever his "brain-fags" and terrors of The Void, Hanuman House was always the "monkey house. . . . Eh, monkey, bull, cow, hen. The place is a blasted zoo, man. . . . You have one concrete monkey-god outside the house and two living ones inside." It is Biswas who turns his back on "the Hindu delight in tragedy" and jeers at the cremation songs of the Tulsis. Jolting the sancrosanctity of Arwacas, Biswas the madhouse voyeur, jerrybuilder, parodist, journalistic jongleur, "insuranburner," amateur impersonator with a repertory extending from Quasimodo and the Scarlet Pimpernel to Samuel

Smiles and Huckleberry Finn, prevails by the grace of Naipaul—and vice versa. For all his European glooms Naipaul presses his fantasy of an ancestral "stick-fighter" waging his "little wars" in the shadow of Marcus Aurelius and Epictetus, and trailing the panache of his "Mr." from one end of the chronicle to the other, unsullied.

Yet it would be wrong to settle for a Cervantine mutation of the Knight of the Mournful Countenance with Hindu overtones. Apocalyptic comedy is not the concern of Naipaul; but the grinding pieties of survival in the world's "craziness" is; and in this respect the example of Cervantes has not been wasted. Readers of *A House for Mr. Biswas* are not likely to remember it as a "divan" of a thousand-and-one fables, but as a tragicomedy of the picaresque and a search for one man's privacy. The whole heraldry of "accommodation" is there, with its collective emphasis on archetypes of "shelter," "status," "sanctuary," and the rest of it; but it is the burrowings and the night-sweats of an unaccommodated man that give the fiction of Naipaul its special reverberation. One remembers Lear's: "Unaccommodated man is no more but such a poor, bare, forked animal as thou art." The novel frightens as well as entertains, piling the terrors high in chapter after chapter; it works over and under the comedy, deadly serious, turning everything *solitary* and holding all to the scale one expects of a deeply conservative masterwork in a major genre. For all the amenities and endearments of its unemphatic hero, it is Biswas *alone* in a "black void" mauled by a tropical downpour that one remembers:

> Wind swept through the room with unnecessary strength and forced open the door to the drawing room, wall-less, floorless, of the house Mr. Biswas built.

Biswas *alone* in the aftermath of his expulsion:

> The darkness, the silence, the absence of the world enveloped and comforted him. At some far-off time he had suffered great anguish. He had fought against it. Now he surrendered, and this surrender had brought peace. He had controlled his disgust and fear when the men had come for him. He was glad he had. Surrender had removed the world of damp walls and paper-covered walls, of hot sun and driving rain, and had brought this: this worldless room, this nothingness.

Biswas *alone* in his last confrontation with the Tulsis:

> "The old bitch can't throw me out like that," Mr. Biswas said. "I still have some rights. She has got to provide me with alternative accommodations." And: "Die, you bitch!" he hissed towards the verandahs. "Die! . . . The Tulsi sleeping-bags! Patents applied for! Die, you old bitch!"

The fact that he keeps blithe in the midst of corroding vicissitude, that he pounds away on his yellow typewriter the very caricature of the headline his death might elicit from "The Trinidad Sentinel" in its "more boisterous days": "ROVING REPORTER PASSES ON"; the whole spoor-trail of his earned or vicarious "housings"—including the smashed dollhouse bought for his daughter, Savi, in the Green Vale phase of his dispossession—cannot lighten the gravity of a harrowing dénouement. It must be more than a coincidence that "B/is/was" conceals the third person singular of the verb "to be" in both its present and its past tenses and plays back like a pun on "Finn/egan's/Wake"; that both Hanuman House and his given name of Mohun are virtual anagrams of the word *human*. In the House of Biswas necessity and accommodation have been played to a dead heat, and the keystone to a total *oeuvre* has been laid in the concrete and corrugated iron of a life's fiction.

A House for Mr. Naipaul

What remains to be said for that fiction at this point, or, more crassly, what's in it for the next generation of Naipaul's readers? Nothing less, I would say, than a vaulting perspective on the vocation of a novelist for whom character and obsession are interchangeable principles, and accomplish marvels of orientation. Read in the light of *A House for Mr. Biswas*, all Naipaul's novels—or at least those chosen at random for this essay—begin to show their "houses" or converge in a central wasplike configuration, like a Mohammedan ceiling. The permutations of the unaccommodated man are too intricate to labor further; but, somewhere, graduate students are computing the further heraldry of Biswas's dispossession. They will see, for example, that the "little wars" of James Ahmed in *Guerrillas* are inseparable from the basic demand for accommodation in the world's rotundity that embodies Mr. Biswas's dream of "freedom." Searching the successions of Ahmed's fiction, they will come upon "Thrushcross Grange" (out of Brontë, of course!) and his "People's Commune for the Land and the Revolution," and know they are in another of Naipaul's whimsical houses, circled by "unpainted boxes of concrete and corrugated iron already returning to the shantytowns that had been knocked down for this development." They will watch for the expected incursion of magic on the general "wrongness of the world," the addition of "succubi," unplaceable islands, schizophrenic journals, to the raga-tune of Biswas, and recognize the enlargement of solitude and the politicalization of terror. It should not surprise them to come upon precisely the passage any non-Islamic pietist would invoke in the name of Biswas, midway in the mock-fiction of Jimmy Ahmed:

> In my father's house there are many mansions. . . . But the house is full up, now, Roy, there are no more mansions. I suppose like everybody else I fooled myself that there was a mansion waiting somewhere for me, but I didn't really fool myself. . . . Even when I was a child going to school from the back room as the only place I come from in the great wide world, it wasn't mine, I always knew I was fooling myself, I didn't believe there would ever be any mansions for me. . . . I knew there was no mansion, it was all going to end in smoke.

Similarly, *The Mimic Men* may be viewed as a veritable constellation of houses, rooms, private hotels, pensions, colonies, ancestral plantations that bound the exile of a Caribbean colonial living "between the alarm of a world without end and a world without point," writing from "a tall, multi-mirrored, book-shaped room with a coffin-like wardrobe" in London. Ralph Singh's image for his predicament is the islander's image of "shipwreck"; but the heraldry of dispossession repeats the same, multifaceted longing for sanctuary that haunted the fantasy of Mr. Biswas and brought him to the house on Sikkim Street. For Ralph Singh, the search for "that center of stillness, that withdrawal" begins with a hallucination far removed from the minimal needs of Mr. Biswas:

> It would have been, as I have said, in the evening of my days. Life lived, endeavor past, the chances taken. My place of retirement an

old cocoa estate, one of our rundown former slave plantations blighted by witchbroom, not bringing in an income likely to revive any acquisitive anxiety. Myself installed in the old timber estate, house grey, its corrugated iron roof painted in stripes of faded red and white, the wide, low-eaved verandahs hung with cooling ferns, the floors dark and worn and shining. Everywhere there would have been the smell of old timber and wax; everywhere the eye would have found pleasure in fashioned wood, in the white fretwork arabesques above doorways, the folding screens between drawing room and dining room, the tall panelled doors.

Midway in the story it collides with a child's memory of the island haven of his grandmother:

> I tested it whenever I went there for the weekend. I jumped on the floors when I thought no one was looking; and sometimes I lay flat on them to gauge their level. I leaned against walls to assess their straightness. The precautions made me feel safe and sent me to bed without fear. I did not like returning to the physical dangers of my own house, about which I could talk to no one. I longed for the time when I would not have to make that particular journey. I thought that this absurd disorder, of placelessness, was part of youth and my general unease. . . . It was unease of just this sort which came to me when I began this book. There was then no fear of the collapse of either the hotel or the public house between which I divided my time—as I still divide it—but I sickeningly recognized that sense of captivity and lurking external threat, that pain of a rich world destroyed and rendered null.

For his "accommodative" center, Singh chooses the "Roman House" at Crippleville—just as Jimmy focused his disgust and nostalgia on Thrushcross Grange, or Biswas was periodically devoured and disgorged by Hanuman House:

> It was one of those large timber townhouses of the old colonial period, slightly decaying in spite of its modern kitchen. We both thought it attractive but for some reason we had never succeeded in colonizing it. Large areas of it remained empty; it felt like a rented house, which was soon to go back to its true owner. It had never seemed important to us to have a house of our own. . . . Still, to build a house seemed the thing to do; to continue living in an old rented house was beginning to appear ostentatious. I was looking through a picture book about Pompeii and Herculaneum.

> I was struck by the simplicity of the Roman house, its outward austerity, its inner private magnificence. I was struck by its suitability to our climate; I yielded to impulse.

In all cases, the Biswas syndrome repeats itself—aggrandized to multinational proportions and projected upon "the contamination of the wider world"—with obsessive repetitions of the old motifs: "failure," "deficiency," "disorder, placelessness, collapse," "shipwreck," "a house reduced to rubble," "radical danger"; and its complementary dream of "decorum, calm, order of a sort," "a placidity at the heart of celebration."

Even when Naipaul stoops to pastiche as in his "fantasy for a small screen" "specially written for a film company"—something "musical and comic set in the Caribbean" with "much sex and much dialogue"—the cynical reprise is unmistakable. On page two of *A Flag on the Island*, the middle-aged Frankie, revisiting his island base twenty years after its American occupation, confesses himself "jumpy, irritated, unsatisfied, suddenly incomplete": "All landscapes are in the end only in the imagination," he writes; "to be faced with the reality is to start again. . . . This is part of my mood; it heightens my anxiety. I feel the whole world is being washed away and that I am being washed away with it. I feel my time is short." Taking a cab to a forgotten address where he "expected and feared to find a house," he finds only "an *empty* lot."

> "What are you looking for?" the taxi driver asked.
> "My house."
> "You sure you left it here? That was a damned careless thing to do."
> "They've pulled down my house."
> "The house not here," the taxi driver said.
> "What you looking for?"
> "An explanation."

Or he recalls the dismantling of an islander's house in the old days, with an eerie sense of "degradation" and "fairy tale":

> The pillars were knocked down, and where the old wooden house stood there presently began to rise a house of patterned concrete blocks. The house, I could see, was going to be like hundreds of

others in the city: three bedrooms, down one side, a verandah, drawingroom and dining room down the other side, and a back verandah . . . frame by frame, jalousie by jalousie, the house was dismantled and reerected far away by the man who bought it, somewhere in the country.

Here it is a fellow tourist who is left to repeat the exasperated epilogue of Biswas: "'It's like a zoo!' the woman said"; while the connoisseur in Naipaul, reading over her shoulder, is likely to add: "or a 'shipwreck!'"

Obviously, fiction is a house of many mansions, and somewhere there must be a house for Mr. Naipaul; but where? Does the vision of V. S. Naipaul choose the "mansion" of Mr. Biswas as its model, and is there any evidence of that "placidity at the heart of celebration"? Up to now, Naipaul's critics, including those who consider him "the finest living novelist writing in English," have stressed only the negative consequences of his commitment and flinched at its unaccommodating rigors. In varying keys and degrees, they have noted the ingrown recalcitrance of his stance as a comparativist concerned with the conscience of the world and a novelist who owes it an ameliorative vote of good will—as Biswas felt he did, They have dwelt at length upon the exacerbations of V. S. Naipaul, the "bitterness" of his fictive equations, the Swiftian misanthropy of his insistence on the unteachability of the species. For some, his virulence has constituted a kind of heroism in the face of utopian compromise, a determination, like Timon's or Coriolanus's, to reject all token offers and stand by the letter of his implacability. For others, it has squarely blocked the way to the fulfillment of a global talent and limited the efficacy of its philosophical options. The increasing perversion of Naipaul's vision, some would say, is apparent in the curious addition of sexual deviance to both sides of the Asiatic equation—Jimmy Ahmed in *Guerrillas* and Bobby of the English Collectorate in *In a Free State*: the polyglot rapists, sodomists, and pederasts of the colonies whom Biswas, for one, never dreamed of.

Apparently, the little raga-tunes of Mr. Biswas, sad and plucky by turns, are not for Mr. Naipaul. On the whole, he has preferred to live "in a free state," like Bobby and Linda in the little masterpiece that bears that name—constantly on the go between the compounds and the hinterlands, threatened by guerrillas and incomprehensible ash-covered runaways, placelessly fleeing the fallout, in jeopardy. In the anonymous islands he has conjured out of the Caribbean and colonial Africa, there is always news of warring kings and miscegenative messiahs tunneling under and over "the free state": a no man's land between the capital and the compound where petty officialdom thrives in comparative safety and tastes the sanctuarial joys of sexual license and martinis. At large, however, on the open road to the "free state," Naipaul reminds us, there are roadblocks, rumors, armies on the move, regicides. "In the end you don't know what you feel about anything. All you know is that you want to be safe in the compound."

It is there, at the furthest possible remove from Hanuman House, that Naipaul has taken his stand and multiplied his unregenerate fictions in the free state of his discontents. But even Hanuman House, it will be remembered, "stood like an alien white *fortress*" in the omniscient third-person of its narrator. The house on Sikkim Street was seen by Naipaul as "a squat *sentry box*," a booby-trap of architectural perils, and the newspaper for whose pages Mr. Biswas invented the "amazing scenes" of his island universe, was called "The Trinidad *Sentinel*." Similarly, Naipaul has prepared his threatening fables as Bobby, in his nondescript hotel between the capitals and the compounds, prepares his emergency "getaways":

> Intruders: there might have been a crisis, and he might have been without his car, trapped. He decided then to pack, to be ready at any time for a swift getaway. He arranged, around a chair, everything he would need: packed suitcase, trousers, the yellow native shirt, shoes and socks. He went to bed in his vest and underpants. It was pointless, even a little deranged; it was the behaviour of the compound.

If readiness is all, Naipaul's posture in the changing hazards of his narrative is always *Qui Vive?* as is proper for the constitutional guerrillista. All his fictive accommodations are provisional; and he would probably say in the end, with Saint Augustine, in the same exigency of spirit: "Place there is none. We go backward and forward, and there is no place."

It would appear from his most recent novel, *A Bend in the River* (1979)—extraordinary for the saturative detachment of its fictive procedure and the systematic annihilation of every human option for collective and individual enfranchisement—that even the "little wars" of the polyglot man are destined for extinction. Here, the accommodative vacuum is confined no longer to a single house or a compound, but to the satrapy of the Big Man and his "radicalized" flunkies—the new "Domain" in "the bend in the river," in which models of jerrybuilt "progressivism" ostensibly devoted to the good life and European high-rises, wither into tropical disuse. The very first sentence of the opening page sounds the note of doomed initiative which consumes each of its protagonists in turn and delivers whole households to the "trusteeship" of their subordinates, the commissars of "preventive detention": "The world is what it is; men who are nothing, who allow themselves to become nothing, have no place in it."

Similarly the façades of the "new Domain," for all their specious modernity have the recognizable look of all the halfway houses in the repertory of V. S. Naipaul:

> The larger buildings of the Domain were startling—concrete louvres, pierced concrete blocks of great size, tinted glass. The smaller buildings—houses and bungalows—were more like what we were used to. But even they were on the large side and, with air conditioners sticking out in many places like building blocks that had slipped, looked extravagant. . . . But what was the Domain to be used for? The buildings gave pride, or were meant to, they satisfied some personal need of the President's. Was that all they were for? But they had consumed millions. The farm did not materialize. The Chinese or the Taiwanese didn't turn up to till the land of the new model African farm; the six tractors that some foreign government had given remained in a neat line in the open and rusted, and the grass grew high about them. The big swimming pool near the building that was said to be a conference hall developed leaks and remained empty, with a wide-meshed rope net at the top. The Domain had been built fast, and in the sun and the rain decay also came fast. After the first rainy season many of the young trees that had been planted beside the wide main avenue died, their roots waterlogged and rotted. . . . The Domain, with its shoddy grandeur, was a hoax.

Again, the protagonist who presides over a contained and unsparing narrative in the first person singular, Mis' Salim, describes himself as a "foreigner, someone from the far-off coast, and an English-speaker"—a Muslim whose forebears had called Africa their home for centuries but who were "really people from the Indian Ocean," "distinct from the Arabs and other Moslems of the coast," and, indeed, "closer to the Hindus of Northwestern India," at large in the mongrelized limbo of an "Arab-Indian-Persian-Portuguese place." Salim's mood is, again, one of ambivalent "pessimism" and "insecurity"; he writes as an alien with "no family, no flag, no fetish," picking his "unprotected" way in the police state of Bigburger franchises, polytechnic cadets, in the aftermath of the Second Rebellion, in search of a "middle way."

In the end his liquidation achieves an epitome of deracination unmatched in the fictions of Naipaul. The small shop in which for six years he has dispensed "pencils and copybooks, razor blades, syringes, soap and toothpaste and toothbrushes, cloth, plastic toys, iron pots and aluminum pans, enamel plates and basins" is confiscated by a demotic ploy of the President's, and the two youthful charges for whom he has functioned as master, employer, and guardian, are dispersed. Visiting a London to which he "had come back for relief and rescue, clinging to what remained of our organized life," he is driven "back to my hotel room in an agony of solitude and dread"; and returned to the Domain, he is jailed by a "free state" from which the last vestiges of suffrage have been bled dry. The final page finds him, literally adrift on a small steamer, with its searchlights turned off, a "foreigner who was leaving" an unplaceable "bend in the river," within earshot of its custodial guns, on his way to nowhere.

Perhaps the widest possible extension of Naipaul's grievances as a prodigal in search of accommodation occurs in his chronicle of *India: A Wounded Civilization*. Of India itself, which he visited for the first time at the age of thirty in 1962, he says:

> India is for me a difficult country. It isn't my home and cannot be my home, and yet I cannot reject it or be indifferent to it; I cannot travel only for the sights. I am at once too close and too far. My ancestors migrated from the Gangetic plain a hundred years ago . . . and established in Trinidad, on the other side of the world, the community in which I grew up.

Re-examining with a skeptical eye the Islamic amalgam of "nonviolence or non-doing," "karma, the Hindu killer, the Hindu calm," the "old equilibrium" of Indian theosophy, "the religious theater" of beggary, the excremental vision of a world of gnats and chawls and cremations in which "100,000 people sleep on the pavements of Bombay," the "nullity of labor" and the "school of the bullock cart, a mixture of mimickry and fantasy"; rejecting the "cruelty and injustice of dharma" as a "forensic game" which "can accommodate bonded labor as, once, it accommodated widow-burning," he unconsciously repeats Mr. Biswas's contemptuous word for the "monkey-house" of the Tulsis: *"We are a zoo!"* As the *fliegender* son of a *fliegender Indianer*, however, he brings things up to date. He mocks the political clichés of the Gandhian pretenders like Desai as "exhibitionist and hollow as the Gandhianism of the men he opposed: it offered nothing. . . . At its core were the old Indian attitudes of defeat, the idea of withdrawal, a turning away from the world, a sinking back into the past, the recovery of old ways, 'simplicity.'" He deplores the "intellectual secondrateness of India," the "childlike perception of reality" that fosters "the negative way of perceiving" and the "bliss of losing the self," the "caste vision" that postulates "What is remote from me is remote from me," the fixation upon "magic, the past, the death of the intellect, spirituality annulling the civilization out of which it issues, India swallowing its own tail." He not only writes it off as a "Paradise Lost," but commits an ultimate heresy in the spirit of Biswas: "The past has to be seen to be dead; or the past will kill."

As an essayist writing in a medium where the mansions of the novelist are denied him, he returns to that last house of the unaccommodated artist at large in a disinherited world: the house of fiction itself. It occurs in his detailed examination of major Indian novelists like R. K. Narayan (*The Vendor of Sweets, Mr. Sampath*) and the post-Gandhian playwright Vijay Tendulkar (*The Vultures, Sakharam Binder*) or custodians of a social vision. His concluding equation of Gandhi with a failed "imaginative novelist" who "splits himself into his characters unconsciously setting up the consonance that gives his theme a closed intensity" may be regarded as a conscious *profession de foi*. Paraphrasing one of Tendulkar's protagonists with obvious satisfaction, he updates an old credo of Biswas's: "He insists on being a man when he has closed the door on the outside world and is in his own two rooms." In a whole chapter devoted to the New India as "A House of Grain" he focuses on the *sarpach* of the village as "shopkeeper, money-man, landowner" in a kind of apotheosis of Hanuman House:

> The house of Patel . . . was indeed the grandest in the village. It was on two floors, and painted. Bright paint colored the two peacocks carved over the doorway. The blank front wall was thick. Within that wall (as in some of the houses of Pompeii) stone steps led to the upper storey, a gallery repating the raised verandah around the courtyard at ground level. . . . Part of the verandah with the bed and sofa was for receiving visitors. Visitors did not go beyond this to the courtyard unless they were invited to do so. . . . On the raised verandah to the right of the entrance there was no furniture, only four full sacks of grain, an older and truer symbol of wealth in this land of rock and drought. It was a house of plenty, a house of grain.

The transubstantiation of the Hanuman monkeys into peacocks, the mysterious persistence of Pompeii, the blank frontage, the public verandahs and the private recesses beckoning toward their little caliphates of Islamic privacy, will all be noted. But the gaze of the visiting Naipaul fourteen years after the completion of *A House for Mr. Biswas* remains that of the unaccommodated man viewing the world's uncertainty in Promethean isolation and saying in behalf of the street-sleepers of Bombay: "*We are wronged!*"

6
The Depth Factor: Saul Bellow

> It is no longer dreaming and story, for literally there is flying. . . .
> All human accomplishment has this same origin, identically.
> Imagination is a force of nature. Is this not enough to make a
> person full of ecstasy? Imagination, imagination, imagination! It
> converts to actual. It sustains, it alters, it redeems!
>
> —*Henderson the Rain King*

NOVELS, UNFORTUNATELY, HAVE NO LAWS OF PERSPECTIVE, like paintings, to guide the vision to its vanishing point and fix our attention on the depth factor in literature. For painters, the presence or absence of depth seems an equally breathtaking phenomenon. They can either cover the painting with an exegetical overlay of grids to demonstrate manifest depth; or they can give us painterly reasons for rejoicing in its liquidation. Apparently, the destruction of depth is as crucial to the painter's poetics as its invention was to the humanist of the Renaissance. Today, we are free to choose between Picasso's "hoard of destructions," the cubing of planes, the granulation of light, or the total erasure of memory that delivers non-representational man from the eluctible "modality of the visible."

With fiction, it is otherwise. Somehow, we flinch from the premise that depth is expendable, and we constantly rediscover it at both the minimal and the optimal ends of the fictive spectrum: in the secret interiority of Gertrude Stein, or the conspicuous profundity of Joyce. Literature remains steadfastly substantive and insists upon depth as the test of the functional fiction: *immer lichter* is *immer tiefer*; but the taxonomy of depth as an index of fictive procedure has so far eluded systematic scrutiny. From time to time, heretics of the enigmatic like Kafka and Borges have arisen to challenge the premise of depth, or construct epistemological parables to prove it illusory—only to conclude, in the end, that "in parable, you have lost."

But what, apart from our overwhelming conviction that it is *there*, can be said about the depth factor in literature? Are events in themselves naturally "deep" or "shallow"—or, as phenomenologists tell us, are they all merely *faits accomplis*, each identical with each in the sense that, as an event, it has come to be? Is suffering, for example, "deep"? And if so, is it deeper than happiness? Is paranoia deeper than leukemia? Is depth an innate attribute of living, accessible to all who have the wit and clinical virtuosity to retrieve it—or is it an invention of our humanity, like the atom or the myth of the cube? Where and what is the "burden of the mystery," or the "thought that doth often lie too deep for tears"?

It is possible to argue, in purely speculative terms, that depth in either Dostoievski or Joyce is "merely" a fabrication—a pathetic fallacy or an ethical necessity; yet, empirically, readers of both would insist that the depth was intrinsically there, and a measurable "descent" had been made: at exactly "full fadom five" the search for the father had been accomplished, and the "sea-changes" of Ariel were apparent to all. But how does one "descend," and what has been penetrated there at the uttermost depth of things where "bone" turns to "coral" and the "richness" and "strangeness" of things take over? One myth would say: *circuition* is depth—the cyclical mode that gives us eternal returns; or a labyrinthine spiraling toward an unknown outcome: abysses, minotaurs, dragons, the anthropologists' decapitating god in a shed in the forest, the eschatologist's split-level world, with its Dantean circles leading downward or upward; or purely medical circuitions leading into or out of the psyche, in a pathology of nausea and catharsis.

Another fiction would stress *reversal*: the making and unmaking of assumption: contradiction, contrariety, paradox—Penelope's gambit of weaving by day and unweaving by night to keep the suitors at bay and subvert an imminent answer. Those partial to the hermetic, like Borges, would opt for a synoptic rather than a serial mode of thinking: the maximizing of the *heterogeneity* of things (Machado's favorite word) as the criterion of the storyteller's depth. Here narrative procedure would reject the unilateral way and insist on the pluralism of *Roshomon*, Joseph

Conrad, the prophetic books of Blake, E. M. Forster, the Four Gospels—or, for that matter, the courtroom, with its express intent of subverting the single vision and its terminal outcome. It would favor a fiction of universal outcomes as the consequence of particular instances, archetypes rather than individuated protagonists, circumstantial plots that operate charismatically and turn the quotidian into the fabulous; that is, the fiction of generic or mythic storytelling. Here depth would seem to lie in the tension of irreducible co-existence: the anguish of the multiple vision, or the "negative capability" of Keats's "man of Genius" who adds doubt to doubt "without any irritable reaching after fact and reason."

It is these considerations that lead me, almost against my will, to dwell on the depth factor in Saul Bellow and single him out as our "deepest" artist in fiction since Faulkner and Henry James. Every reading of my favorite fictions of Bellow's—*Dangling Man, Henderson the Rain King, Seize the Day, Herzog, Mr. Sammler's Planet*—returns me to the seminal adjective of his very first novel to suggest the stance of his total *oeuvre*: The Dangling Man, or, better still, The Dangling Imagination. My choice, were there world enough and time, would be to stress the extraordinary persistence of both the dangle and the sensibility of Bellow's irascible little diarist as a clue to both the poetics of depth and the continuity of Bellow's vision. Even the surname of Joseph is left to dangle throughout that novel, without the Kafkan hint of a final initial, and has the faculty of drawing into the orbit of its dangling anonymity the ambience of all the other protagonists of Bellow who characteristically function as *surnames*: Henderson, Sammler, Herzog. All of them "dangle"; all of them have reason to say, with Joseph, "I'm not fit company. I'm up in the air"; or "For months I have been angry with my friends. I have thought of them as 'failing' me. . . . I have been brooding over this failure"; or "How should a good man live; what ought he to do?"; or "I was still an apprentice in suffering and humiliation"; or "How was I to become a whole man alone, without aid? In what quarter should I look for help, where was the power?"

Which of Bellow's presiding *personae*, waiting in the blinds of his personal entrapment to "seize his day," would not have said of himself, like Joseph: "I feel I am a sort of human grenade whose pin has been withdrawn," or yearned for a "colony of the spirit," "a group whose covenants forbade spite, bloodiness, and cruelty," brooded over "the least penetrable part of me, the seldom disturbed thickets round the heart," and dangled in the balance of a double allegiance to "The mind. Anyway, the self that we must govern. Chance must not govern it, incident must not govern it. It is our humanity that we are responsible for it, our dignity, our freedom"; and, conversely, to "the craters of the spirit—to know what we are and what we are for, to know our purpose, to seek grace?" Was it Henderson, Sammler, Herzog, or Joseph who elicited the affectionate reproach of a friend: "'What a change! What a difference! You used to be an absolutely reasonable guy!'" and returned the gingerly answer: "'Wait. I'm collecting all my feelings and my misgivings. I am somewhat afraid of the vanity of thinking that I can make my own way toward clarity. But it is even more important to know whether I can claim the right to preserve myself in this flood of death that has carried off so many like me, muffling them and bearing them down and down, minds untried, sinews useless—so much debris"?

At this point the affinities not only escalate rapidly, but begin to disclose the persistence of larger fictive configurations in Bellow—total narrative enclaves rather than the inflection of isolated protagonists. One begins to perceive the "dangle" of total books. For example, in the entry for December 22nd, Joseph (1944) overtakes Herzog (1964), and suddenly the basic metaphor of the "late Bellow" flashes its *donnée* across two decades:

> "I sat down [says Joseph] and wrote Jane Addams a letter of apology. She was still alive."
> "Did you?" he said looking at me curiously.
> "I never mailed it," I said. "Maybe I should have. Don't you believe me?"
> "Why shouldn't I?"
> "I changed my mind about redoing the world from top to bottom à la Karl Marx and decided in favor of bandaging a few sores at a time. Of course, that was temporary, too."

and two pages later:

> To have invented a letter to Jane Addams was, however, clearly wrong. Why on earth had I done that? I had a point to make, yes; but I should have thought of a better way.

Or consider the metaphor of homosexual rape that crackles through its positive and negative connections in both *Herzog* and *Mr. Sammler's Planet*. What is one to make of the spiritual rape by the black pickpocket of Sammler, who

> unbuttoned himself. Sammler heard the zipper descend. . . . He was directed, silently, to look downward. The black man had opened his fly and taken out his penis. It was displayed to Sammler with great oval testicles, a large tan-and-purple uncircumcised thing—a tube, a snake. . . . Over the forearm and fist that held him Sammler was required to gaze at this organ. No compulsion would have been necessary. He would in any case have looked.

Precisely what is its bearing on the literal assault on the youthful Herzog "on Roy Street where the vermillion tickets fluttered, lettered with black symbols"?

> Herzog's heart began to pound; he felt feverish—he was overtaken by a man one dirty evening. The man had clapped his hand over his mouth from the back. He hissed something to him as he drew down his pants. His teeth were rotten and his face stubbled. And between the boy's thighs this red, skinless, horrible thing passed back and forth, back and forth, until it burst out foaming.

What is the depth value of the metaphor of negritude in both its criminal and its benevolent guises—as the kindly police sergeant of *Herzog*, the "lordly" and "serenely masterful" pickpocket of *Mr. Sammler's Planet*, and, finally, the doomed philosopher-King Dahfu of the African desert plateaus in *Henderson the Rain King*? In what concordance of hyperbole can we construe its imaginative importance for fiction here?

My guess is that the total *oeuvre* of Saul Bellow cannot be approached in terms of single books alone, but demands to be viewed, as Sammler viewed his planet, as a vast system of cancellations, reversals, repetitions, pulsars, contradictions—a fictive phenomenon inseparable from the Romantic premise that it is the function of the imagination to "dissolve, dissipate, diffuse" whatever seems given or gratuitous—to hold it implacably *at bay*, in order to "create anew." Not for nothing has Herzog moved from "the brilliant start" of his thesis "on *The State and Nature in 17th and 18th Century English and French Political Philosophy*, to a minor academic classic on *Romanticism and Christianity*, to that harrowing impasse of all skeptical vulgarians: 'Foo to all those categories!'" It is a terminal insight of the immobilized Herzog that all reflection should somehow "end with a new angle on the modern condition, showing how life could be lived by renewing universal connections; overturning the last of the Romantic errors about the uniqueness of the Self; revising the old Western Faustian ideology; investigate the social meaning of Nothingness." Like Joseph the Dangler (whose preserve was "the philosophers of the Enlightenment"), he yields to imaginary dialogues with the "Spirit of Alternatives" when he should have been mailing letters to Jane Addams; or meditates on the "question of risk" with Nietzsche, Whitehead, and John Dewey, reads Hocking on "Creative Suffering," Mermelstein on "Millenarianism and Paranoia," or contemplates the "fall of the quotidian" with Heidegger.

"'*The human soul is an amphibian*,'" Herzog cries out in the modern Elizabethan of Saul Bellow, "'*and I have touched its sides. Amphibian! It lives in more elements than I will ever know.*'" Like Marlowe's Doctor of Wittenburg, whose aging eroticism he translates into demotic American (Ramona, Sono, Madeline), Herzog has finally "sounded the depths of that thou would'st profess," and divided the intellectual history of mankind into phases of spiritual immersion: the Grecian, the Magian, the Christian, and the Faustian ages. He has rejected both the "spilt religion" of Hume and the "bottled religion" of Rousseau, drawn up a pharmacopoeia of the "traits of paranoia" and "studied it like the plagues of Egypt:" "Pride, Anger, Excessive 'Rationality', Homosexual Inclinations, Competitiveness, Mistrust of Emotion, Inability to Bear Criticism, Hostile Projections, Delusions," and called for a "moratorium on the definitions of human nature." Fictively and philosophically, he has opted for the metaphysics of The Dangling Imagination ("Why does she want to make me *dangle* like this?" asks Moses Herzog of the implacable Madeline). His cry at this point is the cry of all suspended protagonists in Saul Bellow: "Oh, for a change of heart, a change of heart—a true change of heart!"

In the same way, the prototypal dangler, Joseph, midway in the philosophers of the Enlightenment, is "stopped on Diderot." Awaiting a change of heart that will reveal "the ephemeral agreements by which we live and pace ourselves" and deliver him to the military, he sounds the ironist's exacerbated razzberry of self-abnegation: "Hurray for regular hours! Long live regimentation!" He talks Rousseau and Locke as well as Herzog does, and is equally aware that "The world was crude and it was dangerous, and if no measures were taken, existence could become—in Hobbes's phrase, which had lodged long ago in Joseph's mind—'nasty, brutish, short.'" Like Herzog, he is left to dangle equivocally at the vanishing point of "danger and crudity." His ultimate repudiation of the autonomous life would merit an epistolary nod from Herzog himself: "Alternatives, and particularly desirable alternatives, grow only on imaginary trees."

For this reason, I think it is beside the point to ask, with Robert Boyers, for ethical flatness or ameliorative passion in a fiction like *Mr. Sammler's Planet*, which holds the mirror up to an incompetent and unameliorative Nature, and postulates a fallen, rather than a perfectible, world. It is no negative insight of the seminal Joseph's to explain, as prologue or epilogue to Sammler's vision: "I do not like to think what we are governed by. I do not like to think about it. It is not easy work, and it is not safe." It is the devastating premise of the dangling imagination that "our senses and our imaginations are somehow incompetent" (Joseph); that "people of powerful imagination, given to dreaming deeply and to raising up marvelous and self-sufficient fictions, turn to suffering sometimes to cut into their bliss, as people pinch themselves to feel awake. I know [says Herzog] that my suffering, if I may speak of it, has often been like that, a more extended form of life, a striving for true wakefulness and an antidote to illusion, and therefore I can take no credit for it." "It is no longer dreaming and story," says King Dahfu, "for literally there is flying. . . . All human accomplishment has this same origin, identically. Imagination is a force of nature. Is this not enough to make a person full of ecstasy? Imagination, imagination, imagination!" And as prayer, rather than premise, he concludes: "It converts to the actual. It sustains, it alters, it redeems."

On the other hand, Herzog is no stranger to Mr. Boyers's enlightened ethical grievances: "To introduce into serious discourse considerations and perspectives that banish to irrelevance the central issues or insistently terminate them, is to opt for confusion."

In the opinion of Mr. Boyers, "These confusions point to more than a split in the central character, a radical ambivalence the likes of which most of us surely know and share. I am concerned with *a failure of imagination* that refuses to work through the problems it posits on the level on which they are originally conceived." Yet it is precisely the triumph of Bellow's imagination, I would contend, that he has built into the working plasm of his fiction this Promethean negation, along with all his other misgivings and demurrers, and, in effect, drafted an Herzogian letter addressed to all who would construe it as "confusion" or "failure," or "not sufficiently historical":

> Dear Professor ———————.
> A curious result of the increase of historical consciousness is that people think explanation is a necessity of survival. They have to explain their condition. And if the unexplained life is not worth living, the explained life is unbearable, too. 'Synthesize or perish!' Is that the new law? But when you see what strange notions, hallucinations, projections, issue from the human mind you begin to believe in Providence again.

Paradoxically, the effect of this "letter" is to arouse in Herzog "a deep, dizzy eagerness to *begin*." Having distinguished between "potato love," "the victim bit," and the fallacy of the historical consciousness, having superseded even the Kierkegaardian postulate that "As soon as thought begins to deepen it reaches death first thing," thanks to Herzog, Bellow uses fiction to override history, as Aristotle used tragedy to override epic, and affirm the autonomy of the imagination. "Our own murdering imagination," says Herzog, "turns out to be the great power, our human imagination, which starts by accusing God of murder."

It is this power, which an earlier Romantic called "esemplastic," or Nietzsche might call magic, that helps us to measure the distance between the work of genius and the work of talent, between "a marvelous Herzog," and a nominally "great Gatsby," between the expedient and the ungratified vision. If Bellow nevertheless appears to some to "dangle," rather than to commit himself usefully to some alternative sociological mandate, his pejorative posture has its ironical and biological appropriateness. While others wait on the stairs for the "*Trepwörter*" that might give them some belated advantage, this fiction, saying "Foo to all those categories!" forges ahead to envelop all in an aura of uncanny persuasion and convince us that, in a fiction, at least, the illumination has been major. Somewhere at the center of the depth factor, Bellow has assembled all his protagonists in a single zone of magical immunity. There Herzog dangles mesmerically and concludes with "no messages for anyone. Nothing. Not a single word." Brooding on "useful duties" and "creative suffering," he says: "But we know this. We know, we know, know it!" In the same way, Sammler directs his gaze hypnotically beyond the "degraded life through which we are speeding" and its inadequate polity, to the planet which is *his* by right of imaginative pre-emption. It is the same planet, however, that Moses Herzog sees, swinging in his hammock in Ludeyville, wrapped in his overcoat, at five in the morning: "The stars were near like spiritual bodies. Fires, of course, gases—minerals, heat atoms. . . . Thus humanized, this planet in its galaxy of stars and worlds goes from void to void, infinitesimal, aching with its unrelated significance." And Mr. Sammler's planet is equally inseparable from the night sky and the African desert of Henderson the Rain King, with its "stars flaming like oranges, those multi-million tons of exploding gas looking so mild and fresh in the dark of the sky." To be sure, Sammler's state is no match for Herzog's, with the latter's "mixture of clairvoyance and spleen, *esprit de l'escalier*, noble inspirations, poetry and nonsense, ideas, hyperesthesia—wondering about this, hearing forceful but indefinite music within, seeing things, violet fringes about the clearest objects." But he repeats, to a word, Herzog's epistemological formula for illumination and mystery: "That we know, that we know. We know, we know."

What is it we know we know we know? Lear would say: We know: "Who loses and who wins, who's in, who's out / And take upon's the mystery of things / As if we were God's spies." E. M. Forster would say: We know we have "only connected," and will straightway be reabsorbed into the cosmological muddle. Mann's Gustave Aschenbach would say: "Knowledge is forgiving. It takes no position. . . . it has compassion with the abyss—it is the abyss." The rest of us, spying for God with less conviction, perhaps, than Sammler or Herzog or Joseph or Henderson, know, at the very least, that history is merely a fiction which we manipulate daily with the conspiratorial intention of propitiating social necessity. We build our systems as others pile the furniture against a door that will not lock securely, forgetting that such doors are only buffers against the intransigency of a universe which did not take the Darwinian way out of chaos in order to be historical. We know that all fiction is, at best, celestial espionage. Its function, at its deepest, is to haunt us with Wordsworthian intimations that knowledge offers no abiding equivalence with the nature of things, and Nature owes nothing to Social Reality; that causality is an ingenious extrapolation which explains only our obsessive preoccupation with continuity in a discontinuous world. A sunflower by Van Gogh, or a bedroom in Arles, or an equation by Einstein, we know, are other, and stranger, than we thought; once the brush is lifted from the canvas or the ink has dried on the number, we are left with only an ideogram for which there is no universal grammar. Angling our spy's eyeglass, we know that we live within the enclosure of a parenthetical convenience, on each side of which the "burden of the mystery" stretches on to infinity, like Mr. Sammler's planet, like Henderson's jungle plateaus, like Herzog's psalms of abandonment in his hammock in Ludeyville, New Jersey. We know from fictions such as Saul Bellow's that fiction differs from history in that it registers the galactic stresses of the unknown pressing in on us from both sides of the parenthesis, as an arch exists to support the strains invisibly brought to bear upon it. Dangling in the center of the depth factor like a plummet, "That we know, that we know. We know, we know."

7

Memoir as Myth: The Odysseys of Pablo Neruda

ONE OF THE BEQUESTS of Walt Whitman to his American "*élèves*" is an economy of conspicuous redundancy. The solipsistic theme which divinizes the Self and enlists the "cosmical artist-mind lit with the Infinite" to "confront his manifold and oceanic qualities" is nothing if not repetitious. In the case of Whitman, it led to the loose-leaf dynamics of an infinitely expandable work-in-progress into which the divagations of the Self are made to debouch, as a single exercise in extension. There, the repetitions of the "Me in the center" seem inseparable from a "quality of Being, in the object's self, according to its own central idea and purpose, and of growing therefrom and thereto," like a "lesson in Nature." In the case of Neruda, committed to "the positive hero" of "the North American Walt Whitman and the Soviet Mayakovsky," the Song of Myself has seemed fragmented, ancillary, disparate—an improvisation in search of its center, whose effect has been tentative and narcissistic, rather than "positive."

Readers of Neruda are already well acquainted with his autobiographical repertory. They have seen it in its purely erotic guise in the "despairing" singer of his *Twenty Love Poems and a Desperate Song* (1923). It emerges again in the epilogue to his compendious *Canto general*, as "*Yo Soy: I am*," a geopolitical blend of both Villon and Whitman, starting from the rain-forests of Temuco, as Whitman started from Paumanok, sketching in his "residence" in the Far East, Mexico, Spain, and his exile from Chile, and concluding with last wills and testaments to his party and his *tierra* (1950). Thereafter, it deviates into autobiographical and occasional prose, much as Whitman accumulated the entries for his *Specimen Days*: scattered pages on oceanography, conchology, bottles and figureheads, gastronomy, Quevedo, the artifacts and gewgaws of Isla Negra, and one highly stylized essay of some length on "Childhood and Poetry," which launches Chapter 1 of the present *Memoirs*.[1] As a serialized autobiography in ten chapters published between March and June (1962) by the Brazilian *revista*, *O Cruzeiro Internacional*, it resumes the pageants of the Self with the epoch of the *Residencias* and concludes in a Byronic epiphany of exile, studded with nostalgias, the capitals of Europe, and the orders and salutations of the Iron Curtain countries, as "Lives of a Poet" ("*Las vidas del poeta*"). Two years later, on the occasion of his sixtieth birthday, the Song of Myself reappears in the guise of yet another autobiography in verse, entitled *Memorial de Isla Negra* (*Black Island Memorial*), symbiotically scattering the "lives of the poet" throughout five volumes devoted to the fortunes of Neruda and the peninsular bastion that he claimed as his meditative domain in 1939.

The volume of posthumous *Memoirs* draws upon all these antecedent "lives," "memorials," epilogues, "songs," and miscellaneous *hors d'oeuvres*. Refining and expanding in some cases, dilating, compressing, realigning in others, hurtling over the riches and disasters of a final decade in an effort to overtake what history and cancer compelled him to foreshorten, the *Memoirs* concludes with "some quick lines only three days after the unspeakable events took my great comrade, Allende, to his death." The title chosen by Neruda for his valedictory volume is no longer "The Lives of a Poet," but the unlovely and ominous declaration: "I Confess I Have Lived," which his American publishers, for reasons of linguistic incompatibility or the search for an elegance absent in the original, have encircled—in Spanish—in the "o" of *Memoirs*, like a mandala. Yet Neruda's true signature for his autobiography, after years of reflection and the addition of some 150 pages, is bound to bemuse those in search of his total legend as a personal historian.

What is the meaning of this confessional posture? Why the past perfect of the verb "to live" rather than the plural of the noun, "lives"? The question is an important one, insofar as it casts new light on a terminal Song of Myself conceived in the twilight of a failed polity and the shadow of physical disaster. "Confession" is a word with either a forensic or a eucharistic ring: in a court of ecclesiastical or secular law, it stands for a public acknowledgment of guilt, and in its religious sense it constitutes a sacramental bid for absolution. Thorny and gauche though it may be to English translation, the confessional posture is the last of Neruda's musical signatures—defiant, ironic, unrelentingly heretical: a vitalist's profession of faith in the life-force which acknowledges only the sanctity of existence and "confesses" nothing but the integrity of its ongoing *élan*. Neruda recants nothing, regrets nothing, extenuates nothing, trims nothing. His translation of the pietist's "I confess that I have *sinned*" into the revolutionary's "I confess that I have *lived*" is, in the loftiest Spanish sense, quixotic and parodistic. It calls to mind the premise of yet another of his admired precursors who sought to marry Hell and Heaven in the enigma of a "mental traveler" at large in a "dangerous world" of innocence and experience where "all Act is Virtue."

It would be easy to write all this off as the brag of a militant egoist. Readers of the *Memoirs*, however, moved by the Life in a way that they have not been by the previous *personae* of his *oeuvre*, will welcome it as a clue to that "poetics of amplitude" which is the special provenance of the epic. For despite all its shortcomings as a "confession" in the grand manner of the saints or the updated style of the clinically bedeviled, the sheer majesty of the Life comes through with a dazzle that deserves to be called charismatic. Behind the dropping of names, cities, continents, oceans, and cataclysms, the inexhaustible derring-do of geological displacement, one is haunted by a *déjà-vu* which piques the attention. Somewhere, one has met this combination of vastitude, geographical mobility, and fatality before. Neruda is right to caution his readers that "what the memoir writer remembers is not the same thing the poet remembers. He may have lived less, but he photographed more and he re-creates for us with special attention to detail. The poet gives us a gallery full of ghosts shaken by the fire and darkness of his time. Perhaps I didn't live just in myself, perhaps I lived the lives of others." The quick of the matter is touched when Neruda goes on to remark, "From what I have left in writing on these pages will always fall . . . yellow leaves on their way to death and grapes that will find new life in the sacred wine."

It is then that one says: "But the word for the life is—*Homeric!*"

II

I do not mean to suggest by this any comparison, substantive or hermeneutical, of the *Memoirs* of Pablo Neruda with the *Odyssey* of Homer. What I mean to suggest is that the *stature* of Neruda in awesome ways already known to readers of his *Residences*, his *General Song*, his *Black Island Memorial*, and his *Odes*, is everywhere implicit in the "photographic" particulars of his "lives." If there are latter-day Homers, as there are latter-day prophets, then the *Memoirs* of Pablo Neruda comprises a lower-case odyssey that discloses a dimension of the modern imagination measurable up to now only in a succession of "failed epics": a "shoring up of fragments," ruins, Bridges, Cantos, and American Selves already written into the North American canon of our century.

For the effect of the *Memoirs*, without seeking to be so, is oversize, grandiose, *fabulous*. It helps us to understand how the late purveyors of myth come by their magical commodity when the matrix of a new "enlightenment" provides no confirming canons of sanctity—encompassing personalities, transcending history, and writing their vision *large*. It undertakes the re-invention of Homer not as an anachronistic exercise in scale, as Joyce might be said to do, but as the unconscious recapitulation of a great phylum committed to the dynamics of "eternal return." It makes clear that the *oeuvre* of Pablo Neruda, for all his fondness for the "positive hero" of Whitman and Mayakovsky, was never merely a "song of myself" written for the "Me in the center," but a search for his species.

If, as would also appear, Neruda's "true Penelope" was Chile, he wove and rewove a fabric that was epical rather than personal or patriotic. Least of all can it be said that "politics" was the exclusive or principal concern of the Neruda of the *Memoirs*. As the last of many ostensible "songs of myself" in the teeming plenty of his *oeuvre*, his autobiography is equally concerned with enigmas, mysteries, ethnic and global wars, demi-gods, captains, kings, cosmological and zoological fantasies, as well as the old Homeric staples: Eros, Mars, and Themis, who presides over the destiny and justice of things. I should like to undertake in the remainder of this essay—whimsically or tediously as the occasion may require—a reading of the *Memoirs* in the "Homeric" mode.

My concern, as I hope to make clear, is nothing so jejune as the transformation of an Iliad into a Chiliad; but with the persistence of Homeric staples—Eros, Mars, and Themis—and their aggrandizing force in the evocation of "noble" utterance. What is at issue, to borrow the nomenclature of Wallace Stevens, is "the noble rider and the sound of words."

Readers coming to the prose Life after the Complete Works of the poet need not be reminded that the letter of Pablo Neruda anticipates the Life in its pervasive mingling of both the crepuscular and the erotic themes. They are aware of a twilight melancholy, with its Hispanic mask of *soledad* and its gravid professions of sensuous and indefinable despair that drenches Neruda's first phase as a poet of landscapes and *amores*. The results, inconsequential in *Crepusculario* (*Book of Twilight*) (1923), were sufficient in his *Twenty Love Poems and a Desperate Song* (1924) to launch his reputation as a poet just entering his twenties and ensure a circulation of more than a million copies by the time he was fifty-seven. In 1952 there were more passionate avowals under the title of *Los versos del capitán* (*The Captain's Verses*), published anonymously to maintain the poet's double allegiance to a wife and a mistress. By 1953 he was able to provide a whole anthology of Ovidian metamorphoses under the title of *Todo el amor* (*Total Love*). In 1960 he added a century of sonnets to his third wife, Matilde Urrutia, entitled *Cien sonetos de amor* (*One Hundred Love Sonnets*), and in 1967 a cycle of "barcaroles" in which uxorious adulation and a sequence of sea chanteys were similarly intended as epithalamia for the pleasure of his lady.

The provenance of Eros in the works of Pablo Neruda is, then, at least as consuming and diverse as it is in the *Odyssey*; but its persistence into the Life of the *Memoirs* is no less "Homeric." There comes to mind, in the first third of his chronicle, the anonymous thresher in the haylofts of Hernandez; the menstrual Marisol-and-Marisombra of the *Twenty Love Poems*; the stranger from the *boîtes* of Les Halles who "got into my bed sleepily and obligingly" to preside over the erotic mysteries and conduct the poet "to the very origins of pleasure"; Josie Bliss, the "Burmese pantheress" whose "jealous tantrums turned into an illness" that threatened the life of the poet, taxed all his sexual prowess as an American sensualist, and provoked his most acerb and exacerbated masterpieces, the "*Tango del viudo*" (*Widow's Tango*) and

"*Las furias y las penas*" (*The Woes and the Furies*); Patsy, with her cadre of Boer, English, and Dravidian "girls of various colorings" who "went to bed with me sportingly and asked nothing in return"; the Ceylonese pariah who balanced great buckets of excrement on her head like a matutinal goddess of the privy, and submitted to the solicitations of her clients "with eyes wide open, completely unresponsive"; Kruzi, the Jewess "who had been given a choice between a maharajah, a prince, and a wealthy Chinese merchant" with a trunkful of panties, and was intercepted at the door of her Rolls Royce by the Dutch authorities who "considered it a grave offense for her to live as a concubine of a Chinese."

All serve, in any "epical" reading of the Life, as permutations of Eros, like that triptych of enchantresses whom Homer immortalized in his quadrant of "*belles dames sans merci*," as if to give visceral and numinous force to the vitalism of his protagonist before returning him to his web-weaving spouse. All elicit avid episodes to themselves in Neruda, as in Homer. Here, in effect, Calypso, "that lady of the lovely locks,"[2] "singing in a beautiful voice," moves again in an ambience of caverns, "birds of the coast whose daily business takes them down to the sea"; Nausicaa flicks a "glistening whip" over her wagon-load of ambrosial laundry on a seacoast in Phaeacia, en route to her rendezvous with the naked Odysseus; Circe of the floating islands, "singing in her beautiful voice as she went to and fro at her great and everlasting loom," prepares her philtres of "yellow honey flavoured with Pramnian wine," and, at the entrance to the twin whirlpools here, also wait those deadliest singers of all, "the Sirens who bewitch everybody that approaches them." As archetypes of erotic enchantment each serves to launch the Odyssey of Homer's much-displaced campaigner precisely as the assorted hookers and odalisques of the Orient launch the long exile of Neruda in a picaresque chronicle of deracination, perfidy, and legitimate restorations that mingle the sacred with the sensual and the martial with the political.

III

It is not surprising, therefore, that Neruda's chronicle of Levantine "solitude" should end in a paradox that was to polarize his allegiances as a poet throughout the remainder of a crowded and contradictory career: the affirmation of "mystery," and the irreversible commitment to a militant and quotidian world of man's bread and man's labor. Specifically, it is a *musical* factor that Neruda extrapolates at the conclusion of the first third of his autobiography to epitomize that "secret" ingredient which, in his opinion, had hitherto eluded "the critics who have scrutinized my work":

> Although my poetry is not "fragrant or aerial," [he writes] "but sadly earthbound," I think those qualities, so often clad in mourning, have something to do with my deep feelings for this music that lived within me.

It is that "music," at once daily and alien, heard, at one point in a Cambodian jungle when Neruda "for a terrible moment" believed himself transported "to the spot where I should die" and left to "the fury of my killers" by strangers, and at another, in the casbahs of Colombo, where he stopped his rickshaw while

> a mysterious human voice sang on in the dark; the voice of a boy or a woman, tremulous and sobbing, rose to an unbelievable pitch, was suddenly cut off, and sank so low it became as dark as the shadows, clinging to the fragrance of the frangipani, looping into arabesques and suddenly dropping with all its crystalline weight

which remained crucial in a spiritual diaspora that took him to Rangoon, Ceylon, Batavia, and Singapore from 1927 to 1932. At one extreme it compelled an erotic and solitary confrontation with the ineffable—an encounter which was thereafter constantly to force the poet "to find this music so that I might listen to it" at moments of incongruous political engagement, and invite the special angularity and privacy of his *Odes*, his *Book of Vagaries*, and his *Skystones*.

At the other extreme, Neruda explains, it was precisely in the epoch of his *Residences*—a limbo of maximum sensuality and maximum introspection when he had "never read with so much pleasure or so voluminously": Joyce, Lawrence, Rilke, Blake, Leonard and Virginia Woolf, "kilometers of English novels," the *poètes maudits*—that he found himself "returning to Rimbaud, Quevedo, or Proust" to track the enigma of his "voices" to an unexpectedly rational conclusion.

Swann's Way made me experience all over again the torments, the loves and jealousies of my adolescence. And I realized that in the phrase from Vinteuil's sonata, a musical phrase Proust referred to as "aerial and fragrant," one savors not only the most exquisite description of sensuous sound, but also a desperate measure of passion itself.

With the aid of musicologists and musicians he pursued the phrase from Vinteuil through Schubert, Wagner, Saint-Saëns, Fauré, and d'Indy, to its source in César Franck's "Sonata for Piano and Violin" where, Neruda was convinced, there was finally "no room for doubt. Vinteuil's phrase was *there* . . . ," "losing itself in the depths of the shadows, falling in pitch, prolonging, enhancing its agony . . . building in anguish like a Gothic structure, volutes repeated on and on, swayed by the rhythm that lifts a slender spire endlessly upward."

Very fittingly, the theme that concludes his chapter on "Luminous Solitude" is the same that led Odysseus to the islands where the Sirens "who bewitch everybody that approaches them" cast their spell on the unwary mariner "as they sit there in a meadow piled high with the mouldering skeletons of men": the theme of unearthly devastation, primordial melancholy, sonal enigma—the poetics of the inscrutable, which is the pervasive signature of his *Residencia en la tierra* (*Residence on Earth*). "No seaman," sing Homer's fatal sisters, "ever sailed his black ship past this spot without listening to the sweet tones that flow from our lips, and none that listened has not been delighted and gone on a wiser man." Similarly Neruda observes:

> In his sharp-sighted narrative about a dying society he loved and hated, Proust, the greatest exponent of poetic realism, lingered with passionate indulgence over many works of art, paintings and cathedrals, actresses, books. But although his insight illuminated whatever it touched, he often went back to the enchantment of this sonata and its renascent phrase with an intensity that he probably did not give to any other descriptive passages. His words led me to relive my own life, to recover the hidden sentiments I had almost lost within myself in my long absence. I wanted to see in that musical phrase of Proust's magical narrative and I was swept away on music's wings. . . . Savage darkness came down like a fist on my house among the coconut trees of Wellawatte, but each night the sonata lived with me, leading me on, welling around

me, filling me with its everlasting sadness, its victorious melancholy.

The justice of this extraordinary gloss on the "bitter style" of the *Residences* that "worked systematically toward my own destruction" can hardly be overestimated. It is one of the major *données* of the *Memoirs* that students of the "lives" and the *oeuvre* of Neruda will have to reckon with in evoking the amplitude of his vision. For the whole Proustian-Homeric mix of "poetic realism and a dying society" with the meanderings of that most lachrymose and accident-prone of exemplary exiles, Odysseus of Ithaca, is *there*: wars, usurpations, betrayals, geographical and sexual peril, "the woes and the furies," the Sirens, the mysteries. Elsewhere in his *Memoirs* Neruda pauses for another of his typical reversals of context, in the service of a dialectical counter-myth. Of his first book he says, in italics: "I have always maintained that the writer's task has nothing to do with mystery or magic, and that the poet's, at least, must be a personal effort for the benefit of all. The closest thing to poetry is a loaf of bread or a ceramic dish or a piece of wood lovingly carved, even if by clumsy hands." Polemicists have already elevated this rubric of the *lares* and *penates* to extravagant heights of the sacrosanct; but Neruda's mandate to his interpreters is clear.

For all his repudiation of the Far East as an "influence on the poems" of *Residencia en la tierra* ("I say that this business of influence is mistaken"), it is the Siren-song of the mysteries (the phrase from Vinteuil or César Franck or the androgynous singers in Colombo)—which in India and Malaysia were never far from the human misery of things—that stayed with Neruda to the end. "The esoteric philosophy of the Oriental countries," one may readily concede, can be dismissed as a "by-product of anxiety, neurosis, confusion, and opportunism of the West," or a "crisis in the guiding principles of capitalism." The music of enigma, however, exactly placed in Homer, as in Proust and Neruda, as a tutelary episode to convey his hero through the epical threshold that led him, with the aid of some stout twine and exemplary seamanship, to the restorations of Ithaca, cannot be overlooked.

It is the *music* that one hears, in any number of keys and baffling registers, all explicitly professed, in the later work of Pablo

Neruda: in *Odes*, in the chants of his *Cantos ceremoniales*, the sea chanteys of his *La Barcarola*, the "sonatas" of his *Memorial de Isla Negra*, the "chansons de geste" of his *Canciones de gesta*, his *One Hundred Love Sonnets*, or little love songs "hewn out of wood," and, finally, his posthumous *Elegia*. This *scoring* and rescoring of whole volumes to engage sonal intangibles of the ordinary is never absent from the *oeuvre* of Pablo Neruda; nor is its function a purely cosmetic or programmatic one. Its effect is to alter the pitch and intensity of a vision, skew all the wavelengths to higher frequencies of the irrational, and invite all the permutations of oddity, vagary, and "extravagance" of his "late" style. Its intonation, wayward or droll at some times, delphic and incantatory at others, psychologically dense or colloquial at others, pays homage to the abiding priorities of mystery, bewitches by bafflement and surprise, and denies the reader the linear consolations of historicity.

More subtly and equivocally, it leads to that special provenance of islands and oceans that mingles process with enigma, materiality with the inscrutable, evanescence with the unalterable, which one associates with both Homer and Neruda. No reader of the lives of Pablo Neruda can miss the singing of his Sirens. It clings to the seascapes, the citadels, and the geological fantasies of Isla Negra, dominates his watery perspectives, and constitutes the very axis on which the evocations of the *Memoirs* are made to revolve in the Eternal Present. His insular and oceanic gods work themselves into the very fabric and time of his story as persistently as Poseidon and Athena weave their theophanies into the fortunes of Odysseus:

> Immersed in these memories [Neruda writes, as if to a Muse], I suddenly have to wake up. It's the sound of the sea. I am writing in Isla Negra, on the coast near Valparaiso. The ocean—rather than my watching it from my window, it watches me with a thousand eyes of foam. . . . Years that are so far away! Reconstructing them, it's as if the sound of the waves I hear now touched something inside me again and again. . . . I shall take up those images without attention to chronological order, just like these waves that come and go.

And midway in his concluding chapter, pathetically fragmented by the ravages of cancer and the perfidies of his "Cruel, Beloved Homeland," he notes:

Solitude and multitude will go on being the primary obligations of the poet in our time. In solitude, the battle of the surf on the Chilean coast made my life richer. I was intrigued by and have loved passionately the battling waters and the rocks they battled against, the teeming ocean life, the impeccable formations of the "wandering bird," the splendor of the sea's foam.

IV

Compared with that of Eros, the provenance of Mars does not seem to require the labors of an exegete to make its pertinence felt. It has been thrust on the total accomplishment of Neruda by partisans of all political faiths over the years, bearing down from every direction; and in South America it still passes for the operative context of a simple-minded poetics of "the poet in the streets." To think of Neruda is to think of wars, revolutions, slogans, presidiums, dictators, falanges, duces; to be Marxist, Communist, Popular Unitarian, consul, senator, ambassador, presidential incumbent; to walk with Stalin, Nehru, Ho Chi Minh, Allende, and Frei. Despite all his later disclaimers, Neruda materializes for his countrymen again and again, cap-a-pie, on the battlements of Europe as in his native Chile, rattling sabers and dispensing a poetry of the barricades that would put Homer to global shame. For South American and Soviet readers, he remains the poet of an *Iliad* rather than an *Odyssey*; and his *Memoirs* make it clear that he is in part accountable for these confusions.

Almost too neatly, the odyssey turns into an iliad on the final page of his chapter on "Luminous Solitude": "And this Hitler, whose name appears from time to time in the newspapers," Neruda asks the Jewish consul of Batavia:

"—this anti-Semite, anti-Communist leader, don't you think he can assume power?"

"Impossible," he told me.

"Why impossible, when history is full of the most absurd incidents?"

"But you don't know Germany," he stated flatly."That's the one place where it is absolutely impossible for a mad agitator like him to run even a village."

The chapters that follow drum up a veritable fanfare of militant subtitles. Their rhetoric is martial; their pace, stertorous; their rapid dispersals and regroupings in "another part of the field," melodramatic: Chapter 5: "Spain in My Heart," Chapter 6: "I Went Out to Look for the Fallen," Chapter 7: "Mexico, Blossoming and Thorny," Chapter 8: "My Country in Darkness," Chapter 9: "Beginning and End of Exile," and so on, to Chapter 10 recounting his "Voyage and Homecoming" like a nephew of Odysseus or Agamemnon. All is seen in either the stopped motion of hallucinatory close-ups of García Lorca, Arellano Marin ("a diabolical character,") Napoleon Ubico, González Videla ("a Chilean Judas," an "amateur tyrant on the saurian scale," "an acrobat who played to all sides"), Ilya Ehrenburg, Miguel Asturias, Jules Supervielle, Nehru, Mao Tse-tung, etc., etc., or in frantically accelerated time-lapse, where one catches glimpses of the hero between flickery and snowy subtitles: "A Congress in Madrid," "The Masks and the War," "Nazis in Chile," "Anthology of Pistols," "Macchu Pichu," "The Nitrate Pampa," "A Road in the Jungle," "The Andean Mountains," "In Paris with a Passport," "In the Soviet Union," "India Revisited," "My First Visit to China," "Wine and War," "Palaces Retaken," "Era of the Cosmonauts."

Here the crosscutting becomes almost too clipped for comfort. Neruda's nightmarish flight over the Andes, for example, is picaresque rather than "Homeric": there is more freight than the *Memoirs* or the enforced escalation of its recovery can bear. Nevertheless the epical intonation remains. Episodes and identities fade in and wipe out like swamp gas, replete with villains, braggarts, demi-gods, princes, champions and the place-gods who preside over battlefields and destinies. Elsewhere, the heroes sulk in their tents—Pandit Jawaharlal Nehru (a "man with a bilious complexion" who "must be going through a bad physical, political or emotional experience") Mao Tse-tung ("I saw hundreds of persons waving a little red book, the universal panacea for winning at ping-pong, curing appendicitis, and solving political problems"), Stalin ("Stalin cultivated his mysteriousness systematically"; he was "a man who was his own prisoner")—while the battle broadens, or idles, or sweeps to a fratricidal climax. Most conspicuous and passionate of all are the two minor holocausts which recapitulate each other with eerie identity of detail: the

Spanish Civil War, in which Neruda's "House of Flowers" in Madrid, "caught between two fronts," was eventually "smashed to smithereens" by Falangist artillery, with shrapnel "on the floor among my books"; and the civil war in his native Chile, in whose aftermath, we are informed by a Chronology, "his house in Valparaiso and the one in Santiago, where his wake was held, had been ransacked and vandalized."

Curiously enough, the global paroxysms of Kapital, like World War II, register as little more than a premonitory murmur: according to Neruda, he was in possession of information, while still Consul General of Chile in Mexico, that led him to anticipate Japan's entry into the War one week before the bombing of Pearl Harbor. The ghastly duration of that war, however, seems as remote to Neruda as Achilles's or Hektor's awareness of the wars of Rameses II and the rise of Tiglath-Pileser in the time of Ilium and Achaea. For Neruda, the operative front, apparently, was elsewhere: in the New Russia or the New China, or those mini-nations of Spain and South America where the readings on the Richter scale were still only symptomatic, or Hispanic, or provincial. Behind, and to one side of the Iron Curtain, Neruda's busy-ness was incessant: red carpet deputations of inquiry or adulation in which Éluard or Aragon or Alberti was elevated, Allende and Castro canonized, Stalin apotheosized and then extenuated, Nehru and Chairman Mao regarded with a fishy eye, and González Videla and Francisco Franco consigned to the nethermost circle of obloquy in polar blocks of rhetoric.

A second front, often as deadly and intimate as the permutations of Eros, was the professional front on which Neruda's genius was drawing to itself the lethal fire of the envious: persecutions from within and without by *criticones*, poetasters, trend-setters, vandalous international factions: a punishing ordeal of implacable and venal detraction. Here also Neruda intervenes to consign his old malefactors to their appropriate circles of damnation and posthumous ignominy. On the other hand, there are sinecures and orders of merit, almost equally political, which Neruda confers upon talents of good will: Paul Éluard, called "The Magnificent," the ubiquitous Ilya Ehrenberg, Quasimodo, Italian translator of Neruda, Gabriela Mistral, Alberti, Picasso, Siqueiros, Rivera, Darío, and the novelists of the South American "boom." Whitman is mentioned rather minimally on four occasions, Baudelaire on six, Proust at great length and with conspicuous fervor on two. Of Eliot, Neruda records that he had to lock himself into a bathroom to escape the bewitchment of his verses, much as his Homeric namesake lashed himself to a mast to neutralize the music of the Sirens, while Eliot went on reading through the door.

> Eliot used to read my poems. . . . And I was flattered. . . . No one understood them better. . . . Then one day he started to read me his own, and I ran off, selfishly, protesting: "Don't read them to me, don't read them to me. . . ." I was depressed. . . . Eliot has so much talent. . . . He can draw. He writes essays. . . . But I want to keep [my] reader, to preserve him, to water him like an exotic plant.

On César Vallejo, tiresomely paired with Neruda as continental contenders for the Hispanic Fleece, Neruda is characteristically astute and acerb. He addresses himself to the whole protocol of vogue and exposes the tactics of Vallejistas both at home and abroad:

> Vallejo was serious and pure in heart. . . . I have written two poems, on different occasions, about my dear friend, my good comrade. . . . In the last few years, during the small literary war kept alive by little soldiers with ferocious teeth, Vallejo, César Vallejo's ghost, César Vallejo's absence, César Vallejo's poetry, have been thrown into the fight against me and my poetry. This can happen anywhere. The idea is to wound those who have worked hard, to say, "This is no good; but Vallejo was good." If Neruda were dead, they would throw him in against Vallejo alive.

V

Finally, there is the equivocal domain of Themis—that Themis who, according to Telemachus, "looseth and gathereth the meetings of men," and, in Homer, serves the double function of convening assemblies and presiding over feasts. How has the goddess of assemblies apportioned Neruda his desserts, and where does her weight fall in the *Memoirs*? Anthropologists like Jane Harrison and Gilbert Murray have been hard put to penetrate the mysteries and prerogatives of her office; but all are agreed that her enclave is societal, oracular, normative. Themis is at once a keeper of the destinies and proprieties. According to Miss Harrison, she is "prophecy incarnate," the summoner to the agora and the sacramental banquet, "the stuff of which religions are made," the "herd instinct, custom, convention slowly crystallized into Law," the keeper of the mysteries to which man "owes obedience, to which he pays reverence," the "social imperative," the guardian of the *polis* and the collective consciousness of men. Miss Harrison goes on to explain that "The Greek word *Themis* and the English word, *Doom* are, philology tells us, one and the same. . . . Out of many *themistes* arose Themis. These *themistes* stood to the Greek for all he held civilized. They were the bases alike of his kingship and of his democracy . . . the ordinances of what must be done, what society compels. . . . They are also the prophecies of what shall be in the future: they are also the dues, the rites, the prerogatives of a king, whatever custom assigns to him or any official."

One is tempted to translate the word straightway into the philosophical and political vulgate: for "Themis," read "categorical imperative," or "dialectical materialism," or Hegelian due process of History. However, the "phrase from Vinteuil" demands a magical rather than a Marxist rendering. In the spirit of "Homeric" mystery, Neruda's operative word for it in the Complete Works was "*deberes*," or "responsibilities." Its persistence in the total canon of Neruda as the bard's mandate to render unto Moscow the things that are Moscow's, and unto Art the things which are Art's, is resolute, low-keyed, and non-negotiable. It is Neruda's way of serving notice that he will write a partisan pastiche like *Las uvas y el viento* (*The Grapes and the Wind*, 1954) or an *Incitación al Nixonicidio y alabanza de la revolución chilena* (*Incitation to Nixonicide and Praise for the Chilean Revolution*, 1973) whenever the occasion calls for one, and an *Estravagario* (*Book of Vagaries*, 1958) or a *Piedras del cielo* (*Skystones*, 1970) whenever the vagaries and solitude of things move him to listen to his Sirens.

Similarly, his *deberes* to Themis in the prose Life are reaffirmed in a massive penultimate chapter called "Poetry Is an Occupation." The Spanish here rendered as "occupation," "*oficio*," is pure Jane Harrison, and embraces such private and sacerdotal "occupations" as "The Power of Poetry," "Living with the Language," "Critics Must Suffer," "Short and Long Lines," "Originality," "Literary Enemies," "Criticism and Self-Criticism," and, finally, when all the stables have been swept and justice administered to friend and enemy alike, a glimpse at Elysium itself, "The Nobel Prize." Reflecting on "Short and Long Lines" he writes:

> I started life more naked than Adam, but with my mind made up to maintain the integrity of poetry. . . . Poetry, with a capital P, was shown respect. Not only poetry, but poets as well. . . . The poet who is not a realist is dead. And the poet who is only a realist is also dead. The poet who is only irrational will only be understood by himself and his beloved, and this is very sad. The poet who is all reason will be understood even by jackasses, and this is also terribly sad.

And he concludes the section as a whole with a resounding invocation to the *polis* of the "social imperative" of poets:

> Poetry is a deep inner calling in man; from it came liturgy, the psalms, and also the content of religions. The poet confronted nature's phenomena and in early ages called himself a priest. In the same way, to defend his poetry, the poet of the modern age accepts the investiture earned in the street, among the masses. Today's social poet is still a member of the earliest order of priests.

It is precisely here that the significance of these stock-takings needs to be anchored as a culminating "permutation of Themis." The pattern that emerges from the whole of the *Memoirs* is ritual, conservative, reverential, rather than "revolutionary"—a comely and civilized insistence on the decorum of the poet's obligations to his state, to his self, and to biological process. For all his "bohemian" penchant for "eccentrics," it is the decorum of the constitutional way and the old sacrament of marriage—a kind of ethos of spiritual seemliness—that Neruda came to affirm, just as Homer divinized the legitimacy of his hero's functions as exemplary husband, house-cleaner, and Prince of Ithaca. Even in the conduct of his favorite revolutions Neruda everywhere implies the constitutional and responsible way: polls, plebiscites, and peace, rather than assassinations. Nothing was more abhorrent to Neruda, it is clear, than the mindless subversion of consent by hooligans, cynics, and conspiratorial anarchists—the cartoon of a Beard with a Bomb in its pocket:

> When the reactionary right had to depend on terrorism [he writes], it used it unscrupulously. . . . General Schneider, the

army chief of staff, a respected and respectable man who opposed a *coup d'état* to prevent Allende's succession to the Presidency of the republic, was assassinated. . . . The gang was made up of young members of the social set and professional delinquents. . . . Blocked everywhere by diabolical and legal obstacles, the Chilean road was at all times strictly constitutional.

Elsewhere he writes of "Extremism and Spies":

Former anarchists—and the same will happen tomorrow to the anarchists of today—very often drift off toward a very comfortable position, anarcho-capitalism, the refuge of political snipers, would-be leftists, and false liberals. All those individualist rebels are delighted, one way or the other, by the reactionary know-how, the strong-arm method that treats them as heroic defenders of sacrosanct principles. . . . I saw all this in Spain during the war.

Of guerrilla tactics in the abstract, he notes:

Guerilla methods in Latin America opened the floodgates to all sorts of squealers. The spontaneous character and the youth of these organizations made it hard to detect and unmask spies. . . . this cult of risk was encouraged by the romantic spirit and the wild Guerilla theories that swept Latin America. . . . For a long time the supporters of this tactic saturated the continent with theses and documents that virtually allotted the popular revolutionary government of the future, not to the classes exploited by capitalism, but to all and sundry armed groups. The flaw in this line of reasoning is its political weakness: it is sometimes possible for a great guerilla and a powerful political mind to coexist, as in the case of Che Guevara, but that is an exception and wholly dependent on chance.

And of the Achilles' heel of Soviet protocol, he concedes:

The existence of Soviet dogmatism in the arts for long periods of time cannot be denied, but it should also be mentioned that this dogmatism was always considered a defect and combatted openly. . . . Life is stronger and more obstinate than precepts. The revolution is life; precepts prepare their own grave.

It is in this sense that the true title of his *Memoirs* comes full circle, insists on itself, and achieves its full force as a confessional affirmation of the Virtue of all Action. "I have *lived*!" is the "*oficio*" of the activist. For Neruda, as for Blake, the rites of the *polis*—whether it be Santiago, Stalingrad, or England's "green and pleasant land"—and the hierophantic service of Themis, were no fossilized barrow of bones. On the contrary, they comprised an autonomous *life*—life Homerically conceived as a movement from herd instinct to Law, a convening of feasts and assemblies, a commitment to the mysteries and the prerogatives of a "social imperative," a ceremonious embodiment of fidelity. The simplicity and comeliness of Neruda's lifelong *deberes* as a card-carrying summoner to the congresses and calling of his party is finally as obvious as the piety of Odysseus. The tone of his chapter on "*oficios*" is millenial, messianic, pacific, as in Book 24 of the *Odyssey*, when

> Athene called out at once to Odysseus, by his royal titles, commanding him to hold his hand and bring this civil strife to a finish, for fear of offending the ever-watchful Zeus. Odysseus obeyed her, with a happy heart.

Similarly, Neruda writes in a late poem of "Summation":

> I am glad of the great obligations [*deberes*]
> I imposed on myself. In my life
> many strange and material things have crowded together—
> fragile wraiths that entangled me
> categorical, mineral hands,
> an irrational wind that dismayed me,
> barbed kisses that scarred me, the hard reality
> of my brothers,
> my implacable vow to keep watchful,
> my penchant for loneliness—to keep to myself
> in the frailty of my personal whims.
> This is why—water on stone—my whole life has
> sung itself out between chance and austerity.

In the same chapter Neruda, after "the death of the Cyclops of the Kremlin" (meaning Stalin), when the "human jungle shuddered," quotes from a page of Ilya Ehrenburg: "Pablo is one of the few happy men I have known." He goes on to invoke the delights of Themis in an uncluttered assertion that "We poets have the right to be happy, as long as we are close to the people of our country and in the thick of the fight for their happiness. . . . In my party, Chile's Communist Party, I found a large group of simple people who had left far behind them personal vanity, despotism, material interests. I felt happy knowing honest people who were fighting for common decency, for justice." It was, for Neruda, a happiness not unmixed with the mischief of loyal insubordination, as his preference for his *Book of Vagaries*, above all its competitors in the canon of his *Obras*, makes clear:

> Of all my books, *Estravagario* is not the one that sings the most, but the one that has the best leaps. Its leaping poems skip over distinction, respect, mutual protection, establishments, and obligations [*las obligaciones*] to sponsor reverent irreverence. Because of its disrespect, it's my most personal book. Because of its range, it is one of the most important. For my own taste, it's a terrific book, with the tang that the truth always has.

In more reverential guise, the last word in any Homeric reading of the works of Pablo Neruda must be reserved for the poet himself, who, in a sonnet to his Greek namesake, reaffirmed the uncertainties and sanctities of Themis in a concluding sestet:

> Whoever sees you and never guesses all
> that was given you to know, will never know
> the magic of your tranquillity in motion.
>
> Compared to you, all arrogance is paltry,
> the rich, impoverished, and your constant honor, this:
> always to be secret and sonorous as the wind is.
>
> (To Homer)

Notes

1. Trans. Hardie St. Martin (New York: Farrar, Straus, & Giroux, 1977).

2. All quotations from the *Odyssey* of Homer are from the translation by E. V. Rieu (Harmondsworth: Penguin, 1946).

C. Translation: Grammars and Consciences

8
The Translator as Nobody in Particular: Faiths and Fidelities

ANY BILINGUAL TRANSLATION of the complete text of *Residence on Earth*[1] is so crucial an occasion for the canon of Pablo Neruda in this country that it might almost be termed a liberation. It delivers a talent, Homeric in its vision of a continent and a cosmos, from anthologists (like me) who have been preparing the way by mapping the relative densities and dimensions of the poet's itinerary during five prodigious decades of spiritual wandering. Presumably, it restores the poet *intact*—with his longueurs, his obsessions, his idiosyncracies, and his native language—and compels the reader to inhabit the *time*, as well as the continuum, of a singular commitment, without abridgment or intervention. It also presents us with an artifact in English in which the translator professes to "as much fidelity to the author's words and intent as is permitted by the difference between the two languages," and requires us to weigh that against its original.

What does one have when one has a "literal" translation of *Residence on Earth*? The question is a haunting one for poetry, with a history that concerns not only the "fidelities" of Mr. Walsh's reading of Neruda's *Residencias*, but also the semantics of translation as such. Ideally put, the question is not: How I Sat Down to Translate the *Residencias*, or even a method and esthetic of translating Neruda, but whether, in the words of Saint Paul, "there be *knowledge*"—what needs to be known by reader and translator alike, and the extent to which it is knowable. Ideally answered, the question would engage the poetics, linguistics, and epistemology of translation, as well as the particulars of two texts confronting each other *en face*, across the binder's seam. At its most squalid, the occasion could descend to the level of a cockfight or a provincial *alternativa* between literalist and liberalist—a trading of readings in which two irreconcilable premises devour each other and nothing is left but the sneer on the face of the Sphinx.

Let me say what I can regarding the epistemology of "literal" translation and its consequences for the truth of the *Residencias*. "Truth" of translation, "accuracy" of translation, or, in the moralized jargon of the trade, "fidelity" of translation, is generally assumed to be cognate with the practices of the sedulous literalist. Indeed, the effect of matching simultaneously printed texts in two languages, the author's and the translator's, in parallel columns is to induce a positivism with regard to poetry and the imaginative transfer of languages that is both misleading and illusory. It assumes, in the first place, that the original itself is knowable in a version which is innately and univocally available to all, as a kind of *Datum-an-sich* which should induce all responsible translators to render the poet's paradigm in identical terms. Its attitude toward the dynamics of language itself—toward the behavior of one verbal symbol in relation to another, and their outcome—follows a premise of scientific optimism which even the sciences have come to outgrow. In the romantic pattern of the "microbe-hunter," the literal translator would take his foreign text into the laboratory of the pure scientist, subject it to a science of absolute communication, a semantic bombardment of its fissionable phonemes, and emerge with basic transmutations into English. A simplistic semantics and a misguided analogy with scientific method have led him to identify the truth of a poem substantively with its "words," and its "intent" with its data. Yet the "science" of translation is often no better than a science fiction of translation, and the weapon of "accuracy" merely a magical change of clothing, in which the mild-mannered reporter emerges from the telephone booth minus his specific gravity, in the accouterments of Superman.

There will be few to question the premise that a poem is made up—apparently—out of words, as a truth is made up out of "facts"; but a collection of facts does not constitute a truth, and a collection of words does not constitute a poem. It is the *relationship* between facts that determines a truth, and the relationship between words—sonal, formal, textural, affective, latent, asseverative—that determines a poem. Coleridge would say that in the beginning was a *passion* rather than a word; and that the source of all poetics is properly a "balance in the mind effected by that spontaneous effort which strives to hold in check the workings of passion . . . consciously and for the foreseen purpose of *pleasure*." It is to this relationship that the translator of poetry addresses himself—a relationship which he soon discovers does not gratuitously spring into place, as an effect follows its cause, once the English word has followed "literally" upon the Spanish. A fine translation is not a Rosetta Stone decoded, but always has something confidential about it.

Certainly, literal translation has a right to exist along with all the other fictions and ploys of the translator: mimicry, superimposition, imitations, equivalences, mouth-to-mouth resuscitation, and lexicographical and syntactical "high-fidelity." All partake of the gift of tongues, all are part of the hubbub. All have their pieties, their shortcomings, their bigotries. In the case of *Residence on Earth*, however, the search for criteria is haunted by another factor which compounds the enigma: the poet's choice of an irrational medium in which words no longer offer guarantees of "intent," and intents are no longer "normative commodities" accessible through systematic transliteration. I refer to the celebrated "surrealism" of the poet's address: a "tormented poetry" in the words of Amado Alonso, in which "poetic meanings subjectively intuited do not disclose themselves as nameable and describable things, but through the mediation of images and metaphors—that is to say, slices of reality constructed *ad hoc* by the poet and valid only as symbols, indirect expressions of affective intuitions."

Here, at least, it would appear that the literalist's tactic of fingering the upraised *words* of the original like a kind of Braille in the total blindness of poetry might offer an alternative to the overawed translator. It is the procedure preferred by Mr. Walsh—a kind of hard-core stenography described by himself as "transparent," in which the poet writing in Spanish achieves the impossible feat of "speaking for *himself* in a new tongue." Of course, the poet speaks for himself only once—in the tongue which anchors his psyche and his syntax to the language of the original. His only mode of existence is the mode of the original: everything else is apocryphal. Antonio Machado, a teacher of

French as well as a poet writing in the language of Neruda, has said that "The only living language is the language in which we think and have our being. We are given only one. . . . we must content ourselves with the surfaces, grammatical and literary of all the others." Similarly, the translator, on the other side of the binder's seam, is forced to confront the alienation of his own tongue and speak for its character as a process commensurate with the original; he can never be diaphanous. The binder's seam is there to remind us that the translation of poetry is not a systematic plagiarism of the original, under cover of a second language; it is an act of imagination forced upon one by the impossibility of the literal transference or coincidence of two languages, two minds, and two identities, and by the autonomy of the poetic process.

The role of "being nobody in particular" is the least interesting of the available roles of the translator of poetry. But does it nevertheless *work*? To return to the question originally proposed: What does one have when one has a literal translation of *Residence on Earth*? In the first place, one would have to say that instead of "transparency" or fidelity, one has a usable, if sanctimonious, opacity. We have a venture of conspicuous diligence and good conscience which holds the whole of a baffling undertaking to its course, pursues its literal bias with only occasional lapses into presumption, and registers its reading not so much on the other side of the binder's seam, as in the spaces over the Spanish reserved for the undergraduate trot, rather than the "poem itself." We have, that is to say, a kind of English "kenning," or dubbing, or *skinning* of the poem—the disengagement of a verbal epidermis to suggest the total integument in which the poet's discourse was initially embodied, like the bladder for a metaphysical blood pudding. The accomplishment ought not to be underestimated. Insofar as the Spanish words are *there*, we need to know what would happen if they were transposed in a kind of basic English resolutely committed to a premise of anonymous deference, thought by the translator to constitute the morality of his whole enterprise. Not only do we have a total surface which directs us undemonstratively to the depths—the skin for a musculature present only in the organic transactions of the original—but we have a resolute continuity of scale which suggests at least that the translator was faithful to *himself*. Unlike more fanciful translators who often deviate into literalism, Mr. Walsh rarely ventures a chary or a whimsical reading. Indeed, it becomes a kind of event when Mr. Walsh, breaking the lock-step of literalism, renders "*el vendido*" (the sellout) as "the Judas"; "*diamante*" (diamond) as "flaming jewel"; "*el funesto alegorico*" (the somberly allegorical) as "the metaphorical doom"; or mistakenly turns "*mi sangre*" (my blood) into "my brow," and "*alegres disparos*" (happy explosions) into "gay nonsense" (sic). One wonders whatever possessed him. He is not curious or tentative or reversible. For Mr. Walsh, there is no nonsense or misgiving about the moving of the verbal counters, even when the poet himself, midway in a poem called "*Arte Poética*" questions whether all might be rendered "possibly in another even less melancholy way," and alludes to a "swarm of objects that call without being answered," a "*nombre confuso*" (a jumbled name)—which, through another mishap, Walsh has rendered as "*hombre confuso*," "a bewildered man."

We have, in short, another kind of "equivalence," as the freer modes of translation are generally said to give us equivalences rather than literal equations—a body of information useful to readers and clerks, who may choose to remain ungratified. It is the helpful function of Mr. Walsh's translation to show us how shallowly we have penetrated into the imaginative retrieval of a poem by a policy of abstemious literalism. In the realm of pure research, it leaves us surveying the undoing of creation, like Michelangelo in *The Last Judgment* with his own autographed skin in his hand: a posture important for eschatology, and the comic distance essential to humane translation.

Nevertheless, in a way that is the by-product of the awesome scale of the original itself, it *does really work*. Parsimony, in the face of so many temptations, becomes a kind of saintliness. Prolonged exposure to the English of Mr. Walsh, without the stereophonic distractions of the original, creates a *patois* of its own—a monaural pick-up of the explosive changes of texture and pulse of the original and a metronomic leveling of the full orchestration. All remains predictably bleak, while the Spanish goes on being unpredictably shaken by seismic changes of intensity and direction in the volcanic interiors of the imaginative process. For a time one is almost ready to suspend the admonition of Nerudists like Amado Alonso that: "To understand and savor the poetry of Pablo Neruda, it will not do to first understand intellectually the external constructions and then penetrate to the feelings by this means, but quite the reverse. . . . one must first engage the affective climate that is the spirit of this poetry, submit to the contagious suggestivity of the images encountered, to the insistence of the poet's motivation and the sure power of the sonorous constructions." Reconnoitering on the short leash of the literalist, one forgets that the nonesuch English of "I ceaseless from clothes to clothes come sleeping from far away" is a sophomore's parody of Spanish; that in English one does not "weep with health, with onion, with bee"; that only Emily Dickinson dared speak of "each invisible water" in sober earnest. At other times, the entrapments of a chicano syntax and word order seem more incorrigible and ungainly: "in my guitar interior" for—of course!—"*en mi interior de guitarra,*" or "It's not true so much shadow upon your hair" for the Spanish underpinning: "*No es verdad tanta sombra en tus cabellos.*" The latter, carried into a further stanza, turns into a tonedeafening disaster:

>It's not true so much shadow pursuing you,
>it's not true so many dead swallows,
>so much region dark with laments:
>you come flying.

Even at the moments when the language is most molten with direct, psychological discharges, the low frequency of the literalist produces an obsequious jargon that sets one's teeth on edge; Mr. Walsh comes limping:

>You my enemy of so much sleep broken
>just
>like bristly plants of glass, like bells
>destroyed menacingly, as much as shots
>of black ivy in the midst of perfume. . . .
>If there is someone that pierces
>a wall with circles of phosphorus
>and wounds the center of some sweet
>members
>and bites each leaf of a forest giving shouts
>I too have your bloody firefly eyes

>and can impregnate and cross through the
>   knees. . . .

Certainly, this is not the voice of Pablo Neruda "speaking for himself in a new tongue"; it is not even the voice of Donald Walsh speaking out of Madison, Connecticut. It is only literalism at its most supine and myopic, reaping the wages of anonymity: a translator's option of poverty, chastity, and obedience transposed into a crucifixion of self-abnegation. If the whole text persisted in this vein of jaw-breaking asceticism, we would have to dismiss the venture of a "literal" translation of *Residence on Earth* as a catastrophe for poetry. More often than not, however, Mr. Walsh steers an intelligible if uneventful course, provides acceptable readings, and works within the syntax and inflection of an English with which we can basically concur. Significantly, it is in the *Third Residence*, devoted to categorical denunciations and invective—the essentially assertive discourse of a patriot and propagandist—that the literal yield is most productive and the language most plausible. Mr. Walsh's translation of the anathemas of "Almería" or the eulogies of "Antitankers" leaves no bubbles between the literal English and the passion of the speaker: direct translation is functionally appropriate, and anonymity is no longer equivalent to anemia. The effect, for once, is visceral. The distinction is an important one, since it helps us distinguish a mode compatible with the literalism of Mr. Walsh, from a modality in which he is likely to appear grotesque and catatonic. Translation is exigent as well as pietistic; and literal translation is especially ill at ease with a poetry where the pressures of language are multiple, disruptive, suspended. It does not cling naturally to the contours with which the syntax and velocities of the original invested its intentions. This is particularly true of the *Residencias*, where the thrust is not merely open, as the mode of Whitman may be said to be open: it yaws in all directions with craters and cicatrices, splinters like shrapnel, makes a fine art of its vertigo. It compels risk, curiosity, impurity, *poetry*.

The fate of a single word—"*ronco*"—may serve to suggest the inertia of the literalist and its consequences for translation. It is a word of considerable character and piquancy in the Spanish: an onomatopoeic adjective to which Neruda is oddly partial in his surreal tilting of the actual. Being an adjective, it is never a substantive entity like a noun: it does not lie flat on the page, or say itself only *once*, like "ball-peen hammer" or "phenolsulfonate." Cassell's Spanish Dictionary will define it for us as "hoarse, husky, rough-voiced," and suggest its proximity to *"roncar"* (snore). Sonally, it relates to the timbre of human and animal utterance rather than its decibels: nasal, throaty, gutteral, gutsy. Its range throughout the *Residencias* is curiously non-representational: we have *ronco cerezo, ronco paso, roncas bocinas, canto ronco, roncas gargantas, ronco arbol, ronca aguja, ronca cesta, ronco peciolo, roncos rayos*, etc., etc.: cherry trees, footsteps, horns, songs, throats, trees, needles, baskets, leaf-stalks, rays or stripes—all are *ronco* in the encompassing obliquities of Neruda. All force us to wonder about their place in a spectrum of contexts and synonyms. Mr. Walsh, however, is not bemused. In every case his English falls heavily like a brand on a maverick. He says: *"raucous,"* from one end of the book to the other, as though he were in possession of some universal solvent lost to the rest of us.

Actually, of course, he is as much in the dark as any newcomer to the pageants of the surreal; actually, there is no univocal solution, no least common denominator. He is only more cursory and servile. By some law of diminishing returns, moreover, the rigors of the literalist force him constantly to bear witness against himself whenever he is at fault or semantically immobilized. We *know*, for example, that Walsh is wrong when he says "abacus" for *abecedario*, since the former is a device for counting numbers and the latter a primer for spelling words. We know that a sacramental reading of *"licor extremo"* as "extreme unction" (*extremaunción*) is an utterly inappropriate invention; that though a *viejo verde* is a dirty old man there is no reason for assuming that *"cuchillo verde"* (green knife, here rendered as "a sexy [!] knife") has anything to do with dirty old knives; that he has committed howlers in mistaking *"buzos cubiertos de ceniza"* (divers covered with ashes) for *"buhos cubiertos de ceniza"* ("owls covered with ashes"), transliterating *"aguas de espaldas"* as "back waters," and rendering the homicidal humors of *"dar muerte a una monja con un golpe de oreja"* (kill a nun with a punch in the ear) as "slay (!) a nun by striking her with an ear." Similarly we are everywhere aware of inept choices in bizarre contexts to which they could not apply—"surreal" or not. It is plain someone has blundered when *"las dulces tarjetas de larga cola,"* which recalls the lavishly upholstered picture postcards of Neruda's "Poetry and Childhood," turns "sweet cards with long trains" into "sweet calling cards" (*tarjetas de visita*); when "*arañas de mi propriedad*" (spiders of my property) become, of all things, "inherited chandeliers," and a "*golpe de plata*" metamorphoses into "my silver set" (*vajilla de plata*) rather than "a quantity (or windfall?) of money" in downright South American. It is equally obvious that the force of "*documentos disfrutados*" has not been penetrated by calling them "benefited documents," which means nothing at all; and the impersonal grammar of "*sea lo que soy*" which follows unmistakably through the final stanzas of "*Significa sombras*" is badly skewed by replacing the poet's appraisal of his own shadowy obligations with some other shadowy intruder's. And so on.

All this bookkeeping would be secondary if the mode of the translation had been qualitative rather than categorical; if the translator had given a pulse to his language, a style to his utterance, a point of view to his choices, and held our attention there: if he had, in short, made a poet's demands on the emerging English rather than a pedant's or a proctor in Intermediate Spanish. In the words of Neruda (and Mr. Walsh), it is here that all that is

> foreign and hostile begins . . .
> the names of the world, the frontier and the remote
> the substantive and the adjectival too great for my heart
> originate there with dense and cold constancy.

In the last analysis, the failure of the literalist is a failure of curiosity, nuance, initiative, engagement, *poetry*—a preoccupation with predictable "fidelities" rather than an act of imaginative faith. "To ask with infinite interest," Kierkegaard somewhere says, "about a reality that is not one's own, is faith." In the present case, the faith was little, the interest all too finite and inflexible, and the reality no one's—least of all Pablo Neruda's.

Note

1. *Residence on Earth*, trans. Donald D. Walsh (New York: New Directions, 1973).

9
Lowell's *Imitations*: Translation as Personal Mode

IT WOULD APPEAR that the domain of Robert Lowell's *Imitations*[1] is public rather than private in character: a "small anthology of European poetry" from Homer to Pasternak and Montale, drawing upon five languages, including the Russian; with the curious omission of the Spanish. To some extent the concessions to Homer and Sappho are perfunctory: lip-service to the museum of the sixth century B.C., except in some fragments from Sappho which engage Lowell's lifelong preoccupation with cosmic and personal deprival. As a "small anthology of European poetry," however, the collection is obviously sparse and crotchety; what is important is the poet's readiness to explore the European intonation, try the agonies and the vagaries of the European subject in a way that his American contemporaries have not, and prove them by translation on his pulses. The effect of his anthology in the long run is to draw the reader's attention constantly to the person of the translator, and away from the ambience of "Europe." It would appear that Lowell, like Pound and Hölderlin, has employed a mode of translation to enact a repertory of *personae* native to his irascible and inquiring genius; that what we have is, in fact, not an anthology of European poetry, but a species of dramatism: an artist's mimicry of other artists.

It is Lowell's startling expectation that all—Homer and Sappho, Der Wilde Alexander and François Villon, Leopardi, Hebel, Heine, Hugo, Baudelaire, Rimbaud, Mallarmé, Valéry, Rilke, Saba, Ungaretti, Montale, Annensky, and Pasternak—"will be read as a sequence, one voice running through many personalities, contrasts, and repetitions." To this end, the mimetic brio of his assault upon the initiating voices is nothing short of ruthless. Sappho has been supplanted by "poems [that] are really new poems based on hers"; Villon has been "stripped"; Hebel has been "taken out of dialect"; Victor Hugo's "Gautier" has been "cut in half"; Mallarmé, Ungaretti, and Rimbaud have been "unclotted" at the translator's pleasure; a third of *Bateau Ivre* has been jettisoned; two stanzas have been added to Rilke's "Roman Sarcophagus": "And so forth! I have dropped lines, moved lines, moved stanzas, changed images, and altered meter and intent."

The scandalized purist need not search long for a vantage point from which to sink his knives where self-righteous pedantry has always found fair game; indeed, Mr. Lowell in his Introduction delivers himself up to would-be assassins with the resolute fatalism of Caesar in the Roman Senate. His admissions and omissions seem almost willfully suicidal. In that European cemetery of noble utterances and awesome identities which he inhabits, his actions appear vandalous and his appetites necrophilous. The question of Conscience, so touchy to critical moralists, seems never to have occurred to him. What remains is only his need, which is apparently insatiable, to "find ways to make [my originals] ring right for me"; to make Montale "still stronger in free verse"; to "keep something equivalent to the fire and finish of my originals"; to be "reckless with literal meaning" and labor "hard to get the tone"; "to write alive English"; "to rashly try to improve on other translations"; and, most significant, to *keep writing* "from time to time when I was unable to do anything of my own."

Connoisseurs of the translated word have every reason to ask where such willful gerrymandering may not lead the professed translator: or *why* it is that certain translators translate. Taking Lowell at his own word, one would have to say that the cause is everywhere personal and solipsistic, as well as feral. More than ennui, certainly, must be postulated in his candid admission that he turned to "imitation" when the real thing was for a time denied him and he faced the virility of the world's eloquence "unable to do anything of my own." In the hard school of "*Sauve Qui Peut*" the cannibalism of the large talent at bay must be applauded for finding other means of dining "with Landor and with Donne"; and I count translation among the most taxing counsels of expedience. It requires, in the first place, an expenditure of self equal to the banquet set forth on the rich man's table. It deploys every skill given the poet's hand in the service of identities and prodigies not his own. As such, it is a form of austerity which emulates the hard morality of Blake: "All Act is Virtue." Incidentally, it also accomplishes a kind of homeopathic therapy for purging past excesses and preparing for exertions yet to come, as when Lowell informs us that his Baudelaire, for all its stunning accomplishment, was "begun as exercises in couplets and quatrains and to get away from the longer, less concentrated problems of translating Racine's *Phèdre*." At its worst, for which Lowell is also accountable, it "imitates" the bittersweet and the mistletoe in its search for symbiotic equivalences, attaching itself to a forest of host-plants to gratify its voracious determination to survive.

This is as much as to say that translation may serve the translator as a form of surrogate identity, as well as a labor of love. In the "parasitology" of translation, it is true, there are certain crustaceans that castrate their hosts, others that attach themselves to large aquatic mammals for the ride and prestige, others that strangle and infect: but the vitalism of Robert Lowell is another thing. I dwell upon it here precisely because his talent is massive enough to invite each of the dangers mentioned, in the service of a commanding identity, and survive. Modesty will get us nowhere in the attempt to arrive at any criteria of translation which may be said to underlie Lowell's accomplishment as intermediary for the European mind. The "one voice" "running through many personalities, contrasts, and repetitions" is unmistakably the voice of Robert Lowell—the most eventful and passionate voice of our epoch, whose voracity matters because it helps to give character to our century. Its impersonations, collapses, reassertions are never parasitical in the morbid sense of enacting flights from the poet's responsibility, or providing lines of least resistance in a peripheral struggle for survival.

On the other hand, little is to be gained from rushing to the defense of the *Imitations* with toplofty disclaimers which pay the poet the dubious compliment of removing him from the imputation of translation entirely. When Professor Alvarez informs prospective readers that the *Imitations* of Robert Lowell is "*not a book of translation,*" that what we have is a "magnificent collection of new poems by Robert Lowell, based on the work of 18

European poets . . . in that constantly expanding imaginative universe in which Lowell orbits," no one is likely to benefit, least of all the translator. Robert Lowell cannot be dismissed as the space-man of recent American translation, circling the European scene in a rubbish of old sandwiches, astronautical weightlessness, and "expanding imagination." Doubtless, he winced, somewhere in the lower gases, to find his "small anthology of European poetry" hyperbolized as "the most varied and moving book that this leader of mid-century poetry has yet produced" and "oddly, one of the most original." Edmund Wilson's equivocation is not much better: that the *Imitations* is probably "the only book of its kind in literature," whatever that happens to be. Nor can I, despite my mistrust of literalists dedicated to the subversion of inquiry and realism in translation, call the "complaint that Lowell has not followed Baudelaire literally" an "absurd" one, with Mr. Wilson. The gift of absurdity is precisely what the literalist has not got; and it is possible that absurdity may do more than sanctimony to justify the deeper claim on our imagination for the passionate integrity of utterance which characterizes the finest of Lowell's "imitations."

What must be asked in the long empirical run is another question: what are we to understand by "imitation"? Precisely what or who is being imitated in the *Imitations*—Robert Lowell? his great originals? or "due process of translation"? Is the essential premise of imitation: (1) "I will now proceed to English this poem *as though I were* translating it"; or (2) "I will now English this poem as though it were part of my own sensibility, moving from element to element inside my own identity rather than the translator's, assembling and disassembling all inside my own nervous system, committed at all points to my own language rather than the language of the original?" Does the "imitator" differ from the "translator" in that he performs as a kind of versifying dowser, sensitive to the indicated pulls of a *terra incognita*, and capable of turning all into *faits accomplis* of prosody? Is he a virtuoso asked to re-invent at second- or third- or fourth-hand (at times he has no direct access to the language of the original) the occasion that was uniquely the poet's and the habits of mind and language that originally invested it? Are we concerned with fabrication rather than *mimesis*?

Current practice has no easy answers to these questions, and none is forthcoming in the term given the reader by Lowell. The word itself—imitation—has a notorious history of private and public misdemeanors from its awesome beginnings in Aristotle up to the present. Life has been "imitated," Nature has been "imitated," Action has been "imitated," with nobody much the wiser. Indeed, the provenance of the "mimetic" factor is almost a certain guarantee of the surrender of the issue to polemical metaphysics and has helped to expose the bias of whole centuries. Thus, one generation talks of copies, phantoms, deceptions, in the name of imitation; another "holds the Mirror up to Nature"; another divinizes its literary models: "To copy Nature is to copy them"; another chooses "the mind's self-experience in the act of thinking" and re-invents Fancy and Imagination. Our own century has benefited by the combined assaults of I. A. Richards, the debunkers of I. A. Richards, Butcher's preface to the *Poetics*, Francis Fergusson's bid for the "histrionic sensibility," and the long vista of verbal and compositional "dramatism" central to the poetics of Kenneth Burke.

None will serve to crystallize for us the intent of Robert Lowell in this volume. Among more recent symposia on the subject—notably, the barrage of eighteen voices out of Harvard *On Translation*[2]—Jackson Mathews's "Third Thoughts on Translating Poetry" comes closest to the issue at hand, in decidedly cautionary terms. "The temptation," he writes, "is much greater in poetry than in prose to fall under the spell of the model, to try to *imitate* its obvious features, even its syntax, or to *mimic* the voice of the other poet. The usual mistake is to believe that the form of the model must somehow be *copied*." The spectrum remains the same—*imitate, mimic, copy*—but the paradox accomplished here is to force Lowell's word to account for all that he has repudiated in the name of "imitation." For whatever its shortcomings, Lowell's *Imitations* is no mockingbird in an aviary of European originals.

II

Where, then, are we to turn for clues to the criteria of license and translation in Robert Lowell's anthology? In the absence of a "philosophy of composition," I would like to propose a direct reading of the "imitations" into which all has been metamorphosed by the translator himself—a collation of *his* choices, without any hint of paradigms known or imaginable to me, to which they might conform. Among the eerie truths learned by practicing translators is the fact that the One True Translation, which all pedants seem to have to hand and consult at will, exists nowhere at all. The particulars of Lowell's originals and the particulars of his "imitations" do exist, however, and together they may help us to construe the personal venture he has undertaken in behalf of his great models. For this purpose I have chosen two poems of Eugenio Montale's—"Dora Markus" and "*Piccolo Testamento*"—for reasons that seem serviceable enough to me, though I am aware that all acts of translation are unique to themselves, especially where the range of voices and epochs is as orchestral as in Lowell.

Lowell's special fascination with Montale is already apparent in his prefatory remarks on his distinguished contemporary. "I had long been amazed by Montale, but had no idea how he might be worked until I saw that unlike most good poets—Horace and Petrarch are extremes—he was strong in simple prose and could be made stronger in free verse." Here is both the admirer's profession of engrossment in an appealing and powerful talent, and the translator's discovery of a stance from which he might attempt an Archimedean moving of two worlds. Apart from such assurances—which are never idle in Lowell—there are a number of other considerations which confirm the appropriateness of such a choice. Despite Lowell's preference for Baudelaire as a *semblable* in spleen, guilt, and "*l'Inconnu,*" despite his taste for the nostalgias and demoniacal historicity of Rimbaud as an artist "*maudit,*" despite the neoclassical atavisms of Rilke and the delphic contemporaneity of Pasternak which he openly courts, the intonations and textures of Montale perhaps come closest to the temper of Robert Lowell himself. Like Montale's, Lowell's prevailing cachet, after *Lord Weary's Castle,* is hard-bitten, melancholy, psychologically dense, with a subject that keeps curiously fluid despite the relentless pressure of despairing intentionality. Poem after poem in *For the Union Dead,* for example, eludes one in the midst of its restless thrust and circuition, as is also the case in Montale's "*Mottetti,*" "*La Casa dei Dognani,*" "*Iride,*" "*La Primavera Hitleriana,*" and countless others. For all Montale's declared predilection for "occasions" (he is content to call a whole volume *Le Occasioni*) what puzzles the reader most in both Montale and Lowell is the nature of the poetic occasion itself: *where* the poem's center was supposed to fall in the midst of the seething interplay of scruples, particulars, recriminations, and insurmountable rejections.

The Italians, with their civilized tolerance of the ineffable, have an admiring word for this phenomenon which they apply like a watermark to Montale: *hermetic*. The American reader has only the giddy afterthought: but what was it all about? Similarly, both Montale and Lowell carry a dense burden of personal and historical wretchedness, failed loves, psychological landscapes, existential incongruities inseparable from persons and places and electric with the pulsation of the moment. We have the unplumbed exacerbations of Montale's Bellosguardo, Eastbourne, Finistère, Proda di Versilia, to place alongside Lowell's Dunbarton, Nantucket Graveyard, Nautilus Island, Rapallo, and Boston Commons as stations of a spiritual itinerary. Like Lowell, Montale has written a "Ballad in a Clinic," watched storms from "The Coastguard's House," untangled the oddities of a "gnomelike world" from a "Café at Rapallo," scouted the ironies of "A Metropolitan Christmas," turned mordantly upon his own failed purposes in city parks, orchards, on trains and on beaches, leaving an inconclusive savor that troubles the attention without wholly disclosing itself. As in Lowell's volume by that name, a whole genre of heraldic "life studies" is opened up in Montale's "Dora Markus," "To Liuba Leaving," "Arsenio," "Carnival for Gerti," and "Visit to Fadin"; and it is hardly necessary to point out the "confessional" bias of poems like "Little Testament," "Letter Not Written," "Two in Twilight," "To My Mother," and the whole sequence of "Motets." The uncanny impression remains, after many readings of Montale's "Eastbourne," that it is a poem that might well bear the signature of both poets.

As an instance of "life study" Montale's "Dora Markus" is especially noteworthy. Here we have not only "one of the most poignant love elegies of all time" (in the opinion of Glauco Cambon) but a counterplay of intimacy, psychological divination, and the displaced "oriental" mind moving between Porto Corsini and the Austrian Alps. As a study in exile it combines a rich texture of deprival and unrest ("*irrequietudine*") in a shimmering context of suspended outcomes: the poet's implacable vision of a "voice, legend, destiny" already "exhausted" or manhandled; the "*antica vita*" of a Jewess miraculously surviving from one day to the next by talismanic powers whimsically attributed to an ivory mouse in her jumble of lipstick, powder puff, nail file; and an immediate scene—majolica interiors, seaside *pensiones*, complete to the bay leaf that "survives for the kitchen." The aim of the poet is, above all, to recover the peculiar "*ansietà d'Oriente*" (Oriental anxiety) at once so fascinating and appalling to the Italian's appetite for melodrama: the capacity of Dora Markus to drift without outcome in a Levantine haze, instead of opting for fatality like a heroine in an opera by Verdi or Puccini.

Formally, it is among the most expansive and readily accessible of Montale's great set pieces: open, conversational cadences undisturbed by the intrusion of eruptive afterthoughts—the "*dolce stil*" rather than the "*rime aspre*" of Montale's many voices, riding on its phrases, pauses, assonantal depths and graces with an unflinching objectivity. As such, it would not appear to offer the thorny talent of Robert Lowell an ideal vehicle of "imitation"; and it is hard to see how he was persuaded that Montale was either "strong in [the] simple prose of Kay's *Penguin Book of Italian Verse*" or "could be made stronger in free verse." The verse form chosen by Lowell is indeed free to the point of crudity: a prosody without pulse or that factor of inner rhyme which so often limbers the tensions and deepens the resonance of both Montale and Lowell. In comparison with the supple elegance of Montale, it is peculiarly shrill, prosy, angular, without reverberations. Its effect is that of an intermediate, rather than a final, draft, as though Lowell were still mired in the prose of *The Penguin Book of Italian Verse* or preliminary renderings of his own. The presence of Robert Lowell, sometimes playing at "imitation," sometimes pressing for the bare sound and the tough reduction of intricate matters which is his true signature, comes and goes; the equivalences of Montale do not.

Nevertheless, the fact remains that "Dora Markus," for all its ineptitude, is a *translated*, and not an "imitated" poem. Every sequence of Montale's thinking has been retained intact, every image has been confronted, for the most part, in its own context; every effort has been directed with scrupulous and laborious integrity on unfolding the progressions of the poem as they are given the reader by the poet himself—with one maddeningly tone-deaf exception. The last line of all, indispensable to both the pathos and the symmetry of the poem—what Sergio Solmi calls "the special curvature of Montale"—weighted with the total charge of Montale's induction of a "voice, legend, destiny," is suppressed: "But it is late, it grows later and later." Characteristically, Lowell has preferred to bleed off into suspension points and ignore the Dantean return to inexorable judgment of the original.

The digressions of Lowell's Montale deserve close scrutiny because they encompass whatever remains of the purely "imitative." It would be pointless and tedious to attempt an exhaustive collation of the two texts, since this is not a study in detection but a glimpse at the propinquities and equivalences of translation. Turning to the most harmless deviations first—the permissible variants or extensions of meaning forced upon the poet by exigency or "inspiration"—one might note the following in the first section of "Dora Markus." A "wooden pier" (*ponte di legno*) becomes a "plank pier": all to the good. The "almost motionless" (*quasi immoti*) fishermen become "dull as blocks"—possibly as extensions of the same plank pier; a "sign of the hand" (*segno della mano*) becomes a Lowellesque "toss of your thumb"; a dockyard (*darsena*) becomes "outlying shipyards"—very Bostonian; what was "shiny" (*lucida*) in Montale becomes "silvered" in Lowell; an impassive spring (*primavera inerte*) is a "depressed spring," and a way of life called "dappled" (*si screzia*) by Montale is curiously "subtilized" in Lowell. In a key phrase to the poem as a whole, the "soft Oriental anxiety" of Dora Markus is diagnosed by Lowell as "nervous, Levantine anxiety"—and surely "Levantine" is a triumph of the *mot juste*: one of those windfalls of which one says the translator has pinned down what the original could not. The "stormy evenings" (*sere tempestose*), on the other hand, are leveled into "ugly nights," the admittedly equivocal "*dolcezza*" (a word intransigently foreign to English) turns into "ennui" rather than "sweetness" or "blandness"; and the "lake of indifference" (*lago d'indifferenza*) invoked by Montale as the heart of Dora Markus, is modified somewhat myopically into a "puddle of diffidence," as though the word had been read wrongly by the translator.

In most cases, the changes noted are legitimate ventures in interpretation, in which, as Valéry has pointed out, the translator not only presses for language, but "reconstitutes as nearly as possible the *effect* of a certain *cause* (a text in Italian) by means of another *cause* (a text in English)." More arbitrary departures, however, follow fast. Lowell elects to turn the simple "lowlands" or "flatlands" (*bassura*) of Montale into a "patch of townsick country"—his own invention—and renders "its calms are even rarer" (*i suoi riposi sono anche piu rari*) with the heavy-handed "the let-ups are nonexistent," pre-empting what the author has left suspended. Other modifications seem merely inept or gratuitous to the quizzical reader: why, for example, "full of amnesia" for *senza memoria* (without memory)? Why clutter the "*antica vita*" (old life) of Montale with the needlessly explanatory "old world's way of surviving"?

Similarly, there are some troublesome admixtures of interpretation and fabrication in Part II of "Dora Markus." It is of the essence of Lowell's temperament and, as such, allowable that the "ragged peaks" or pinnacles (*gl'irti pinnacoli*) of a seascape should turn up as "frowsy shorefront" in Lowell, the geese's cry (*gemiti d'oche*) turn into "catcalls," the "throbbing of motors" (*palpito dei motori*) metamorphose into "the put-put-put of the outboards," American-style, and "the evening that stretches out / over the humid inlet" (*la sera che si protende / sull'umida conca*) contract into "night blanketing / the fogging lake coves." There are also less allowable thrusts, however, which represent not "due process" of interpretation, but random piracies on the part of an "imitator" writing as he pleases, precisely as Lowell declares he intended to. Carinthia "of flowering myrtles and ponds" (*tua Carinzia di mirti fioriti e di stagni*) takes a curiously baroque turn of fancy: "*Your corsage is the crescent* of hedges of flowering myrtle." Where Dora Markus merely "stoops on the brink" (*china' sul bordo*) Lowell's text explodes roguishly into "sashay on the curb of a stagnant pond"—certainly a strange outburst for the "exhausted" and "indifferent" Dora of Montale's legend. Similarly, there is a revving-up of the "big gold portraits" (*grandi ritratti d'oro*) which preside over her legend, into "ten-inch gold frames / of the grand hotels," as well as their subjects, whose "looks of men / with high [set] weak whiskers" (*quegli sguardi / di uomini che hanno fedine / altere e deboli*) shape up luridly as "the moist lips of sugar daddies / with weak masculine sideburns."

The passages cited, I repeat, constitute passing deflections, digressions, personal readings, and renderings of detail; or incidental collapses and fumbled opportunities. Their telltale abundance in the case of "Dora Markus" constitutes a record of imprecision that forces one in the end to dismiss it as inept or provisional; the matrix of Lowell's English text itself, however, remains a *translated* rather than an "imitated" one. As such, "Dora Markus" presents a hard assay that need scandalize no one, however much it may disappoint the admirer of Robert Lowell who *asks* (as would I) for the sound of his voice and delights in following it as an attending presence through the translation it has chosen to inhabit. The failures of touch, the incidental occlusions of intent and tone, the occasional overacting, overposturing, overreaching, the rare pratfalls into prosy approximations, are those of all poet-translators busy at their trade in the ordinary way, probing through that double identity which is the *néant*, the nothingness, from which all true translation begins.

III

Precisely the same must be said for the modality and effect of Lowell's *"Piccolo Testamento"* (Little Testament). Here the translator's total encompassment of his original—his overall felicity of touch, texture, compositional detail—is as impressive as the botched approximations of "Dora Markus." Perhaps one ought look no further for causes to such propitious effects, but merely acknowledge their existence as *faits accomplis* and pronounce the union of minds and languages fortunate. The nature of the original, in this case, however, in itself promises more compatible outcomes. In comparison with the pure line of "Dora Markus," the "Little Testament" is a poem more deeply scored with all the idiosyncratic merits of Montale—denser, stranger, nervier in its turns of rhythm and fancy, less immediate in its disclosure of the complex matters touched upon, more obdurate in its hermetic self-scrutiny, more oblique in its confidences. As such, it offers continuous resistance to all that is merely manipulative or "imitative" on the part of the translator and insists on its retention *intact*. At the same time, it is full of glancing turns of direction, texture, metaphorical and stylistic alignment, forging through its transpositions with a driving pulse, without the forfeit of a single misgiving or anxiety.

Presumably, this brings us closer to the vein of Lowell's "Skunk Hour," "Colloquy in Black Rock," "The Flaw," and "The Severed Head"; there should be less need, under the circumstances, for the translator to punctuate, revise, delete, and transpose matters to his satisfaction. Deviations from Montale's original persist here as in "Dora Markus," and one might even wonder about the justice of passing incursions. When Lowell gives us a "pearl necklace's snail's trail" for Montale's "snail's trail of mother-of-pearl" (*traccia madreperlacea di lumaca*), the visceral exudation of the snail is falsely represented by a necklace which has nothing to do with the context and omits the special iridescence sought by the poet. Similarly, when Montale, in the "crepuscular" vein of Italian modernism, writes the powder and mirror (*la cipria nello specchietto*) of a lady's compact (probably) into his poem as another instance of talismanic delusion, the poignancy of the ordinary is lost in the "*spectrum* of a pocket-mirror." I see no good reason, moreover, for turning the "soft coal wings" (*l'ali di bitume*) of Montale's descending Lucifer into "hard coal wings," his shadowy Lucifer (*un umbroso Lucifero*) into a "torch-bearing Lucifer," his dance (the "*sardana*") into an "orchestra," even if one grants that the Greek *orxestra* was actually a dancing-place. Lines 5–7, that universal stumbling-stone of translators of the "Little Testament"—and there are many—will of course please no one familiar with the elliptical fascinations of the original, and resist the best efforts of Lowell to improvise on his own. The "light of church or workshop / that neither the black nor the red cleric (acolyte?) / may nurture" (*lume di chiesa o d'officina / che alimenti / chierico rosso, o nero*), breathes heavily in Lowell's version: "The lamp in any church or office / tended by some adolescent altar boy / Communist or Papist, / in black or red." The question of which is the red and which the black, remains, as well as the improbable orthodoxies of the adolescent Communist.

With every allowance made for near misses and far reaches such as these, I should still insist that the "Little Testament" of Lowell's Montale follows through from beginning to end as a *translated* venture of considerable beauty, intact in its own rhythms, illuminations, skills, and integrity: a meeting of minds and imaginations where they intersect in two artifacts—or Valéry's Italian "cause" wedded to his English "effect" which provides the reader, in turn, with a cause in itself. If this metaphysic is too hard or casuistical for the hasty to construe—and I suppose it is—the fault is not wholly Valéry's or Lowell's, or mine. It is part and parcel of a modern semantic bias which expects the croupier's handy transformation of blue chips into cash at the prevailing international exchange at each turn of the translator's wheel. For positivists such as these, the dropsical linguistics of Nabokov's "poetics" in the aftermath of his Pushkin "translations" is a fitting crucifixion.

Debate on such matters is likely to be bottomless, discussion badtempered, and scholarship usurious. I prefer, instead, to dwell on the appropriateness of Lowell's continuing pursuit of translation as personal mode, in the years which have followed his initial *persona* as the castlebound Lord Weary. Unlike the guerrilla nationalists, professional bridgeblowers, rooftop snipers, and nocturnal infiltrators and assassins of the translator's domain, he has steadily gone on learning his trade by open assault in a variety of skirmishes and full-dress battles, in full view of the enemy, cap-a-pie, in single combat. It is already a very far cry from the glowing fabrications "after Rimbaud," "after Valéry," "after Rilke," in *Lord Weary's Castle*, with their reticent preface: "When I use the word *after* below the title of a poem, what follows is not a translation but an imitation which should be read as though it were an original." The author of *Imitations* and the translator of *Phèdre* and the *Oresteia* need never apologize for poems which presumably "come after" his sumptuous models. His English now lives *simultaneously* with the tongues and talents to which he is beholden.

Similarly, it can be said of his "dramatism" that translation has made it increasingly possible for him to depersonalize his penchant for heroic and patrician *personae* (Jonathan Edwards of the spiders and the "surprising conversions," the memoirs of General Thiebault, the confessions after Sextus Propertius, Valéry, Rimbaud, Rilke, Cobbett—all out of Lord Weary's castle) and move on to the province of drama as such. Here, Lowell's activity has been dazzling in both the pomp and the diversity of its passion for transformation. More and more his medium has become theatrical in the literal sense that Lowell has increasingly sought out the provenance of the *played play*, rather than the pirated or inhabited identity of European masters. He has taken a craftsman's pains to "translate" Melville's *Benito Cereno* into an objective theatrical artifact, instead of appropriating the identity of Melville himself. He has translated the *théâtre* of Racine, rather than turning Racine into an impersonation of Robert Lowell. More recently he has thrown his total force against the full weight of Aeschylus's *Oresteia* in a bid for total theater.

It is to be hoped that with the passing of time and the channelization of a sensibility that hindsight now shows to have been constantly "histrionic," Lowell will continue to leaven the integrity of his translation. Ultimately, there should be no need whatever for him to remove himself from the rank and file of translators as such, or work in a special aura of privilege, in the name of "imitation." I say this without much hope that translators are ever any the wiser for having translated for a decade or a lifetime, or that they can ever hope for "Adam's dream," who "awoke and found it true." Indeed, Babel is always with us. The moralist will say, for example: Translation is a long discipline of self-denial, a matter of fidelity or betrayal: *traduttore, traditore.* The vitalist will say: Translation is a matter of life and death, merely: the life of the original or the death of it. The poet will say: Translation is either the composition of a new poem in the language of the translator, or the systematic liquidation of a masterpiece from the language of the original. The epistemologist will say: Translation is an illusion of the original forced upon the translator at every turn because he has begun by substituting his own language and occasion for that of the poet and must fabricate his reality as he goes. The Sibyl sees all and says: Translation is the truth of the original in the only language capable of rendering it "in truth": the original language untouched by translation.

Notes

1. (New York: Farrar, Straus & Giroux, 1961).
2. Ed. Reuben A. Brower (Cambridge, Mass.: Harvard University Press, 1959).

10

The Vanishing Original: Transvaluations

THE LAUGHING NERUDA

CRITICISM OF NERUDA both in this country and in South America has long paid homage to the fact—a profound rather than a peripheral one—that whoever touches his work touches Chile; and that, ultimately, whoever touches Chile touches the whole ambience of Spanish letters. With the passing of time, however, it has become clear that appraisal has languished as well as prospered on this account; for while the achievement of Pablo Neruda has gone on crossing boundaries and denying "establishments," comment has remained singularly narrow, inbred, and positional. Too often the effect has been to decant the total essence of a much-displaced identity into a "Chilean Indian from Parral," chemically inseparable from the stones, the forests, and the coastal waters of his own country. Both his admirers and his detractors dwell obsessively on particulars of Chilean landscape or Chilean politics which diminish rather than enlarge an intransigent personal vision. Compiling a long index of placenames and public occasions, they have turned a poet's dispensation to the world into a family quarrel or a South American property.

To be sure, any program that includes the *Canto general de Chile*, *Las piedras de Chile*, and *Memorial de Isla Negra*, and teems with anecdote and personal history, requires a glossary for North American readers. An overlay of continents, jungles, rivers, cities, and oceans seems to cover Neruda's world like a cartographer's isinglass; and much of *La arena traicionada, Crónica de 1948*, and *Las oligarquías* will require the fine print of topical Hispanists to be wholly intelligible to readers in 1995]. Nevertheless, it is a fact that the *Canto general de Chile* was ultimately absorbed into a *Canto general*, and as the poet went on to explain: "Amidst all these visions, I wanted to paint a portrait of the struggles and victories of America as part of our very zoology and geology. . . . It is a lyric attempt to confront our whole universe."[1] The true range of Pablo Neruda will never become apparent (especially to Swedish Academicians) until one has reckoned with explicit directives furnished us by his titles. His "lyric" mode embraces (1) songs *(Veinte poemas de amor y una canción desesperada*, 1924), (2) chants *(Canto general*, 1950; *Cantos ceremoniales*, 1960), (3) odes (three books of *Odas elementales*, 1954–1959), (4) sonnets *(Cien sonetos de amor*, 1959), (5) sonatas *(Sonata crítica*, 1964), and (6) barcaroles *(La barcarola*, 1968). His range is "general," "elemental," "ceremonial," and "memorial," rather than topical; and his "residence," three times over, is "on earth" (*Residencia en la tierra, I, II, III*)—or when it is not on earth, it is airy, fiery, or oceanic.

A bibliography of Pablo Neruda guides us to these key terms as surely as it detains us en route in Punitaqui, Macchu Picchu, Spain, Asia, and Isla Negra. It is to these terms, as indices to the further range of Pablo Neruda, that I should like to address myself in an introduction intended, for once, not as a translator's primer for non-Hispanic readers, but as one poet's meditation on another. I shall assume, because his essential gravity pulls the depths and meanings that way, that the poetry of Pablo Neruda is part of everything else I know and sense about work of genius everywhere; that it is not a special *barrio* or ghetto of the contemporary mind known only to the case worker and the Spanish-speaking expert in segregated mentalities; that we have wrangled too wastefully about public commitment and thought too little of the solitude of an interior stance; that his work, given "free and innocent passage," resonates against literatures other than his own, including the English, from which he has translated Blake, Joyce, and Shakespeare,[2] and that this resonance is the true measure of his long traffic with the democracy of letters.

Any revaluation of the achievement of Pablo Neruda must, I think, pause for a long, second look at a volume published after four volumes of "odes" under the fanciful title of *Estravagario* in 1958, and apparently more important to Neruda than to his critics and countrymen. Partisans of Neruda's odic and "residential" manner, fellow travelers for whom the "only" book is *Rail-*

Splitter, Awake!, devotees of his *Twenty Love Poems*, and cultists of Macchu Picchu have all tended to set it aside as an interim work, like his youthful *Crepusculario* (1923)—which the oddity of its title may serve to recall. Precisely how to render the neologistic force of the title is a translator's problem that need not detain the reader for long. It is a word of prismatic obliquity, splitting the glancing illuminations of *extraviar*: to get lost, to wander off course, to divagate; *extravagante*: extravagant, eccentric, way out; *vagar*: to loiter or potter; and to English ears, at least, *vagary*, whimsy, caprice. If it is possible to call *Crepusculario* Neruda's *Book of Twilight*, it may be permissible to call *Estravagario* his *Book of Vagaries*.

The titular linguistics are important only because an unplaceable word may also help to locate an unplaceable intonation and suggest the humors that invest it like an aura. The "unplaceable" factor is, indeed, something more than an aura: it is both a destination and a predicament. As "destination," its intent is to throw the complacent reader, for whom Neruda is either a monolith or a public convenience, off course; and as a predicament, it offers a comic bath of "negative capability" in which the poet romps like a water weasel. On the one hand, his "delights are dolphin-like," and "show his back above / The element they liv'd in"; on the other, they toil in the "thick rotundity of the world" for the center of a poet's disturbance, groping for transparency. Neruda's avowed penchant for "impurity,"[3] however, constantly deflects him into private caprice, a *coquetería* of unanswered solicitations, digressions of the mind's finalities into the absurd, the quizzical, and the imponderable. With good reason, he enlists the "camp" of antiquarian steel engravings from an obsolete *Works of Jules Verne*, and the "pop" of a *Book of Illustrated Objects*[4] resembling a Sears-Roebuck for the Mexican provinces, printed in San Luis Potosí in 1883. Against this iconography of persiflage, savored by a mind that shrugs away all fictions of solution, including the political, Neruda enters his defense of ignorance as an aspect of the world's redeeming impurity.

The epistemology of uncertainty is the constantly augmented theme in a work that might otherwise seem a packet of damp squibs rather than the fuse to a spiritual explosion. It begins vaguely with a cluster of unexamined intuitions: "It is dark in the mothering earth / and dark within me"; "the whole world frightens me—death and cold water"; "I am tired of the hard sea and the mysterious earth," of old hens, bad aperitifs, good education, statues, of concessions, of "everything well-made" and "that ages us." Who would have surmised, asks Neruda, that "earth would change her old skin in so many ways?"—with an afterthought out of Wonderland itself: "We go falling down the well of everyone else." His best hunch brings him close to the anguish of his three *Residencias*: "We are crucially alone / I propose to ask questions / let's talk man-to-man. . . . No one knows what he's talking about / but all agree it is urgent."

Meanwhile, a sense of self-loss and the withering away of the known renders both question and answer increasingly remote. There is mockery as well as pathos in his clown's grimace: "My heart is so heavy / with the things that I know / it's like dragging / a dead weight of stones in a sack"; or "No matter how many we are or I am / at the moment / I can never meet up with a soul: they lose me under my clothing / they went off to some other city." At times a child's recalcitrance edges the irony of the poet's denial: "I'm not asking anyone anything / but every day I know less": "Why [do I] recognize nobody / and why does nobody recognize me?" The comedy of the amateur's stage fright, pinned down by spotlight and audience, does not escape him: "I don't know what to do with my hands / and I've thought of doing without them /—but how will I put on my ring? / What an awful uncertainty!" Sheepishly, quizzically, he calls out from his treadmill: "I don't come, I don't go / I don't dress, I don't walk about in the nude / I've thrown forks, / spoons and knives into the well. / I smile only at myself / I don't ask indiscreet questions." "Which is which, which is how?"

The true distress of the poet, however, is never far from his vagaries, and is frequently summed up in a cry: "What must I do to sort myself out? / How can I provide for myself?" The hazards of the absurd show their darkened as well as their lighted side: "A shadow moves over the earth / man's spirit is shadow / and therefore it moves." There are admonitions, cautionary asides: "I don't want to mislead myself again / it is dangerous to walk / backward, because all at once / the past is a prison." In stroboscopic changes of dark and light the poet can only assure others grimly: "From time to time, at a certain remove, / one must take one's bath in a grave"; and himself: "I'm going to open and close myself up / with my most treacherous friend, / Pablo Neruda."

The result is a parody of Socratic quest in which Neruda, committed to the "clarification of things," puts his question to priest, physician, gravedigger, and "specialists in cremation," in turn. No one will miss, under his shifting humors, macabre and impudent by turns, the shock of the poet's concussion with Death, like a roadblock barring the way to the motorist turning a curve at top speed: "The minute vanishes, vanishes over one's shoulder," and "suddenly we have only one year to move on / a month, a day, and death touches our calendar." The responses, as I have tried to suggest, are riddlingly diverse, from the child's game of hide-and-seek: "Let's count up to twelve now / Then: everyone—quiet!" to the radiologist's glare: "Everyone sees / the plight of my shocked viscera / in radioterrible pictures," to spiritual panic: "Help! Help! Give us a hand! / Help us to be earthier day after day! / Help us to be / holier spray, / come airier out of the wave!" Since finalities and outcomes are hardly germane to a *Book of Vagaries*, the answer remains sibylline to the end: "When the wind skims / your skull's hollows / it will show you enigmas / whispering the truth / where your ears used to be." His ultimate impersonations are perhaps three: "I am one who lives / in mid-ocean, close to twilight / and further away than these stones"; "I am he who makes dreams; / in my house of feather and stone / with a knife and a clock / I cut clouds and waves / and out of these elements / I contrive my calligraphy."

The significance of this glancing look backward at Neruda's book of vagaries may not yet be apparent to the casual reader. It is, in the literal sense of the word, a pivotal book: it veers away sharply, like that "swimmer of heaven" in his concluding Testament, from the resolute materiality of his odes and "general songs," and "leaps into transparency." Certain only that "those who would give me advice / become crazier with each passing day"—including the "politically astute" who note down all deviations, who "wrinkle, grow gray, and can't stomach their chestnuts"—our hero of comic impurity, like the celebrated squire from La Mancha, retires to take counsel. In full sight of the utopian dream and the "sad countenance" of his master, he parodies his predicament with the country humors of a yokel: "Now I don't know which way to be—/ absentminded or respectful; /

shall I yield to advice / or tell them outright they're hysterical? / Independence, it's clear, gets me nowhere. / I get lost in the underbrush / I don't know if I'm coming or going. / Shall I take off, or stand firm, / pay for tomcats or tomatoes?" His decision, in the owlish "Parthenogenesis," is stubborn, circular, and mocking: "I'll figure out as best I can / what I ought *not* to do—and then do it. . . . If I don't make mistakes / who will believe in my errors? . . . I'll change my whole person / . . . and then when I'm different / and no one can recognize me / I'll keep doing the same things that I did / since I couldn't possibly do otherwise."

Apart from the immediate drolleries of this soliloquy, which in effect returns a rebellious Sancho Panza to the service of a dream, there would be some somber things to say. Philosophically, it poses questions about the nature and uses of "advice" as a species of knowledge, about the validity of the "independent" stance as a clue to autonomous reality, about standing firm, moving off, and tactical error as a test of identity, about the changeable, the innate, and the learned. All are recognizably "existential" preoccupations; all are recklessly and joyously engaged in on page after page of the *Estravagario*.

In this sense, Neruda at times comes close to the mood of his younger countryman Nicanor Parra, with whose "anti-poems" the harlequinade of *Estravagario* has often been associated by South American critics. Certainly, it would be a mistake to overlook the affinities of the two major talents of Chile who in 1958—the year of the publication of *La Cueca Larga* and *Estravagario*—undertook to scrutinize each other at length in an exchange of *Discursos* concerned with the criteria and intent of poetry in a new decade of the South American idiom. It would be equally misleading to overlook the fact that the "anti-poem" was *always* present in the protean repertory of Pablo Neruda, in poems such as "Walking Around," from the *Residencias*, in the hard-bitten reportage of *Canto general* and the witty emaciations of the *Odas*; and that, indeed, the whole premise of an "impure" poetry invoked by Neruda in 1935 is the true precursor of the "anti-poem" both in Nicanor Parra and in South American letters as a whole. The "anti-poem," after all, is an importation and not an invention, of Parra's: it predates the *Poemas y anti-poemas* of Parra in the work of Corbière, Apollinaire, Pound, Eliot, Cummings, and Brecht, among others, and has been endlessly adumbrated in a genre of "anti-plays," "anti-novels," "anti-worlds," "non-essays," etc., which bear witness to the deflationary trend of the modern imagination in the service of the ignoble, the apostate, and the absurd. In purely Hispanic terms, it is written into the whole of *Don Quixote* where, as another avowed enemy of the baroque, Antonio Machado, liked to point out, the "Cervantine fiction" or anti-romance, calls for a "double time" and a "double space," a "twinned series of figures—real and hallucinatory . . . two integral complementary consciousnesses conversing and forging ahead" in a "book of harlequinade creating a spiritual climate which is ours to this day."

It is equally proper to suppose that the poems of *Estravagario* represent, politically, a kind of "revisionism" by a servant of goodwill, in the aftermath of extraordinary devotion to party lines, dogmas, tactics, and disciplines. In this case, the disengagements of *Estravagario* show both the irreverence and the autonomy of Neruda's commitment to an ideology. Consulting the Presidium of his own pulses, testing the "equivocal cut of my song," he discovers he is no man's Establishment ("rector of nothing"), and, in the realignment of checks and balances, opens the way to a decade of unprecedented self-scrutiny. It is to this later decade that we now turn.

A House of Fourteen Planks

Despite the prominence given it in the title and the body of the sonnets themselves, the key word of Neruda's *One Hundred Love Sonnets* (*Cien sonetos de amor*, 1959) is not "love" but "clarity" (*claridad*). The almost Parnassian abstraction of the term may jog some startled memories of the "*très-chère*," "*très-belle / Qui remplit mon coeur de clarté*" of Baudelaire,[5] with his equally troubled dream of a voyage under "wet suns" and "disheveled skies" to consummations where "*tout n'est qu'ordre et beauté.*"[6] It is significant that, in the protean world of tidal impulses, oceanic disorder, diurnal and seasonal change which shapes the progressions of the *Sonnets*—Neruda's characteristic insistence upon the impurities of function and the unfolding telluric and human improvisations of a lifetime—it is *claridad* that the poet has come to espouse, literally, in the person of the Beloved.

The more closely one follows the word through the poet's calendar of "morning, afternoon, evening, and night" with its intimations of changing seasons glimpsed through the "salt disaster" of water, the "mash of the light," "all that shudders below / underfoot, underground," "the insubstantial fog," "an untimely autumn," "today, tomorrow, yesterday" that "destroy themselves in passing," the more one comes to feel its spiritual rather than its cerebral force in the poem. Only occasionally does it connect with the world of quantitative and syllogistic order, as when, viewing the Southern Cross through the "night of the human," Neruda invokes its "four zodiacal numbers" in an image of cosmological serenity. Even here, the numbers and elements connect "for a passing minute only"; the "green cross" is straightway vegetalized into parsley, animalized into fish and firefly, carbonized into diamond, absorbed into the chemistry of fermenting wine.

However imperfectly seen, it is the *claridad* of Matilde Urrutia that constitutes the poet's vision of love's permanence and the world's changes. It is Neruda's word for the beautiful—just as *integritas, consonantia, claritas* came to constitute a triad of spiritual properties of the beautiful for St. Thomas—with the special anguish of Neruda's passion for the secular way. On the one hand, we have the "waves' shock on unconsenting stone," "the seaweed's sodden aroma," "the towering spumes of Isla Negra"; on the other, we have the "dear Orderer" (*Ordenadora*) who "thrust[s] herself into the subterranean world," bringing definition, the "order [that] apportions its dove and its daily bread": recognizably sacramental images of providence and redemption. In between moves the "flying hand" of the housewife, arranging cups, saucers, casseroles, "walking or running, singing or planting, sewing or cooking or nailing things down / writing, returning"; and in the realm of brute nature, the tides, the breakers, the "ocean's tormented pavilions," the "machinations of the wasp / who toils in behalf of a universe of honey," and the poet's "leaky barge adrift / within a double skyline: dream and order."

The latent "religiosity" of crosses, doves, bread, wine, honey, the "crown of knives," the "scarecrow smiling his bloody smile," "mockers and backbiters" merits some passing notice, despite Neruda's wry disavowal of any "plaiting and peddling of thorns." If the doves of Sonnet LXXVIII have more in common with the doves painted by Picasso for the Second Congress of the Defenders of Peace, and if the bread is the bread written into the traditional slogans of proletarian revolt from the French Commune to the Petrograd uprisings of 1917, the special *claridad* of the *Sonnets* makes them resonate freshly against universal archetypes which have attended the strivings of the spirit in all ages. It is no disservice to the hard-won contemporaneity of Neruda to point out that his mystique of an "impure poetry" for engaged poets everywhere has Christian as well as existential overtones in its insistence on a "corruptible" state upon which imaginative transcendence depends. The impure, the fallen, the perishing, all that "escapes the interstices" when the net of human order has been knotted by the rational orderer, dominate the watery brooding of Neruda throughout the whole of the poet's later oeuvre, since the *Estravagario*.

The task of the *Cien sonetos de amor* is to retrieve an "immaculate day" in all the temporal impurity of its hours, phases, seasons, alternations of feeling and light, fixed in the last, happy *claritas* of love. On the compositional level, the labor begins with a "profanation" of the sonnet form itself, which, despite its careful count of fourteen lines apiece, omits both the end rhymes and the metrical profile which dynamize the "sonnetification" of feeling and argument, and leaves the thought to work its way through tercets and quatrains as an act of nature. Indeed, it is Neruda's intent, according to his dedicatory note to the light-and-dark lady of his sonnets, to turn the sonnet form itself *wooden*. "In proposing such a project for myself," he writes,

> I was well aware that, along the edges of each [sonnet], by deliberate preference and for purpose of elegance, poets in every age have set rhymes to ring out like silver or crystal or cannon shot. In all humility, I have made these sonnets out of wood, given them the sound of that opaque and pure substance, and they should be so heard by your ears. You and I, walking through forests and sand wastes, by lost lakes and cindery latitudes, gathered those splinters of pure timber, beams delivered to the inconstancy of the water and weather. Out of the very smoothest fragments of all I have fashioned, with hatchet, penknife, and cold steel, these lumberyards of love and raised little houses of fourteen planks where your eyes, so sung and adored, may live on.

The seasoned reader of Neruda, aware of the poet's long apotheosis of wood as an image of the strenuous materiality of the world's body, will know how to make the most of this courtly compliment. The poet of the Araucanian forests who wrote:

> Whatever it is that I know
> or invoke again,
> among all the things of the world,
> it is wood that abides
> as my playfellow,
> I take through the world
> in my flesh and my clothing
> the smell
> of the sawyer,
> the reek of red boards . . .

proffers his "lumberyard of love" as confidently as sonneteers of the past have come with their more traditional nosegays and proud disavowals of marble and gilded monuments. The realism of Neruda is not pejorative. It is, however, "impure." His "century of wooden sonnets," while retaining the classical count of Quevedo and Góngora and addressing itself to themes as Petrarchan as the prosody they espouse, keep open-ended, like a paragraph of prose. If they are read against the tailored profiles of his great predecessors, the shagginess and waywardness of his sonnets are constantly apparent. They contract at will to the minimal beat of

> *Trājō ēl amōr su cōla de dolōres*

or spring open like a sonnet by Gerard Manley Hopkins:

> *Nō sōlo por las tiērras desiērtas dōnde la piēdra salīna*

from one sonnet to the next. As little "houses of fourteen planks" unfenestrated by end rhyme, they remain resolutely functional and unadorned: they house only large movements of the mind and show the grain and the knot of the poet's intention rather than the scrimshaw of the prosodist's virtuosity.

On the other hand, it would be a mistake to assume that they comprise a landscape of blockhouses and framed plank, like those pioneering encampments of the poet's childhood which went up in periodic holocausts and were rebuilt by Temucans "who know how to build in a hurry." Viewed against the profile of the wonderfully spindled and granulated *Odes*—or, indeed, from any vantage point along the circumference of poetry as such—his "century of sonnets" registers with remarkable elegance as a city of the mind in which passion and meditation come and go with powerful strides toward a noble objective. Indeed, it is with something of a surprise that one comes to realize—as an afterthought, rather than a concession to the "rail-splitting" Neruda—that the customary stabilizers and parquetry of sonnet are not regularly present in the unfolding poem. This is due, in part, to the "feminine" genius of Latinate discourse as such, with its functional repetition of identical or assonantal slack syllables which makes it almost impossible, at least to Anglo-Saxon ears, for Italian and Spanish not to *seem* to rhyme.

Closer reading reveals, however, the deeply traditional source of both the eloquence and the concord of the *Sonnets*. The density of a quatrain like the following, for example, should be apparent even without the translator's gloss:

> *Ay de mí, ay de nosotros, bienamada,*
> *sólo quisimos sólo amor, amarnos,*
> *y entre tantos dolores se dispuso*
> *sólo nosotros dos ser malheridos.*

The eloquence is there because the elegance is there, the traditional rhetoric of invocation and lament balancing romantic outcry with Gongoristic refinement, parallel syncopation of key words: *sólo, nosotros, amada, amarnos*. In Sonnet LXVI, where all is sparely set on the bones of the sonnet, and end rhyme is regular, Neruda proves that he can, at will, produce a sonnet in the classical vein of the Spanish masters, where the combining elements—marked density, parallelism, repetition, and a "Shakespearean" prosody so adroitly fused with the "Italianate" as to create a continuous texture of two end rhymes used six and eight times respectively—all point the way to the sources in Quevedo and Góngora so highly esteemed by the poet.

On the whole, the effect of Neruda's constant *sauvización* of the lines is to exchange the rail-splitter's hatchet for the eloquence of the cabinetmaker and the artisan. The fact that the eloquence is virile, flexible, intimate, need deceive no one, just as his earlier identification with Lincoln as rail-splitter (*El Leñador*) and Vallejo as "carpenters, poor carpenters" is inseparable from his compositional integrities as an artist. The *Cien sonetos de amor* are a landmark in the literature of the sonnet that confirms again the catholicity of Neruda's genius at its flood tide, at the same time as it breathes new life into dry sticks. It accomplishes the miracle of transforming that most servile and feudal of forms—the sonnet's long complaint of knightly self-denial and court compliment contrived for the express delectation of a patron—into a husband's book of hours, grievances, privacies, troubled meditations. It removes the inamorata, once coy and cruel by turns, from her medieval tower, into the kitchen, with its recognizably bourgeois panoply of "cups and glasses / cruets of oil and oleaginous golds," sets her, sharp as a snapshot, against a background of "blue salt, with the sun on the breakers," as she emerges, "mother-naked . . . taking her place in the world." It eternizes her in "ovens of clay with Temuco adobe," without the Renaissance boast of indestructibility for "this scribbling on the paper." In its fusion of both the elegant and the immediate, it proves again the eventual sophistication of Neruda's premise of the Impure as a species of "pastoral," in which, as Empson once pointed out, the complex man goes to school to the simple man "to mirror more completely the effective elements of the society he lived in."[7]

THE MOURNING NERUDA

The year 1961–1962 is notable, in Neruda's long chronicle of plenty, for the publication of three volumes of verse, each differing from the other in form and subject matter, and all in marked contrast to the special rigors of the *Sonnets*: *Las piedras de Chile* (*The Stones of Chile*), *Cantos ceremoniales* (*Ceremonial Songs*), and *Plenos poderes* (*Full Powers*). *The Stones of Chile*, which the poet with good reason calls his "flinty book," not only follows the format of a volume by Pierre Seghers celebrating the stones of

France, with photographs by Antonio Quintana, but, we are told in a preface, was "twenty years in my mind." During those years, Neruda contemplated the coastland of Chile with its "portentous presences in stone," which he later transformed "into a hoarse and soaking language, a jumble of watery cries and primordial intimations." The result is a "memorial" which organizes Neruda's lifelong fascination with the craggy, the telluric, and the metallurgical into a veritable Stonehenge of exact and monumental fantasy. The dimensions and intensities shift from poem to poem and image to image, from gigantic evocations in the vein of *Macchu Picchu*, to pebbles for the passing delight of a child, to memorial cairns and barrows elegizing the metamorphoses and convulsions of geological time. This is no mere programmatic picture book of curiosities, however, ready-made for the sightseer—no tourist's guide to the stones of Chile as "house," "harp," "hairy ship," "big table," or a bestiary of playful petrefactions including a bull, an ox, a lion, a turtle, and three ducklings. It is a freehand lithography of time and the spirit.

In any other hands, *The Stones of Chile* might well have turned into a marginal rather than a residual book, a mineralized eschatology. What is remarkable is the speed and the certainty with which Neruda, working in sportive and approximate contexts—the profiles which distance and illusion confer on stones—divines a deeper subject twenty years in the making, like antediluvian artifacts in the "corings" of a geologist. The poet's *aficiones* for wood, water, cereals, stars, shells, are already well-known staples of his substantive world, manifestations of his deep purchase on the "impure." His essay on "oceanography,"[8] with its spacy trajectory from the Pillars of Hercules to the *krakens* of Copenhagen and the *narwhals* of the North Sea, his conchologist's passion for the artifacts of the sea floor, his delight in plankton and the sea horse (rendered doubly attractive by the Spaniard's whimsical equivalence: "*unicornio marino*") similarly confirm his passion for the oceanic. *The Stones of Chile* takes a titan's step forward to fix them all in a massive assemblage of images, Medusan in its genius for turning to stone all it gazes upon.

The result, curiously enough, is not frozen Heraclitus or stopwatched Bergson, but a set of poems which yield to the imagination at every turn: which breathe, dissolve, nourish like those visceral deposits secreted by the ambergris whale so often observed by the poet from his Isla Negra window.⁹ Nothing is less static or earthbound than the stones of Neruda's Chile: by his "Great Rock Table" the "child that is truth in a dream / and the faith of the earth" waits "for his portion"; in his Harp, nothing moves but "a world's lonely music / congealing and plunging and trying its changes"; his Ship sails placelessly through deaths and distances; and out of his Blind Statue, he "cut[s] through the stone / of my joy toward . . . the effigy shaped like myself," devising "hands, fingers, eyes." Caliban's world of rock and primordial ooze is transformed into Ariel's domain of light, speed, scintillations, island music, ether:

> In the stripped stone
> and the hairs of my head
> airs move
> from the rock and the wave.
> Hour after hour, that changing of skins,
> the salt in the light's marination.

Despite the frequently "hoarse and soaking language," the "jumble of watery cries and primordial intimations," the impact of the volume is neither sodden nor wooden. Its contour remains, as it should, sculptural, mobile, diaphanous: "weddings of time and the amethyst," "marriages of snow and the sea" which mirror "the heart's whole transparency / in / the boulder / the water."

By contrast, the *Ceremonial Songs*, also dated 1961, is a more diverse work than either the book of sonnets or the book of stones. The title at once directs us to a difference of tempo, scale, intonation. In opting for the "ceremonial," certainly, Neruda is removing himself from the "general"—a designation he was happy to claim for that heroic compendium embracing fifteen volumes and 568 pages in the original edition published in 1950 (*Canto general*). Since the poet himself does not dwell on the "ceremonial" factor as such, one is left to deduce its attributes from a scrutiny of the constituent songs: their content, their form, the whole ambience of the "ceremonious" inflection. One notes, first of all, that it is a book which deals in sequences, concatenations, trains of poems, rather than "taciturn castles"¹⁰ of stone or "little houses of fourteen planks";¹¹ it is a book of long poems—the longest in twenty-two sections and the shortest in four—of a decidedly meditative and exploratory cast. The subjects fall readily into four general categories: commemorative pieces devoted to literary and historical personages (Manuela Sáenz, lover of Simon Bolívar; de Lautréamont); seasonal pieces, embracing midsummer and the rainy season; landscapes (Spain, Cádiz, the cordilleras of Chile, the ocean); and introspective pieces like "Cataclysm" and "Party's End," in which the poet contemplates his world, his person, and his scruples with a characteristic rotation or circuition of the troubled matters it contemplates.

The range of *Ceremonial Songs*, then, is ambitious: there is no attempt on the poet's part to mitigate the gravity and duration of his inductive labors. On the contrary, it seems to be one of the shaping criteria of the "ceremonial" that it aggrandizes and solemnizes whatever it touches. To be "ceremonious," apparently, is to be formal, speculative, unhurried: to build more and more *time* into the unfolding of the mind's apprehension of itself. In the realm of content, it is also, clearly, to celebrate and to elegize. However diversely the subject veers from persons to places, and from places to the things that embody them, the unity of mood, temper, tone, throughout the *Ceremonial Songs*—a kind of spiritual seepage—remains inviolable to the end.

At first reading, the persisting factor is felt to be a pervasive melancholy; but successive rereadings fix the melancholy as profoundly elegiac in origin. Only by adding the elegiac weight of the *Ceremonial Songs* to the cosmic and erotic melancholy of the sonnets and the book of stones can one begin to intimate the distinguishing cachet of the later poetry of Pablo Neruda. What remains to be noted in the whole vista of the late Neruda, from its whimsical inklings in *Estravagario* to the processional densities of *La Barcarola*[12] is the *de-ideologizing* of his subject, and its nervy containment in immediate acts of the poet's mind: his increasing reluctance to terminate existing doubts by rational acts of the will. It is this that imparts to all the hopes, apprehensions, and positional assurances of the poet their penumbral melancholy. And it becomes the task of "ceremony" to mediate between melancholia and the world, summoning up what is left of the old dispensation and casting out despair by reimagining the real in existential rather than ideological terms.

In short, the "ceremonial" songs serve notice that we have to do with a *mourning* Neruda, a *"poeta enlutado,"* not the pusillanimous guise which Neruda rejects both for himself and a perishing world ("The stones do not mope!") but the mourning once deemed "becoming" to Elektra, orphaned exemplar of the world's kinship. Certainly, it would be a disservice to suggest that the "mourning Neruda," like the "music-practising Socrates,"[13] is not sustained and consoled at every turn by political particulars which, in the striker's militant parlance of the 1930s, *organize* in the midst of mourning. Indeed, nothing is more apparent in the spectrum of Neruda's labors as poet and humanist than the energizing genius of both his melancholy and his empirical anguish. On the other hand, the abiding presence of the *poeta enlutado*—to which he testifies everywhere without guile or reservation—is equally apparent as a constant of his imaginative sensibility. If, in 1924, he begins with a ratio of "twenty love poems" to "one desperate song" (*Veinte poemas de amor y una canción desesperada*), the evidence of his work throughout the three *Residencias* makes it clear that the desperate song was actually unending, and determined the "surrealistic" displacements eventually wrought by his pre-revolutionary acedia. ("It so happens I'm tired of just being a man.") And if, as Luis Monguió has suggested,[14] the emergent politics of Neruda turns the world's melancholy into a celebration in which "*every* song is a love song," the seminal reciprocities of love and melancholy remain significant.

A sampling of the progressions of the most ingratiating of the pieces will serve to illustrate both the tactics and the dynamics of the "ceremonial": *Fin de fiesta/Party's End*—the terminal book of the poem as a whole. To all intents and purposes, the occasion of this vortical poem in thirteen parts is scenic and seasonal: the "first rains of March," the seacoasts of Isla Negra, and the omnipresent changes of the Ocean. Underneath this amalgam, however, like a tidal force under a breaker, a deeper theme asserts itself: the confrontation of renewable nature with unrenewable man. It manifests itself first in the motif that gives the poem its ironically lackadaisical title: the theme of "*fiesta.*" By "fiesta," it appears, Neruda intends the gregarious drive that assembles, celebrates, and eventually disperses all things—not merely the single "reveler," but the corporate being of his "words and mouths," the "roads," by which he materializes and disappears.

By Section Two, the poet has accomplished a kind of symbiotic fusion of the Season, the Man, and the Festival into a single aspect of the world's temporality.

The motifs of seasonal rain and the sea return in Section Three, "exploding in salt," ebbing, delaying, "leaving only a glare on the sea," and are churned into a "spray" of eschatological wonderment. On the one hand, the "submerged things" of the universe ask; "Where are we going?" and on the other, the algae riding the currents ask: "What am I?" They are answered by "wave after wave after wave," with Heraclitean enigmas: "One rhythm creates and destroys and continues: / truth lies in the bitter mobility."

The word "bitter" ("*amargo*") is a clue to the encompassing melancholy that thereafter seeps into the matrix of the piece and turns all into an elegiac meditation on the efficacy of human exertion—the people, footprints, dead papers, "transportation expenses" ("*gastos de transportes*") of man's efforts to match the unkillable being of the world with acts of the will and imagination. Here the weariness of the poet is such that he asks for a suspension, if not indeed a liquidation, of the inhabited world: inhabited poems, inhabited beaches, inhabited time, where the "habitable" is construed as the "distinguishing mark" of individual initiative: "for a moment let no living creature enter my verse." For the first time since the *Residencias* of his youth, Neruda, looking away from causes, factions, ideological commitments, into the void where the crystal expands, the rocks climb the silence, and the ocean "destroys itself," restates that heresy of all engaged protagonists: "It so happens I'm tired of just being a man." A more haunting issue, apparently, has presented itself with his returning acedia: it is Antony's enigma of the "marring of energy" and the miracle by which "the ocean destroys itself without marring its energy." The quantitative anguish of things is summed up by Neruda in another outcry, which measures the inadequacy of a world in which "our fathers in patches and hand-me-downs . . . entered the warehouses as one entered a terrible temple": the consumer's outcry of *How much?*

Thus, a third of the way into a shifting and many-sided poem, the backlash of baffled intentionality reasserts itself in political and polemical terms. A new insistence on expedient protestation—on "the whithers and wherefores / wherever it pleases me—from the throne to the oil-slick / that bloodies the world," mounting as the "grains of my anger grew greater," turns the purchaser's *How much?* into the prophet's and the revolutionary's *How long?* There follows another turn of the poet's imagination as a new assault of personal choice on the inequalities of the human condition flows into the voids and pockets of his initial melancholy. It is this systole-diastole of his meditative patterns that is the distinctive mark of the "mourning and organizing" Neruda. Indeed, he seems to breathe as naturally as a sponge on the ocean floor of his exacerbated discomfiture. He absorbs doubts, contradictions, passing flotsam in the great baths of ricocheting images and uneasy afterthoughts which he inhabits, rocking in the play of altering pressures, volumes, thermal densities, speeds. No one has written more vividly than Neruda of the thermodynamics and psychology of the deep-sea diver (See "Ode to a Diver"[15]); and somewhere, at the critical depths that break or sustain the human violator of the oceanic and the subterranean, Neruda has known how to anchor the rational balances that turn chaos into meditative order.

The result is an elegiac poem not unlike the *Elegien* of Rilke in both the discontinuities of its empirical search for hard answers, its preoccupation with "the dead with the delicate faces," the "preciously dead,"[16] and its insistence on "clarity," joy, a strenuous humanism that asks nothing of "angels" in its pursuit of the heart's fears and the spirit's intimations. It differs from Rilke's "ceremonial" amalgam of melancholy, skepticism, and temporal love, of course, in its *visceralization* of thought—its commingling of thought with "the thorn's languages / the bite of the obdurate fish / the chill of the latitudes / the blood on the coral / the night of the whale"—and its pendulum backswing toward "men." The "*Engel-nicht—Menschen-nicht*" ("Not men, not angels"[17]) of Rilke's impasse, glimpsed only briefly in Section Four, is promptly exchanged for "the brutal imperative . . . that makes warriors of us, gives us the stance / and inflection of fighters," as Neruda crosses his "bridge of commitment" (*lo que hicimos*) into the "pride of a lifetime" and its "organized splendor" (*el esplandor organizado*).

If the accomplishment of Neruda in *Party's End*, however, were merely tactical and ideological, one might well prefer to sweep backward to the derogated Rilke for truer confrontations of the human condition. The triumph of *Party's End*, however, is that its oceanic circuits stay nowhere for long, are not positional. The day sought by Neruda, in the end, is neither paradisiac nor ideological: it is an "expendable day," "a day bringing oranges," rather than a day of reckoning—though some hint of the social dream clings to the afterthought: "the day / that is ours if we are there to retrieve it again." At the close of the poem, the "white spindrift," the "ungratified cup of the sky," the "watery autumn" move in again, and, with them, the obdurate mobilities of a poet who remains "just as I was / with my doubts, with my debts, / with my loves / having a whole sea to myself." Apparently, it has been enough to "come back," to touch his "palms to the land," to "have built what I could / out of natural stone, like a native, open-handed," to "have worked with my reason, unreason, my caprices, / my fury and poise." No longer "deracinate" (*sin mis raices*) as man, as poet, as Chilean, clouded and luminous by turns, Neruda can now

> . . . say: "Here is my place," stripping myself down in
>   the light
> and dropping my hands in the sea,
> until all is transparent again
> there under the earth, and my sleep can be tranquil.

This redistillation of serenity clings to the whole of Neruda's *Plenos poderes* (1962), imparting to each of the thirty-six poems that unmistakable "fullness of power" to which its title bears witness. Weary "neither of being nor of nonbeing," still "puzzling over origins," professing his old "debts to minerality," yet wavering "as between two lost channels under water," the poet "forges keys," "looks for locks," opens "broken doors," pierces "windows out to living." What was plaintive or suspended in the *Ceremonial Songs* brightens in the upbeat of re-examined commitment, for which Neruda's distinguishing word is "*deberes*": obligations, and its ancillary variations in *deber*: ought, should, must, owe. Thus, in the introductory poem entitled "*Deberes del poeta*" ("The Poet's Obligations"), his concern is less with possibility than with necessity—the imperatives freely imagined and professed by the poet, to which Yeats gave the name of "responsibilities." The options subsumed under the "responsible" are at once explicit and mysterious: "I must hear and preserve without respite / the watery lament of my consciousness," "I must feel the blow of hard water / and gather it back in a cup of eternity," "I must encounter the absent," I must tell, l must leave, journey, protect, become, be, eat, and possess. Elsewhere, the poet alludes to the "responsibility of the minute hand," the accumulation of "persons and chores," "the imperious necessity for vigilance," "lonely sweetnesses and obligations," "mineral obligations," and "obligations intact in the spume." These, the poet explains, are compelled upon him "not by law or caprice, / but by chains: / each new way was a chain"; he calls for "caution: let us guard the order of this ode," but his mood is blithe: "I am happy with the mountainous debts / I took on . . . the rigid demand on myself of watchfulness / the impulse to stay myself, myself alone . . . my life has been / a singing between chance and resiliency."

Side by side with the theme of resiliency (*la dureza, la dura realidad*) goes a theme of *pureza*, purity, as both a measure of the poet's effectiveness and a reward of his happy "obligation." A table of variations would include not only a multitude of passing allusions—pure waves, pure lines, pure towers, pure waters, pure bodies, pure hearts, pure feet, pure salts—and their variants in *claro* (clear lessons, clear capitals, clear vigilance, as well as "clarities" that are smiling, cruel, and erect) but entire poems like "*Para lavar a un niño*" ("To Wash a Child") and "*Oda para planchar*" ("In Praise of Ironing"). All, says the poet, must be cleansed, washed, whitened, made clear: as in a Keatsian dream of "pure ablution round earth's human shores,"[18] the land's outline is washed by the salt (*sal que lava la línea*) and the land's edge washes the world (*La línea lava el mundo*). Not only does Neruda invoke "a time to walk clean" in the name of the newly washed infant, and insist on "ironing out" the whiteness of the sea itself (*hay que planchar el mar de su blancura*); in the end, poetry itself is made white (*la poesía es blanca*).

Thus, between *dureza* and *pureza* (resiliency and purity) and *deberes* and *poderes* (obligations and powers) the poet "writes [his] book about what I am" (*escribo un libro de lo que soy*) with stunning mastery of all the themes that embody a total identity. The "mourning carpenter" (*enlutado carpintero*) of *Estravagario* and the *Sonnets* is still there, "attending the casket, tearless, / someone who stayed nameless to the end / and called himself metal or wood"; he contributes two of the volume's eulogies, one addressed to the dead "C.O.S.C." and the other, to the nine-and-a-half-year-old "little astronaut" whose "burning car" touches "Aldabaran, mysterious stone," and "crosses a life line." The old preoccupations with the lost and remembered of a poet bemused by the sacramental character of all change are found again in poems like "The Past" ("*Pasado*"); and the old melancholy ("To Sorrow," "*A la tristeza*"): "For a minute, for / a short life, / take away my light and leave me / to realize / my misery, my alienation." So, too, are the dead, "the poor dead" (*al difunto pobre*), the people (*el pueblo*), the nights and the flora of Isla Negra (*Alstromoería, la noche de Isla Negra*), farewells (*adioses*), births (*los nacimientos*), ocean, water, sea, planet, tower, bird—each lending new force to that fullness of power by virtue of which a master of chiaroscuro "in the full light of day" paradoxically still "walks in the shade."

The Burning Sarcophagus

The great watershed of the sixth decade of Pablo Neruda—the work which, at the present writing, soars like the terminal pylon of a bridge spanning four epochs including the *Residencias*, *Canto general*, and the *Odas*—is, of course, the *Black Island Memorial* (*Memorial de Isla Negra*), published in 1964 to solemnize the poet's sixtieth birthday. In effect, it constitutes a fourth gargantuan span over which flows the spiritual traffic of more than half a century, on its way to destinations as hazardous and uncharted as those previously inhabited by a poet who warns us:

> I have never set foot in the countries I lived in,
> every port was a port of return:
> I have no post cards, no keepsakes of hair
> from important cathedrals.

Its trajectory supports the weight, the diversity, and the architectural stresses of everything encountered en route: exile, deracination, embattled ideologies, and the vested enmity of the world. All that the poet has written, imagined, foresuffered in purgatorial changes of forms and allegiances: shapes of the "crepuscular," the erotic, the tentative, the "enthusiastic," halfway houses of wood and stone, and "residences" that metamorphose into bloody bivouacs in Spain, consulates in Rangoon, Ceylon, India, Mexico, France, flights into Russia, China, Mexico, Peru, "voyages and homecomings" to his native cordilleras, all the wanderings of Ishmael and The Prodigal Son, debouch like a great estuary into the pages of *Black Island Memorial*, from whose terminus "Casa La Chascona,"[19] a poet's "house of dishevelment," arises like a hand-hewn Acropolis.

One puts the case a little grandly because the poet's conception is almost orientally pyramidal in its vision of a monument built by the living for a residence *not* of this earth, as well as on it. *Black Island Memorial* is a chieftain's or a pharaoh's personal cenotaph, calling to mind the *alcazares* of Andalucia and the Heorots of Anglo-Saxon myth, hung with shields, talismans, shaggy animal pelts and precious stones, whalebone curiosities of the "seafarer" and "far-wanderer," and encircled by the ocean like a moat. How barbarously or how cunningly Neruda has built his vast *Memorial*, what artifacts, prophecies, legends and gods he has carried over his hearthstone, what enigmas still await him in island, mainland, and ocean, remain to be examined.

The critic's first task, confronted with the grandeurs and *longueurs* of this conception, must be a qualitative one: how to align the "memorial" with the "general," the "elemental," and the "ceremonial" as four phases in the orientation of a talent. I should like first of all to suggest that the "memorial" mode is *nonhistorical*: in Coleridge's words, it "emancipate[s the poet] from the order of time and space,"[20] whereas the general, the elemental, and the ceremonial may be subsumed under it as modes and dimensions of the temporal. The dynamic that gave *Canto general* its unwearying sweep and thrust after three anguished *Residencias* was history: history as the court chronicler and the anthropologist conceive it, and History as the polemical Marxist conceives it in an escalating dialectic of freedom and bondage. It is the historical mode, in this layman's understanding of the term, that induced Neruda to join his private chronicle with the perfidies and restorations of Chile, and the Creation story with a multinational saga of the death of kings, conquistadors, quislings, duces, and assorted "satraps" in a Century of

Perishing Capital. His chronicle is roughly vertical in its sequences: into its rational progressions stream real wars, personal memoir, autobiography, topical villains and saviors, political reportage, global and national disasters, up to the final page, signed, in the poet's own hand, "today, 5 February, in this year / of 1949, in Chile, in 'Godomar / de Chena,' a few months before / the forty-fifth year of my life."

The pentad of Isla Negra, on the other hand, is concerned with memory rather than history. Into its five volumes there tumble a disorganized *recherche* of events, ruminations, obsessive images, words, doubts, allegiances, political mandates, and spiritual recoils in an *ordre du coeur* rather than an *ordre raisonné*. Their point of departure and their point of return are essentially the same: *time present*, in which the poet, brooding daily on the change and the permanence of things from a seacoast in Isla Negra, is induced to evoke an answering dialectic from within. The dialectic is not Marxian, but metaphysical, and its polarizing genius is not History but Memory—the same power invoked by Saint Augustine as "the belly of the mind"[21] in Book X of the *Confessions*. The scene, for all its flashbacks into the displacements of a lifetime, is Isla Negra, to whose sea changes, cloudscapes, and seasonal immediacies the poet constantly returns for a "residence on earth" fixed at last by the heart's choice and due process of mortality.

Visitors to Isla Negra have, between jest and earnest, alluded increasingly to the islanded Neruda as Buddha, guru, and lama[22]—a kind of Latin amalgam of Merlin and Prospero. More often than not, the epithets are irreverently, if affectionately, intended: but the "saintly" Neruda, with his unflinching gaze on the "four perturbations of the mind:[23] desire, joy, fear, sorrow" and his Augustinian assault upon Memory, is an exact distillation of the impact of the *Memorial*. Coming into "the plains, caves, and caverns of my memory" from the secular engagements of a lifetime, he says, almost in Augustine's words ("There meet I with myself and recall myself, and when, where, and what I have done, and under what feelings"):

> I also would see myself coming
> and know in the end how it feels to me

when I come back to the place where I wait for myself
and turn back to my sleep and die laughing.

The laughter of Neruda is a special dimension of the Hispanic—the Cervantine gift of the *quixotic*, in the presence of the Impossible, as it has flowed into the parlance of the world from the uplands of La Mancha. Like both Quixote and Augustine, however, Neruda is called back, out of History to the "reasons and laws innumerable of numbers and dimensions, none of which hath any bodily sense impressed," and to the "deeper recesses" where "all must be drawn together again, that they may be known; that is to say, they must as it were be collected together from their dispersion"; and, indeed, "re-collected." Thus, we have Neruda's:

Memory

All must be remembered:
a turning wind, the threads
in the threadbare event must be gathered,
yard after yard of all we inhabited,
the train's long trajectory,
the trappings of sorrow.

Should a rosebush be lost
or the hare's track dissolve in the night,
should the pillars of memory
topple out of my reach,
I must remake the air,
the steam and the soil and the leaves. . . .

I was always an avid forgetter:
in my two human hands
only the untouchable things of the world
live unscathed,
and the power of comparison
is the sum of their total destruction.

Forgetting, destroying, comparing, the human rememberer, "toiling in the heavy soil" of his being, like Augustine, discovers not sequence and consequence, but the plasm of identity itself, the ego which has been the subject of the poet's wonder in

Whitman, in Hopkins, in Neruda, and in Aurelius Augustinus of Tagaste and Carthage. "What is nearer to me than myself?" asks Augustine. "It is I myself who remember, I the mind." Ransacking the world of "things, either through images, as all bodies, or by actual presence," he comes upon the mind's own testament of what it has committed to memory, "that same memory where before [all] lay unknown, scattered, and neglected." Augustine has suggested the exaltation and despair of the chase, with Nerudian avidity: "Over all these do I run, I fly; I dive on this side and on that, as far I can, and there is no end. . . . Thus do I remember Carthage." And Eliot in our own century has nodded acerb consent: "To apprehend / The point of intersection of the timeless / With time, is an occupation for a saint."[24]

This I take to be both the task of Neruda's *Memorial* and a measure of its "sanctity," for which no fashionable mystique need be sought. Again and again, over the record of personal loves, circumstantial and topical particulars, names, dates, habitations, concretions, a persisting query is heard, turning the knowable into a "dangerous world"[25] of wandering lights and haunted misgivings: "Who was I? What? What were we both?" In a poem taking its title directly from Blake's great archetype of spiritual quest, "Little Boy Lost," Neruda suggests the malaise of the saintly identity:

> Nothing answers me now: let it pass.
> *Being* never was once: we went on being . . .
> All kept on happening,
> one man impurely persisting,
> son of the purely born son,
> till nothing remained as it was . . .
> Sometimes we remember
> the presence that lived with us,
> there is something we want from him—that he remember us, maybe,
> or know, at least we were he and now talk
> with his tongue,
> but there in the wreckage of hours
> he looks at us, acknowledging nothing.

The note is sounded again, plangent and ardent by turns, in "Those Lives":

> "That's how I am," I'll say, leaving this
> pretext in writing. "This is really my life."
> But everyone knows that's not how it happens at all.
> Not only the cords in the net, but the air
> that escapes the interstices matters:
> The rest remains as it was: inapprehensible.

and again:

> I live as I can
> in my destiny's ruthless lucidity,
> between the luminous and the desperate halves,
> disowned
> by two kingdoms which never were mine.

and again:

> Who is that Other I am? He who never
> contrived how to smile and died of his perfect deprival?
> Who outlasted the festival bells and the gala
> carnation, and toppled the lecterns of cold?
>
> Late, it grows late. I go on with it all. I pursue
> this or that paradigm, never guessing the answer,
> knowing myself, in each of the lives I have lived,
> both absent and present, at once the man who I was,
> and I am.
>
> Does the rub of mysterious verity lie there?

The quest for "mysterious verity" is constant throughout these volumes of palpable and impalpable stocktaking, jarring all that clings to the poet's ego, from its moorings in the historical past. In the "memorial" world of Isla Negra, the poet's *verdad* is exactly equivalent to the lover's search for *claridad* in the *Sonnets*—with which it is eventually fused. Keeping "steadfastly triangular," seeing all "at first hand," affirming the "power of the real to augment / and enlarge us," yet "cherish[ing] the equivocal cut of my song," Neruda writes "on the card of our hunger / an order of bread and an order of soul for the table." For this purpose, he returns to that most elusive and obsessive of this themes: the

Song of Myself, and its complementary theme of Non-Being—the *Ser-y-no-ser*, the *Nada*, and the *Sueño* that link him to the great Hispanic tradition of self-contemplation in Calderón, in Unamuno, in Machado, in Guillén. It is in his unappeasable self-absorption, from *Twenty Love Poems and a Desperate Song*, up to the present—his solipsistic meditation on the "water and rock" of "realism and idealism, both parts of my world"—that his love and his desperation have their source.

A closer look at the first of the five volumes of his *Memorial* may help to illustrate. It begins, as did the concluding section of *Canto general* (flamboyantly entitled *Yo soy: I Am*) twenty years before, with a retrospective account of the childhood and the young manhood of the poet. The title of the present volume, however, focuses upon a habitation rather than a name, on a landscape rather than an ego: Temuco of the alternate droughts and rains, the earthquakes, the timberlands, the holocausts—*Donde nace la lluvia* (*Where the Rain Begins*). In his singularly appealing essay on "Childhood and Poetry," published in 1954,[26] ten years before his *Memorial*, Neruda has given us a prose recitative for his Song of Temuco: a personal history from the days of his great-great-grandparents who planted their vines in Parral, to the remarriage of his father, "a nondescript farmer, a mediocre laborer, but a first-class railroader," and his removal to Temuco.

It would appear that Neruda has deliberately set out, in *Where the Rain Begins*, to produce a versified "Childhood and Poetry"—a kind of Wordsworthian *Prelude* to a chronicle of wanderings and revolution, over which the "Spirit of the Place" broods to the end, as the Lake Country broods over the musings of Wordsworth. Where the prose chronicler informs us, for example, that "My mother could pick out in the dark, among all the other trains, precisely the train that was bringing my father into the Stationhouse at Temuco or taking him away," the Spirit of the Place remembers: "The brusque father comes back / from his trains: / we could pick out / his train whistle / cutting the rain, a locomotive's / nocturnal lament / in the dark. Later / the door started trembling." The plank houses, alternately soaking and burning, the mother "dead in Parral not long after I was born," the "tutelary angel" of his father's remarriage, Doña Trinidad Candia, the "glacial" cold of the Temucan schoolhouse, the midsummer forays into the Araucanian forests, the "searing" Cautín and the summits of Nielal, the swans of Lake Budi, the green plums, the beetles, the *copihues*, the secret world of Sandokan and Sandokana,[27] and, above all, the omnipresent whistle of the night train cutting fatefully through flood, distances, and darkness with the wail of a vanished paternity—all are transcribed from the essayist's pages.

Here, it would appear, History and Memory are well matched. The way is vertical, if circuitous, and the elements are in sequence: Birth, First Journey, The Stepmother (*La Mamadre*), The Father, The First Ocean, The Southern Earth, Winter School, Sex, Poetry, Timidity, Swan Lake—such, literally, is the order of his book. Precisely when all is in readiness for a triumphal affirmation of consciousness, however, the Spirit of the Place materializes like a wraith to reaffirm the poet's total disbelief in the buoyant historicity of his chronicle. The pivot that triggers his melancholy significantly takes its title from the poem by Blake already referred to: "Little Boy Lost" ("*El niño perdido*") and the *theme* of loss—"*lo perdido*"—is thereafter never absent from the long circuit of the *Memorial*. As it happens, the word is one of the most multiple—and therefore least translatable—in the rich overlay of its contexts in Spanish. Beginning somewhat lamely with its nominal denotation—"lost"—it traverses an equivocal spectrum from "vanished," "absent," "lapsed," "destroyed," "forgotten," "fallen," to "dead"—always with a nostalgic look backward. Its blood cousin, the multifaceted word to which it generally points, like a needle to a magnet, is *soledad*, or aloneness, loneliness, isolation, self-engrossment, intactness, alienation. Between whirls a mob of grieving mutations: *confuso* (confused), *secreto* (secret), *indeciso* (indecisive), *enlutado* (mournful)—the *no-sé-qué* (I-don't-know-what) of empirical metaphysics on its way to the limbo of the *No-Ser* (Non-Being).

A sampling of the pages of *Where the Rain Begins* must suffice to suggest both the persistence of the lost (*lo perdido*) and its absorption into the spectrum of the solitary (*soledad*). There are *pasos perdidos* (lost footsteps), *fiebre o alas perdidas* (lost fever or wings), *bodega perdida entre las trenes* (shop lost among trains), *grité perdido* (I cried out, lost), *se perdía mi infancia* (my childhood was lost), *perdí los arboles* (I lost the trees), and the *estudiante triste perdido en el crepúsculo* (sad schoolboy lost in the twilight)—which brings the poet up to the publication of his second volume, *Cre-*

puscularío, The Book of Twilight. In between glows an *ignis fatuus* of flickering modulations which are the special illumination of the memory asserting its bafflement at the intersection of time with the timeless. Here, too, the contexts are diverse: *se me confundo los ojos y las hojas* (my eyes and the leaves are confused), *la confusa soledad* (the confused solitude), *una luz indecisa* (an indecisive light), *entro indeciso* (I enter undecided), *la enlutada noche* (the mournful night), *yo, enlutado, severo, ausente* (I, mournful, severe, absent), *volví con el secreto* (I returned with the secret), *en el secreto mundo / caminamos / con respeto* (in the secret world / we walk / with respect), *no distingo entre labios y raices* (I do not distinguish between lips and roots), *no sé, no sé de donde* (I don't know, I don't know whence), *no sabía qué decir, mi boca / no sabía / nombrar* (I did not know what to say; my mouth did not know how to name).

Specification is in order here because the total effect, in *Black Island Memorial*, flickers from point to point like marsh gas, with no expectation of an explosive outcome. It is not given to Neruda. as agonist of the Lost, to shield his eyes in the presence of the mind's transfiguration: neither blinded nor prostrate, he looks steadily into the impurities of duration—animal, vegetal, and mineral,

> while a luster is borne underground, antiquity's princeling
> in his natural grave-clothes of sickening mineral,
> until we are tardily there, too late to be there at all:
> being and not being, life takes its being from these.

Only once is he permitted to see "plainly: one evening, / in India" when, gazing steadily into the flames of a riverside suttee, he sees "something move out of the burning sarcophagus /—call it smoke or a spirit—" and remains until all is consumed, leaving only "night and the water, the dark / and the river, steadfast in that place and that dying." The world's body and the combustion of the world's body: these are the themes of the saint's vigil and man's image of the world's loss.

The point finally to be made, in this uneasy reading of an equivocal legend, is that the *perdido* pursues Neruda throughout the whole compass of his *Memorial*, as a function, rather than a defection, of memory. One could, I am sure, make a tidy case for the first four volumes as the poet's odyssey or hegira through all four elements of the substantive universe—(1) Water (*Donde nace la lluvia: Where the Rain Begins*), (2) Air (*La luna en el laberinto: The Moon in the Labyrinth*), (3) Fire (*El cruel fuego: The Cruel Fire*), and (4) Earth (*El cazador de raices: The Root-Hunter*). Since History and Memory weave themselves equally into his great design, it might be specified for the curious that Water is cognate with the poet's Temucan childhood, Air, with the erotic and the passional, Fire, with revolutionary upheaval and world war, and Earth with the poet's return to his sources on the Chilean mainland: a thoroughly Blakean cosmology. Over this tidy collocation of elements and events, however, as over the burning suttee, moves the Spirit of the Place, surrounded by all the paraphernalia of quantitative optimism, brooding on the Lost, like Dürer's Lady of the Melancholies. If there is any question regarding the persistence of the Lost, one has only to follow the path of the *perdido* into the fifth and final volume, which Neruda somewhat misleadingly has entitled *Sonata crítica* (*Critical Sonata*), as though disengagement and perspective had at last been achieved. Here the tally is no less obliterating than in Book One: Neruda, as card player, "plays for the sake of losing" (*juego /para seguir perdiendo*); he is "lost in the night" (*perdido en la noche*); "there is no longer left [him] a place to lose / the key, the truth, or the lie" (*no hay donde perder / la llave, la verdad, ni la mentira*); we have "all lost the battle" (*todos perdimos la batalla*); "the truth has died" (*ya se murió la verdad*); humanity "loses its way" (*esta humanidad que pierde el rumbo*); the pure being is "lost between words" (*el casto ser perdido entre palabras*); life is "passed or lost" (*cuanta vida / pasamos o perdimos*); memory "trembles in the lost shadow" (*tiembla mi memoria en la sombra perdida*); the "salt is scattered and lost" (*una sal esparcida y perdida*); the wind's sigh remains "lost in the leaves" (*sigue el susurro del viento perdido en las hojas*); but, nonetheless. "I have found my lost roots" (*encontré mis raices perdidos*).

It would be both mischievous and myopic to suggest on the basis of such passages that *Black Island Memorial* is the labyrinthine complaint of a defeated and despairing man. On the contrary, Neruda's steadfast confrontation of the Lost, his avid immediacies and open-ended determination to live "between the luminous and the desperate halves," measure the strenuous vitalism of his position. It is the Muse of Memory, as Keats's Hyperion was also to discover in the fallen world of Titans, sifting the passing event for its "Names, deeds, gray legends, dire events, rebellions, / Majesties, sovran voices, agonies, / Creations and destroyings"[28] that "shows the heart's secret to an ancient power" with an intimacy impossible to History. And it is the double vision of the later Neruda, committed equally to Mnemosyne and Clio, that demands an exact accounting from the poet of "what is past, and passing, and to come."[29] Neruda, looking back at his bulking *Memorial*, unfinished to the very end, declares in the *Critical Sonata*: "He who sings both dies and does not die, he who sings goes on living and dying"; he "sings the earthly and heavenly tower from the abyss." It is thus that the *poeta enlutado*, reading the oceans and weathers of Black Island, construing interstices, gaps, collapses, uncertainties, with a passion that dazzles the imagination, holds in his keeping the plenty and certainty of the world. No poet living has braced the whole of his talent on that "point of intersection of the timeless / With time" with a comparable freedom from cant and preconception, or more resolutely approximated the "occupation for a saint."

Notes

1. Alfredo Cardona Peña, *Pablo Neruda y otros ensayos* (Mexico: Ediciones de Andrea, 1955), p. 40.

2. See *Visiónes de las hijas de Albión y El viajero mental* [*Visions of the Daughters of Albion and the Mental Traveler*] *por William Blake* (Madrid: Cruz y Raya, 1934; repr. Ediciones Botella al Mar, n.d.). His translation of *Romeo and Juliet* was published by Editorial Losada, in Buenos Aires, in 1966, as No. 308 in their Biblioteca clásica y contemporánea.

3. "Sobre una poesía sin pureza," *Obras completas* (Buenos Aires: Editorial Losada, 1957), pp. 1822–23. Translated in *Selected Poems of Pablo Neruda*, ed. and trans. Ben Belitt (New York: Grove Press, 1961), pp. 39–40.

4. See the first edition of *Estravagario* (Buenos Aires: Editorial Losada, 1958). The adornments, profuse in the original edition, are omitted in the more recent *Obras completas* (Buenos Aires: Editorial Losada, 1962; repr. 1968).

5. "Hymne," *Oeuvres complètes*, Bibliothèque de la Pléiade (Paris: Librairie Gallimard, 1954), p. 222.

6. "L'Invitation au voyage," ibid., p. 127.

7. William Empson, "Proletarian Literature," *English Pastoral Poetry* (New York: Norton, 1938), p. 12.

8. "Oceanografía dispersa," *Obras completas* (1957), pp. 1825–27.

9. Ibid., p. 1825: "In this way, the green whale (*Bachianetas glaucus*), enroute to the South Pacific and the warm islands facing my windows in Isla Negra, gets his nourishment."

10. "Algunas palabras para este libro de piedras," ibid., p. 1717—a whimsical allusion to the poems in *The Stones in Chile*.

11. "A Matilde Urrutia," ibid., p. 1649. The "little houses" are, of course, the sonnets of *One Hundred Love Sonnets*.

12. Work in progress, of which a fragment entitled "Amores: Matilde" appears in Volume 5 (*Sonata crítica*) of *Memorial de Isla Negra*. Further "fragments" appear in a pamphlet published by Ediciones de la Rama Florida (Lima, 1966), in an edition limited to 300 numbered copies. The volume itself was published in December 1967 by Editorial Losada in Buenos Aires.

13. Friedrich Nietzsche, *The Birth of Tragedy*, trans. Francis Golffing (Garden City, N.Y.: Doubleday Anchor, 1956), p. 90.

14. *Selected Poems of Pablo Neruda*, trans. Belitt, p. 29.

15. Ibid., pp. 226–33.

16. Cf. Neruda's "*Los muertos de rostro tierno*," "*Los más amados muertos*," with Rilke's "*den jugendlichen Toten*" (*Die sechste Elegie*) and the dead lovers of *Die erste Elegie*.

17. Rainer Maria Rilke, "First Elegy," *Duino Elegies*, trans. Stephen Spender (New York: Norton, 1939), p. 20.

18. Sonnet XX, *The Poetical Works of John Keats*, ed. H. W. Garrod (New York, London, Toronto: Oxford University Press, 1956), p. 372.

19. Neruda's name for his so-called "House in the Sand." The elaborate homage ("*La Chascona*") that concludes the *Memorial*, as a whole, however, seems to synthesize two of the poet's houses—"Casa La Chascona" and "Casa La Sebastiana" in the San Cristobal hills overlooking the Santiago harbor and the right bank of the Mapocho River. Both were vandalized—the latter irreparably—after his death. For a picture book of Isla Negra, with photographs by Sergio Larrain and a text in poetry and prose by Pablo Neruda, see *Una casa en la arena* (*A House in the Sand*) (Barcelona: Editorial Lumen, 1966).

20. Samuel Taylor Coleridge, *Biographia Literaria*, ed. James Engell and W. Jackson Bate, 2 vols. (London: Routledge & Kegan Paul; Princeton: Princeton University Press, 1983), chap. 13, I, 305.

21. *The Confessions of Saint Augustine*, ed. Arthur Symons (London: Walter Scott, n.d.).

22. Thus Selden Rodman, in "A Day With Pablo Neruda," *Saturday*

Review of Literature, July 9, 1966: "I saw him as a Buddha, ageless, perfectly composed, with just the suggestion of a childlike smile around the corners of his sensual mouth." And in a recent issue of *ABC* (Barcelona), "*Neruda como es,*" Luis María Anson writes: "The poet, converted into a living god, an immutable Dalai Lama, reads an ode, heard with all the intentness of a religious prayer."

23. Cf. Neruda's "*las cuatro estaciones del alma*" (the four stations of the soul), invoked in the concluding lines of "*Cuanto pasa en un día*": "How Much Happens in a Day."

24. T. S. Eliot, "The Dry Salvages," *Four Quartets* (New York: Harcourt Brace, 1943), p. 27.

25. "Infant Sorrow," *Blake's Poetical Works*, ed. John Sampson (London: Oxford University Press, 1938), p. 100.

26. Reprinted in the *Obras completas* (1957), pp. 19–30. Translated, with certain omissions, by Ben Belitt, under the title "A Pine Cone, a Toy Sheep . . ." in *Evergreen Review*, 6, No. 22 (January-February 1962), 22–35; repr. in *Evergreen Review Reader* (New York: Grove Press, 1968),

27. Hero and heroine of the piratical *Sandokan* by Emilio Salgari (1863–1911), nostagically invoked by Neruda in his "Childhood and Poetry."

28. "Hyperion," *Poetical Works of John Keats*, ed. Garrod, p. 242.

29. "Sailing to Byzantium," *The Collected Poems of W. B. Yeats* (New York: Macmillan, 1951), p. 192.

II
Toward a Poetics of Uncertainty: Trial Balances

(For Kenneth Frost)

CHARMIAN: Is it you, sir, that know things?
SOOTHSAYER: In nature's infinite book of secrecy
A little I can read.

—*Anthony and Cleopatra*

Preface

Supposedly, grave issues call for grave demeanors; and for some, the pages that follow will appear philosophically foreshortened in their approach to contexts that demand a certain magisterial removal. Nevertheless, I have chosen the private to the pontifical way, with all the oddities of an intimate reading, because I wish to make the most of all the "uncertainties" that compete for the creation of a context. Because my concern is with the *reading*, rather than the writing, of poems, I have addressed myself primarily to readers of good will who ask for maximum proximity to the texts and intent of *poets*; who prefer the questioner's thrust to the answerer's placebos for true access to the challenges of the imaginative process. My concern with the principles and postulates of the "new physics"—to which I owe the homage of an admiring amateur—I would hope, is appropriately chary and quizzical; but since the titans of quantum have beckoned to the poets with a similar reticence, I hope it is allowable to share the quandary of a mutual trespass. If the result is to multiply, rather than diminish, uncertainty, that also serves the purposes of my venture—if, as Niels Bohr has suggested, "Quantum provides us with a striking illustration of the fact that though we can fully understand a connection . . . we can only speak of it in images and parables. . . . When it comes to atoms, language can be used only as in poetry."[1] It needs only the uphill stagger of a Sisyphus to confirm the timeless polarities of a double sanction as a myth for questers on two ascending vanguards: "[Y]ou tell me of an invisible planetary system in which electrons gravitate around a nucleus. You explain this world to me with an image. . . . you have been reduced to poetry. . . . that science that was to teach me everything ends up in a hypothesis, that lucidity founders in metaphor, that uncertainty is resolved in a work of art."[2]

B. B.

Notes

1. Werner Heisenberg, *Physics and Beyond: Encounters and Conversations*, trans. Arnold J. Pomerans (New York: Harper & Row, 1971), pp. 210, 41.
2. Albert Camus, "An Absurd Reasoning," *The Myth of Sisyphus and Other Essays*, trans. Justin O'Brien (New York: Vintage, 1955), p. 15.

11
Toward a Poetics of Uncertainty

i

O fret not after knowledge, I have none.
—John Keats

"WHAT PORRIDGE HAD JOHN KEATS?"

FOR SOME, the negations of Keats[1] may sound like a Pyrrhic surrender of the issue, rather than an epistemological engagement of it, or an unnecessary confusion of "knowledge"—about which we may all be inclined to commend a soothsayer's reticence—with infallibility. "Fret *not* . . . I have *none*": readers of poetry will be quick to counter with the question: "If knowledge is not to be had, why should poets and exegetes raise such distracting expectations of it?" The passing decades have only added to the urgency of Keats's denial and the inflationary raising of expectations; more than ever, the modernities and priorities of poetry press upon the vanguard of all that awaits our re-examination "in Nature's infinite book of secrecy." Browning put the question to his own century with a conchologist's eye for the chemistry of the sub-marine:

> Who fished the murex up?
> What porridge had John Keats?

There are always those who come to the poet with new ruses and alarums for authorial outcomes, "solutions," panaceas—who insist on the shortest distance between two lexical points, closed answers to probabilities and uncertainties, univocal returns; whose stance is acquisitive, confrontational, and categorical, and demands an end to possibility in the name of "knowledge."

That, I think, is the kind of knowledge that Keats is repudiating as a poet and describing as merely "fretful," rather than be-*mused* in the Gallic sense of the word, which prefigures the poet-as-ruminant, with "muzzle uplifted to the air." For the Keats of the Odes, caught between the "vision" and the "waking dream," the "heard melody" and the "unheard," it could never have been the Muse's intent to conclude ontological ventures in knowing with a derogation of wonder, but rather to "pipe to the spirit, ditties of no tone"—to re-enfranchise knowing and press on to its vanishing point; even, if need be, *to destroy it.* Jacob Bronowski, in his essays on the "new" science, tells us that Werner Heisenberg invoked what he called an "uncertainty principle" in the name of the electron, and insisted that "'no events, not even atomic events, can be described with certainty, that is to say, with zero tolerance.'" Bronowski, a Fellow of the Salk Institute for Biological Studies, who was equally at home in his study of *William Blake: The Age of Revolution*, in *The Ascent of Man*, goes on to commend a fellow-mathematician, Niels Bohr, for his twofold role as one of the "founder-fathers of twentieth-century physics" and "consummate artist" in quantum mechanics—because, says Bronowski, his approach allowed of no "ready-made answers." He used to begin his lectures with a cautionary proviso which has been repeated by nuclear physicists in Copenhagen, Vienna, and Los Alamos ever since: "'Every sentence that I utter should be regarded by you not as an assertion but as a question.'"[2] According to Bohr, "Quantum theory provides us with a striking illustration of the fact that though we can fully understand a connection (between mathematical concepts and the body of the world) we can only speak of it in images and parables."[3]

Keats is claiming a similar option for "the man of genius, especially in poetry": the option of remaining negative in a continuum of inexhaustible enablement—of multiplying the unforeseeable to enhance the "unforesayable" in an ongoing dynamics of uncertainty—to all of which he gave the misleading name of "Negative Capability." In pursuing that oxymoron of insatiable dubiety, Keats discovered for the poet, and for readers of poetry, what Heisenberg and Bohr discovered for twentieth-century physics: the volatility of inconclusiveness as a mode of positive empowerment in the search for "what is past and passing and to come" (Yeats).

ii

... it struck me what quality went to form a Man of Achievement especially in Literature and which Shakespeare possessed so enormously—I mean *Negative Capability*, that is, when a man is capable of being in uncertainties, Mysteries, doubts, without any irritable reaching after fact and reason—Coleridge, for instance, would let go by a fine, isolated verisimilitude caught from the Penetralium of mystery, from being incapable of remaining Content with half knowledge.

—John Keats to George and Thomas Keats, December 22, 1817

BETWEEN THE DICE-CUP AND THE URN

Quantum physicists today might well couple the name of Einstein with that of Coleridge in a comparable impasse of imagination[4] that rejects epistemological "mystery" for the spatio-temporal fixities of the finite sciences. For Einstein, there was always the apocalyptical proviso: "*God does not throw dice!*" with the particulars of His gratuitous universe—despite Job's protestations to the contrary and Mallarmé's assurance that "*Un coup de dés jamais n'abolira le hazard*" (A throw of dice will not eliminate chance). In His "new physics" for ontologists of a Third Millenium, God merely "throws cosmoses," in the sense that a potter's wheel "throws" pots, for curators of the cosmic condition. For mages of quantal mechanics like Heisenberg, however, there will always be the haunting rejoinder that "Concepts do not allow a complete description of observed phenomena"—that the Mystery, in effect, is inseparable from the "silent Forms" that "tease us out of thought / As doth Eternity" (Keats).

Although a century of "modernism" now separates the Dice-Cup of Einstein from the Urn of John Keats, it is hardly likely today that a case will have to be made for Samuel Taylor Coleridge as "worker in the Penetralium," despite Keats's precocious disclaimer. It should be abundantly apparent to all, in the ice-caves and dulcimers of Xanadu, the "thunder-fits" and the "rotting seas" of the Ancient Mariner, as it is in the conceptual mazes that have made key chapters of the *Biographia Literaria* inexhaustible to twentieth-century thought, like the equations of Bohr and Heisenberg and Schrödinger. Coleridge's caveat to readers of the "new poetry," emphasizing the "motion of the serpent" and "the path of sound through the air," rather than the ruler's or the razor's edge—a physics of unforeseeable contractions and replications—in a "parable" of the imaginative trajectory, is a case in point.

iii

> The reader should be carried forward, not merely or chiefly by the mechanical impulse of curiosity, or by a restless desire to arrive at the final solution; but by the pleasureable activity of the mind excited by the attractions of the journey itself. Like the motion of a serpent, which the Egyptians made the emblem of intellectual power; or like the path of sound through the air; at every step he pauses and half recedes, and from the retrogressive movement collects the force which again carries him onward.
>
> —*Biographia Literaria*, Chapter XIV

"The Journey Itself": Coleridge, Baudelaire, Rimbaud

For connoisseurs of "uncertainty," the passage is full of warnings, challenges, watchwords, philosophical injunctions and contradictions and postulates, metaphors. But before considering Coleridge's metaphors, I should like to pause for the motif of "voyage" as such—or what Coleridge calls "the pleasureable activity of the mind excited by the attractions of *the journey itself.*" The theme is a constant one in the poetry of nineteenth-century Romantics: English poetry gives us Coleridge's own *Rime of the Ancient Mariner*, and French poetry gives us Rimbaud's *Le Bateau Ivre* and Baudelaire's *Le Voyage*. All three enlarge, with striking similarity of mood and intent, on the theme of "journey" and its gamut of exotic "attractions"; all three are not merely extravagant fantasies of travel, with a global itinerary of places, climates, wonders, horrors, contrasts, prodigies, disasters, and geographical dispersals, but also the great signature pieces of their respective authors—a poetics for their respective visions as masters of their craft.

For Coleridge's Ancient Mariner, the Journey embraces a lifetime of polar and tropical upheavals in behalf of the "attractions" of untried and unanticipated encounters—a sailor's logbook of nautical perils and meteorological accidents and mysteries, which epitomize a lifetime. For Rimbaud, the poet's venture is likened to a "drunken boat"—one of those nondescript, donkey-drawn scows or barges used for menial jobs of transport in the confines of insignificant canals—which breaks its bonds and is swept out to sea in a dizzying escapade of global proportions. For Baudelaire, it narrates the excitements and the marvels, the exacerbations and eventual disenchantment of the poet as globe-trotter or tripper who, in the purest and most inexplicable sense of the phrase, leaves "just for the sake of leaving," to savor the "attractions of the journey itself."

In all three cases, the quest is for a "pleasureable activity of the mind" and an unexamined surrender to the "attractions of the journey itself." There is no thought of any reasoned displacement from ports of departure to foreseeable destinations. All arrivals are inconclusive, frustrating, ungratifying. The *journey* is literally all—viewed by *"ceux-là seules qui partent pour partir"*—and discloses its mindlessness in the end as a journey without a habitation or a name. For all three voyagers, "pleasure" is never very far from terror—a *"dérèglement de tous les sens"* (Rimbaud)—and the world is all the more unfathomable for having been traversed.

Baudelaire, for example, begins by enlisting the faculty of infantile wonder as the source of the traveler's wish to gratify a passion for unforetellable experience and get on with the knowing and naming of a world:

> For the child, in love with maps and prints
> The universe and his vast appetite are one.
> O how tall the world is by the light of lamps!
> In memory's eyes, how small the world becomes!

He stresses only the avidity and naïveté of the child's longing to match the mariner's maps with the pleasures of sensuous contact and personal acquisition. He then opens up the frame to its fullest range in a geography of self-canceling excess—a nautical chaos of perpetual passage, change, unconditional diversity and reversal, disillusion, vertigo, disaster:

> We imitate, O horror! the top and ball
> Waltzing and bouncing even in our sleep.
> Curiosity torments and tosses us about
> Like a cruel angel who flogs the sun itself.
>
> Strange enterprise! in which the goal recedes,
> And, being nowhere, might be anywhere at all!
> Strange that the Man of indefatigable surmise
> Should race on a lunatic quest for peace forever!

Midway in the journey he challenges the voyager to render a true and passionate account of his voyage: "Tell us what you've seen!" and in a further section: "Yes, and what else?" Where Coleridge's Mariner answers piously and submissively, disclosing all to the Wedding Guest who "cannot choose but hear" and turning all to "parable":

> He prayeth best who loveth best
> All things both great and small,
> For the dear God who loveth us
> He made and loveth all

Baudelaire's pieties are demoniacal and emphasize only the vertiginous disgust and ungratified repudiation of the voyager's momentum. It is hardly surprising that the author of *The Flowers of Evil* should finally envision his voyage as "an oasis of Horror in a desert of Ennui." For the voyager in Ennui, only entropy is certain, and each man's death is a lonely contingency without precedent or hope of human accountability.

His final insight is the most disturbing of all and turns the Uncertainty Principle into a poetics of the Insatiable—a diabolism of Quest, in which probability and omniscience confront each other in a demand for the Unimaginable that is as sinister as it is Faustian. Both the tripper's urge to get on to the next port of call and the compass's fixation on Certainty are exposed in their true character as a *death wish*—the poet's (or the reader's) compulsion to "plunge to the bottom of the Gulf—Heaven or Hell, does it matter which?—in search of Something New."

A century later, it was for Michel Foucault, as historian of "insanity in the Age of Reason," to equate the theme of "voyage" with a pathology of madness in which "navigation" delivers "the madman to the Uncertainty of Fate" and "every embarcation is potentially the last." For Foucault the malignity of "embarcation" and the confinement to "water and navigation" are equivalent to self-loss in "that great uncertainty external to everything . . . ":

> It is for the other world that the madman sets sail in his fools' boat; it is from the other world that he comes when he disembarks. The madman's voyage is at once a rigorous division and an absolute Passage. . . . He is a prisoner in the midst of what is the freest, the openest of routes: bound fast at the infinite crossroads. He is the Passenger *par excellence*: that is, the prisoner of passage. And the land he will come to is unknown. . . . One thing at least is certain: water and madness have long been linked in the dreams of European man.[5]

iv

COLERIDGE—METAPHORS OF VOYAGE: THE SERPENT AND THE PATH OF SOUND

Let us return to the passage as a whole with a change of emphasis; let us shift our attention from the theme of "journey" or voyage, to metaphors which adorn or enable it, as Coleridge's directive for the right reading of poetry. Note that Coleridge addresses himself to the *reader* of poetry—to us, you and me, whose function and intent it is to engage the poetic artifact and reflect on its merits as an imaginative datum through an act of *reading*. What he has to say concerns us as appraisers of poetry because it is a poet's mandate about the right reading of poems: how he intended his poem to be read by a seasoned and responsible reader in search of pleasurable outcomes—and who would wish to read a poem otherwise? "The reader," says Coleridge, "should be *carried forward*"; that is to say, the reader has a right to expect a volatile outcome. Poems do not stand still or come to nothing. They get on with themselves, they move ahead and move the reader with them, they proceed, they *create a third thing* out of the union of the reader and the text, which comes to nothing if not read. The premise is a vitalistic one: poems have the power to carry the reader with them, and are at once a vessel to confine and contain and a vehicle to propel. *Both* progress. Both are on-going. But how and where should poems go?

Here, Coleridge, like Keats, chooses the *via negativa*, and tells us how the right reader ought *not* to proceed. He should not, says Coleridge, be carried forward "merely or chiefly by the *mechanical* impulse of curiosity." Mechanical impulses of curiosity, presumably, belong to the syllogistic process of argumentative persuasion: that chain reaction of "Socratic" discourse where right answers to hypothetical questions are obligatory and irreversible to men of good will: that is, if thus and so are granted as acceptable premises, *mustn't* thus and so mechanically and rationally follow, as in a table of algorithmic magnitudes? He then proceeds with a second negative alternative: the on-going reader should *not* be moved by "a restless desire to arrive at the final solution." "Restless desire" is to Keats's purely "fretful" pursuit of knowledge as Coleridge's "mechanical impulse of curiosity" is to Keats's "irritable reaching after fact and reason." The terms are cognate. In both cases, what is repudiated is a determinism that suppresses chance and subverts accidentality, contingency, the random possibility intent on enlarging its options, wherever they might lead, rather than vitiating its outcomes. For Coleridge, as for Keats, the imaginative way is never conclusiveness, finality, arrival, the questioner's domination of his question, but the constant enhancement of the unforeseeable, the augmentation of cognitive power, the excitement of displacements yet to come.

That is to say: Poetry is always *what is on its way to happen, but never overtaken*. The right reader is always concerned with the potential, rather than the terminal, stance—with "the *pleasureable* activity of the mind," he goes on to say, "*excited* by the attractions of the journey itself." His approach is unabashedly hedonistic and tentative: a reaffirmation of the Uncertainty Principle and an identification of uncertainty with the dynamism of "pleasure." In the psychology of pleasure, he assumes, there is always an element of fortuity and hazard; in our own century Rilke went a step further to say "Beauty's nothing but the beginning of Terror we're still just able to bear"; and from her seclusion in Amherst, Emily Dickinson confided to a world at large: "I dwell in Possibility / A fairer house than prose, / More numerous of windows, / Superior for doors." Coleridge himself went on to a further heresy in the name of the Pleasure Principle: The "immediate object of Poetry is *pleasure*, not *truth*." The priorities of the esthetic transaction demand that the mind be excited, pleasured, aroused, *before* it brings its properties as Mind to bear on eventual Truths.

Here, it would appear that for Coleridge this skewing of priorities and wayward shifting of the scales comprised an ontology unique to poetry as a "species of composition opposed to works of science" by its "reconciliation of opposite or discordant qualities" which "subordinate art to nature . . . and the manner to the matter." If so, the poet's priorities invite yet another philosophical risk: that his elevation of the affective over the cognitive returns of his vocation imperils the viability of the imaginative transaction and the autonomy of his medium. It was for Wordsworth to press on to the final presumption that "The knowledge of both the Poet and the Man of Science is Pleasure. . . ."[6] Poetry is the impassioned expression which is in the countenance of all Science."

It may be asked why the same principle of Uncertainty in the realm of nuclear physics, committed to the quantitative and mechanical, should have come to repudiate causality and turn the micro-world of "quantum mechanics" into an oxymoron of incompletion and pure Probability. Here, it would appear, the "impassioned expression" of Quantity—the *certainty* that 2 always precedes 3, as 4 always follows it, as an axiom innate to the algorithmic mode—should work miracles of certitude by the direct calibration of exploding particles in a controlled artillery of *machines* specifically devised to compute the metrics of the observable, with the aid of super-accelerators, cyclotrons, cloud chambers, and a sophistication of geometric equations undreamt of by Euclid or Pythagoras. Yet it is precisely the alchemists of the minuscule who have come to insist on the ephemeral character of their enterprise and embrace the "uncertainties, mysteries, doubts" that Keats claimed for the Kingdom of "the imagining

Man of Achievement." Heisenberg admits that he was "especially attracted by the *mysterious, inexplicable* features of quantum theory." Niels Bohr explains:

> In all previous physics, or in any other brand of science, you could always try to explain a new phenomenon by reducing it to known phenomena or laws. In atomic physics, however, all previous concepts have proved inadequate. We lack a language in which we can make ourselves understood. . . . A theory cannot "explain" anything in the usual strict scientific sense of the word. All I can hope to do is to *reveal connections* and, for the rest, *leave us to grope as best we can*. . . . *When it comes to atoms, language can be used only as in poetry*.[7]

For a moment, one thinks of E. M. Forster's elevation of the principle of "muddle" as a key to the polity of the Britannic protectorate in *A Passage to India* and his choice of the epigraph "*Only connect!*" to plot the disasters of domestic chaos and misprision in *Howard's End*. What is clear, in the new gospel of a "higgledy-piggledy" "law-without-law," with its "observer-participancy" of the "utterly random,"[8] is that a revolution in the physical sciences, which has already overtaken the disciplines of chemistry, biology, astrophysics, oceanography, meteorology, and medicine, has bonded with the poetry of imaginative discourse, much as Wordsworth predicted, and opened the way to a Third Millennium for poets still mindful of the "countenance of all Science." At the bottom of Baudelaire's "gulf" of the unprecedented and the singular lies universal Uncertainty; in an age of interplanetary machines and the fractal microscopy of the metamathematician, "our knowledge of the objects treated in Physics consists solely of readings of pointers. . . . The physical atom is, like everything else in physics, a schedule of pointer readings."[9] It was for John Wheeler to carry the atom to its vanishing point of quantifiable reality with a final flourish of the physicist's pen: "Rock is made of positive and negative electric charges, and more than 99.99 percent empty space. . . . If the stone is someday revealed to be altogether emptiness, 'reality' will be none the worse for the finding." One is left to ponder whether the stone of Sisyphus in its uphill journey to the summit of a gravitational delusion had the weight of a feather's filament, or really required the labors of a Titan to accomplish its fabulous ascent.

V

COLERIDGE AND BLAKE: THE CONTRARIETY PRINCIPLE

From such a paradox, we may deduce a third principle which bears directly on the right reading of poetry, in a triad of imaginative directives: the *Uncertainty Principle*, calling all interpretations into doubt in a search for textual clusters of multiple probability; the *Pleasure Principle* ("the immediate aim of Poetry is pleasure, not truth"); and another which we might call the *Contrariety Principle*—that is, the coexistence of interacting polarities, or oppositions, or contradictions, which, as they move from the polar extremities of their spectra to a center of interpenetration, or collision, no longer cancel each other out as incompatibles, but reinforce one another in what Niels Bohr liked to call a physics of "complementarity." Hegel, that soberest of epistemologists, would say "*Thesis-Antithesis-Synthesis*," and call the total pattern the "dialectical" way to knowledge favored by philosophers of the rational investigation of great unknowns and uncertainties like "justice," "free will," "the Good Life"; that is, if we are to talk about the nature of the Good, let us first postulate the existence of its rational opposite, Evil, and then move forward toward some center that is the consequence of their philosophical interpenetration—what biologists have called the "cross-fertilization of enemy strains," and physicists, the postulate of a "Grand Unified Theory" of "unfoldings" and "enfoldings" (David Bohm).

According to Bohr, quantum mechanics has not touched the quick of its function until it has felt the gravitational pull of its looming contradictions on their way to theoretical resolution in a concept. For Blake, the proposition could be compressed into a single epigram that has come to epitomize the essence of his commitment as a poet who went on to reconcile Innocence with Experience, Energy with Eternity, Imagination with Jesus: "Without Contraries, is no Progression." Coleridge, in his *Biographia Literaria*, patiently restated the premise in the nomenclature of electronic physics, which might almost serve as an Ur-text for quantum mechanics:

> Opposites . . . are of two kinds, either logical, i.e., such as are absolutely incompatible; or real, without being contradictory. . . .

a body, at one and the same time in motion and not in motion, is nothing, or at most, air articulated into nonsense. But a motory force of a body in one direction, and an equal force of the same body in an opposite direction is not incompatible, and the result, namely rest, is real and representable. . . . The principle may be thus expressed. The identity of *thesis* and *antithesis* is the substance of all being; their opposition the condition of all existence or being manifested; and everything or *phaenomenon* is the exponent of a *synthesis* as long as *the opposite energies are retained in the synthesis.*

That, however, is the language of epistemological inquiry into the nature of knowledge, which I have deliberately avoided in my *contextual* pursuit of "poetry and the imaginative process." Let me therefore return to the *imagery*—which is, after all, the root-word for "*imag*-ination," or the encoding of images for concepts—of Coleridge the *poet* in his quest for the imaginative coefficient of a poet's artifact.

vi

Most of my readers will have observed a small water-insect on the surface of rivulets, which throws a cinque-spotted shadow fringed with prismatic colours on the sunny bottom of the brook; and will have noticed how the little animal *wins* its way up against the stream, by alternate pulses of active and passive motion, now resisting the current, and now yielding to it in order to gather strength and a momentary *fulcrum* for a further propulsion. This is no unapt emblem of the mind's self-experience in the act of thinking. There are evidently two powers at work, which relative to each other are active and passive; and this is not possible without an intermediate faculty which is at once both active and passive. (In philosophical language, we must denominate this intermediate faculty in all its degrees and determinations, the IMAGINATION. . . .)

—*Biographia Literaria*, Chapter VII

Coleridge's Water Spider

Note that Coleridge begins somewhat flatteringly—a useful ploy for rhetoricians who seek to disarm their readers before springing the trap of planned analogy!—by identifying with the majority of his readers as an amateur observer of natural quiddities, attributing to them interests and preoccupations identical with his own ("*Most of my readers* will have observed"). He focuses at once on the behavior of the common water spider—"a small water-insect on the surface of rivulets"—as another potential emblem of intellectual power, or totem animal for the "mind's self-experience in the act of thinking." In so doing, however, he "pauses and half recedes" (in the manner of the spider itself) to point up a detail which may very well have escaped the notice of the Sunday naturalist.

Tacticians of suasion might well wonder why he did so, since the detail—a "*cinque*-spotted shadow fringed with prismatic colours on the sunny bottom of the brook"—is not germane to any analogy of the spider with the powers or mobility of the imaginative process, which is his ostensible theme. In effect, he *throws in a kind of dividend* which for a moment reverses the true intent of the passage—actually *immobilizes* the spider and turns the insect at rest on the tensions of the water into a kind of verbal or Newtonian sunburst. To put it another way: he dawdles hedonistically on his way to "facts and reasons and final solutions" for a *pleasurable* digression that confirms the intimacy of his observation and the privacy of his extrapolations. The language becomes odd, special, baroque, the writing denser and more sensuous, *as though* Coleridge were on his way to a poem rather than an entomological datum. He invokes the Pleasure Principle and the Uncertainty Principle to prepare for analogical intensities yet to come, and makes us wonder whether we are looking at a water insect at all, or a "phaenomenon" of alternate rest and mobility. The talk is a strange talk of rainbows, prisms, submarine colors, the "sunny *bottom* of the brook," rather than the "surface of a rivulet," which alone reinforces the physics of ricochet essential to his analogy. He even sends us to the dictionary to discover what we are supposed to understand by a "*cinque*-spotted shadow" (a throw of dice which turns up a 5, or a 5 on dice or playing cards, as well as a fivefold overlap of scintillations).

Paradoxically, it is by this tactic of enticing distraction, this capacity for negative withholding and suspension, that he also proves his authority as observer and engages the reader as surrogate eyewitness. The specificity and pleasure of his digressions prove overpowering: with renewed confidentiality we are ready to accept any further observations on the movement of water spiders from this gambler in rainbows and playing cards. In effect, Einstein's rejection of the God of the Dice-Cup is made to yield to the "hidden variables" of Heisenberg's formula for the physics of Uncertainty. Coleridge has *paid attention*. So should *we*!

vii

> Postpone the anatomy of summer, as
> The physical pine, the metaphysical pine,
> Let's see the very thing and nothing else.
> Let's see it with the hottest fire of sight,
> Burn everything not part of it to ash.
>
> Trace the gold sun about the whitened sky
> Without evasion by a single metaphor.
> Look at it in its essential barrenness
> And say, this is the center that I seek,
> Fix it in an eternal foliage
>
> And fill the foliage with arrested peace,
> Joy of such permanence, right ignorance
> Of change still possible. Exile desire
> For what is not. This is the barrenness
> Of the fertile thing than can attain no more.
>
> —Wallace Stevens, "Credences of Summer"

The Postponements of Wallace Stevens: What Poetry Does

There are at least three profitable ploys for the investigation of poetry which await us at this stage: (1) the *medium* of poetry—the verbal stuff out of which poems get themselves made, and which incarnate "ideas of order": the rhetoric, the prosody, the nomenclature of measuring and reifying language and enlisting the perceptions and passions of poets; (2) the *idiom* of poetry—the factor that gives identity and privacy to the use of a public medium and reveals the expressive mark of "the individual talent"; (3) the *imaginative process* whereby the poet's mind, acting upon language and reality, achieves the compositional transformation of both. Any may serve to provide the reader with intimations of *"what poetry is,"* but I am content with a working premise rather than a table of priorities. I am going to assume that we are constantly and continually interested in *what poetry does*—with poetry as a species of power, an energy in the physicist's sense of a force that enables and transforms, an activity of the mind, the psyche, and the cosmos—as well as with the *means* by which the poet directs his powers and skills upon language, as others direct them upon number. Wallace Stevens, addressing himself to the same problem, hazards a solution in the guise of an exhortation, which provides a convenient beginning—a table of "credences" rather than a methodology for imaginative engineers.

Note that Stevens, like Coleridge, begins with *postponements* and polarities: *"Postpone the anatomy* of summer, as / The physical pine, the metaphysical pine"—more dawdling! more idleness! more procrastination! more negativity! The "anatomy" of things—which many would consider to be seminal as well as skeletal: what the flesh of things needs, if it is to hang properly on the frame of things is always "postponable": there is no royal road to its sources. The tone of the poem as a whole is, accordingly, tolerant and bland, rather than "irritable," though the poet's directives to his reader are far from vague or indolent. The verbs have the urgency of a "methodology," after all: *see, see, burn, trace, look at, say, fix, fill, exile.* The rejected options of "anatomy" bristle with the contrary fascinations that made it a favorite word of John Donne's: *anatomy*: literally, to dissect, or cut up—in order, one assumes, to get at first principles and plain facts of bodily articulation; in other words, investigative looking in the interests of causative knowing. As a word, it belongs to the same orbit as Coleridge's "mechanical impulse of curiosity" and "final solutions," Keats's "facts and reasons," the Newtonian physics of scientific predictability—and is summarily rejected by Stevens. "Physical"/"metaphysical," Tweedledum/Tweedledee—does it really matter?

For Stevens, apparently, the poet does not begin dialectically with acts of preliminary comparison, definition, categories, nomenclature, the naming and manipulation of parts, abstractions, theorems, or discursive computations of relationships by which the mind turns all things mental, and the "physical pine" *becomes* the "metaphysical pine." What is important for poetry is not the looking *for*, or the looking *at*, but the moment of penetrative *seeing*: "Let's see the *very thing* and nothing else." What Stevens is appropriating for poets are the priorities and maximum intensities of the *seeable*; his "very" thing carries the archaic inflection of the visionary's "Verily, verily!" Seeing, for Stevens, involves an undistracted search for the identity of things, the "*Ding*-iness" of the manifest, the idiosyncracies by which a thing is what it is at its maximum intensity—and nothing else.

In stanza 2, there is an almost alchemical transmutation of matter, when the sky is *whitened*, rather than gilded, by the sun: a kind of *halation* in which the seen thing not only is shown in its unique exposure, but is actually "over-exposed" in the photographer's sense of the word, as the photon on the blackened plate reveals the trail of the particle that produced it. Stevens then goes on to repudiate the whole domain of metaphor—all mere similitudes and equations of likeness which distract us by their double referent and subvert the singularity of the seminal. Antipoetically, he demands not equivalence, but identity and idiosyncracy. Only at this point, the white heat of the unsupplantable, can the *seen* be subsequently *looked at*—but looked at, says Stevens, in its essential "barrenness." But what could he mean by equating essence and centrality with "barrenness"—and, in the very next lines, go on to talk of "eternal foliage," "full foliage," "permanence," fecundity, peace? And what is "right ignorance of change"?

Apparently, the serpent of knowledge has stopped to gather itself into coils for the next lunge. We are back with Keats again, somewhere, in the "Penetralium of Mystery"—with "Fret not after knowledge, I have none"; with Negative Capability or the power to relinquish all "irritable reaching after fact and reason." Coleridge is also present in Stevens's injunction to "Exile desire for what is not" ("the restless desire to arrive at the final solution"). The quantum of "essential barrenness" is reaffirmed in the concluding oxymoron: "the barrenness of the fertile thing that can attain no more." In the same spirit, another great contemporary chose the "barren" way to the quintessential—the "enterprise" of "walking naked"—and espoused a modernist's oath of allegiance, with the prayer:

> Through all the lying days of my youth
> I swayed my leaves and flowers in the sun.
> Now may I *wither into truth!*
>
> —W. B. Yeats, "The Coming of Wisdom with Time"

viii

MACHADO AND BLAKE: THE EGG AND THE EYE

Let us pursue further the distinction between *looking at* a thing and *seeing it* as aspects of the poet's attentiveness—sensory epiphanies ensuring imaginative rather than quotidian outcomes. Are they indeed one and the same thing? Is one a prior circumstance of the other; and if so, which is the necessary enabler of the other? Does one *look at* or *look for* a thing in order to *see* it, or must one see the thing first and *look at it* at leisure long after? Which state, or intimation, gives us the truth, rather than the appearance, of "the very thing, and nothing else," and constitutes the imagined or imaginative datum? Or is there no real need to make distinctions of priority or reality between the two and brood on how Tweedledum turns into Tweedledee?

In place of "*pines*," physical and metaphysical, Antonio Machado, one of the twentieth-century masters of contemporary Spanish poetry, in a curious work dealing with the "epigrams, maxims, memoranda, and memoirs of an apocryphal professor" recommends—of all things!—the poet's apprenticeship to an *egg*! What if the poet, like those prestidigitators who employ the common egg for extraordinary feats of mystification and illusion, were to set himself the housewife's task of boiling an egg as preparation for a poem called "Boiling the Egg"?

> I have had occasion to define poetry as man's dialogue with time, and to call certain poets "pure" because they empty themselves of their personal time, in order to grapple alone, or almost alone, with time as such; rather as though one would chat with the buzz-

ing in one's own ears, that most basic sonal manifestation of temporal flux. We agreed, in short, that poetry is the word in its time, and that the task of the teacher of poetics is to teach his students to maximize the temporality of their verse. All our class exercises . . . have been devoted to this end, even our most elementary ventures, one of which I remember: a poem called "Boiling the Egg." . . . We found, in effect, some serviceable images for lyrically transcribing basic culinary procedure—the little alcohol burner flaming bluely, the metal utensil, the agitation of the water, the little hourglass for timing. . . . What was lacking was the *central intuition from which the poem should have started in the first place*: our solicitude for the egg never entered into the matter at all; *we forgot the egg because we never truly saw it,* were unable to live inside the whole process of its cooking and make it our own.

—Antonio Machado, *Juan de Mairena*

Note that Machado, like Stevens, places emphasis on the mysterious "emptiness" (which I take to be another word for "barrenness") of the observer and the "central intuition" from which the poem, en route to the imaginative process, "*should* have started, in the first place." For Machado, the poetry of the egg is inseparable from the *seeing* of the egg—the "very" egg and nothing else, in its primal state before the metamorphoses of its "boiling." Only then can the egg "alone or almost alone" alter its reality to match the changing realities of the anticipating observer. For the poet in pursuit of his poem, there would follow all the indispensable ontology of its boiling: the white and the yolk of the egg (still under its shell) rendered opaque by the physics of its calefaction; the egg turned "medium" at the 3-minute stage, hard at the 7-minute stage (here, "the hourglass for timing" is punctually reversed), the egg rendered divisible into solid or semi-solid entities, etc., etc.

Apparently, the "seeing" of the egg, like its boiling, is drenched in Time, and it is Time that prefigures the hidden multiples of its chemistry. Before sitting down to his poem, for example, the poet may elect to remove his egg at the desired calibration and negotiate the particulars of its consumption: the cracking of the shell, the ingestion of the yolk and albumen, the chemical transformations of the egg by animal enzymes—and so on, to the gourmet's surprises of the omelette, the egg sunny-side up, scrambled, or panned, the egg as quiche, as egg salad, the egg "Benedict" or deviled, the egg poached atop an English muffin—all triumphs of the appetitive psyche, the chemistry of cooking, and the calibrations of the "little hourglass for timing." All await the ministrations of the summoner as possibilities of the Other; all, in the thinking of Machado, "refuse to disappear." The Otherness of the Seen "subsists, persists; it is the hard bone on which reason breaks its teeth. Abel Martín, with a poetic faith as human as rational faith, believed *in the other*, in 'the essential Heterogeneity of being,' in what might be called the incurable *otherness* from which *oneness* must always suffer."

How to put an end to the mutations of the still-imaginable Egg! Even the trick of its balancing—the egg as gravitational rather than thermodynamic equation: the undinted egg stood on its end as a Brunelleschian riddle for the dome builders of Santa Maria del Fiore—has passed into the folklore of transoceanic physics for the "pleasure" of posterity.

Meanwhile, the Platonist, at his games with the Idea of the Egg—the prototypal Egg of Creation Itself, the Egg with the Hen of Us All brooding the Embryo, and the Embryo honing its beak for the mayhem of its encompassing Shell from within—still awaits its appointed epiphany, forgotten by all but the dairyman at his morning rounds of the hen-roost. . . .

ix

We are led to believe in a lie
When we see with and not through the eye.

—William Blake

Blake: The Eye and the Lie

Let us turn to another poet's venture at definition and consign Machado's example to the realm of optical illusions, like the conjurer's egg; let us examine an epigram by Blake for further light on the seen and the unseen. Perhaps the first thing to be said about the above passage is not that it is gnomic or oracular or a couplet, but that its concern is, again, an epistemological one:

that is to say, it focuses attention on the means by which we define and devise dependable data, turn that data into dependable knowledge, and transform that knowledge into dependable belief to confirm and consolidate our sense of enduring reality. I stress the "dependability" of the procedure in all its phases, since it is obviously Blake's purpose to open the way to those eventual "truths" which, according to the poets, should follow immediate pleasures. Blake's implied premise is that no one would willfully expend all this metaphysical anguish upon the creation of *false* beliefs, or "lies." But such indeed would be the case, he argues, if we saw *with* and not *through* the eye.

What would follow, Blake condemns as a total subversion of perception. It is significant, I think, that Blake chooses the eye among the available senses, to epitomize the delusions, falsifications, errors, deceptions, untruths of all sensuous knowing—*not* to discredit the whole sensorium as such, as Plato did, or belittle the eye as an epistemological tool of knowledge-making, but to point up a right and a wrong, a redemptive and a destructive, use of the senses by which knowing, as such, is humanly accomplished. Elsewhere, Blake is to enlist the eye as an adjunct of the prophetic faculty itself—which he reserves for the sonal domain of the *heard*: "*Hear* the voice of the Bard / Who Present, Past and Future *sees*!"

Despite the emphasis placed upon the "*with*ness" and the "*through*ness" of *things*, Blake's real concern is with the spirit in which we appropriate the faculty of vision and the process by which we engage the faculty of observation—vision in its optical rather than its mystical sense—to prepare ourselves for valid acts of imagination. Is the purpose of vision to terminate sensation by arbitrary acts of denotative or descriptive knowing, naming, telling—a knowing that will thereafter exist apart from the knower and the namer, constant and unchangeable in itself, as a mechanical "impulse of curiosity" that has run the gamut of the machine—or is it the function of the eye to open the way to unforeseeable permutations of "possibility"? Is the eye a *tool*, or is it a *thoroughfare* into the personal identity? How do *you* go about, Blake would ask of the visual knower, turning particulars into universals if the intent is to "do good to another in minute particulars"?

Blake's approach in the present epigram is negative, like

Keats's, however much the second of his two operative prepositions implies a positive alternative: "not *with*, but *through*!" He is concerned with patterns of systematic self-delusion and the dynamics of the visual lie: *false* knowledge-making and the mendacity of the visual initiative. He generalizes massively with the first person plural: "*we*"—all of us, anyone of us, all the time, are constantly being duped into the fabrication of false data. We are "*led* to believe" (as the lamb is "led" to the slaughter?) by a great confidence-game of which we remain compulsively unaware: we habitually "see *with*" and not, as real clairvoyance demands, *through* (that is what *per*-ception means!) the eye, penetratively.

What else are we to make of these cautionary prepositions? Are they merely a linguistic quibble to reinforce the gnomic character of an aphorism, or are they crucial directives that truly take us in opposite directions and threaten the integrity of imagination and vision? For one thing, they help us to distinguish between the eye as *eyepiece*, apparatus, optical machine—a device deployed or abandoned at will like a jeweler's loupe or a lorgnette—which predetermines the whole circumstance of the seeing and repeats an identical datum with each usage. In this sense, the whole creation, seen *with* the eye as "eyepiece," merely registers an unchanging datum brought into critical focus by the calibrations of the lens grinder, rather than the exertions of the spectator, and disposes, once for all, of the purely "mechanical impulse of curiosity" deplored by Coleridge.

On the other hand, we have a notion of the eye as part of the seer's self, part of the body which, in Hopkins's words, "each man not only feels *in* and acts *with*, but also feels and acts upon." The eye, in other words (Hopkins goes on to insist), is "*my* eye and *of me* and *me*," and carries into the seen thing the history and sensibility of the seer, as well as a biological faculty of his species. To *see with* the eye is merely to *look at* the *Other*; to *see through* is to penetrate it with the whole psyche of the *Self*. Blake was to say, on an even more luminous occasion, "The eye altering, alters all." For Blake, the difference could be considerable. Asked by a casual sun-gazer whether, on looking at an ordinary English sunrise, he did not see "a round disk of fire somewhat like a guinea," he replied apocalyptically: "Oh, no, I see an innumerable company of the heavenly host crying 'Holy, holy, holy is the Lord God Almighty.'" We may assume that the "guinea-sun" was there to be *looked at*, at will, by every pedestrian Londoner; the "heavenly host," as the phrase goes, "remained to be *seen*."

x

How do you know but every Bird that cuts the airy way
Is an immense World of Delight clos'd by your senses five?

—William Blake

Blake: The Bird and the Airy Way

It is time to proceed to other proverbs and "auguries" of William Blake's which bring the emphasis to bear on the thing *observed* rather than the dilemmas of the *perceiver*, on the object observed rather than the identity of the Observer: indeed, on that "immense World" of substantive "Delights" enclosed or disclosed by our "senses five"—the infinite "reification," as philosophers would say, of all that lies outside the Observer. Coleridge may have put the matter rather too grandly when he pontificated in a single sweep of the pen: "All knowledge rests on the coincidence of a Subject and an Object"; and went on to define Imagination as "the living Power and prime Agent of all human perception . . . a repetition in the finite mind of the eternal act of creation of the infinite I AM."

Blake, however, challenges rather than asseverates, confronts us rather than overwhelms us. The datum he chooses is not a serpent or a water spider or a rising sun, but that airiest of all staples dear to the heart of Romantics: a bird in flight—not Brancusi's chromium abstraction or Yeats's golden singer of Byzantium, but a bird known at first hand by Audubon and Darwin, a bird with a real species, a habitat, and an ornithological phylum known to the birdwatcher, the naturalist, and the man in the street or the fields—a bird out of nature, with no talent whatever for transcendental metaphor.

Yet Blake's epistemological stance is apparent at once from the weight of the opening words, which pose the question classic to all philosophers concerned with the criteria and procedures of knowledge-making: "How do you *know*"? How do you bring your experience to bear on the usable universe and turn it into artifacts of the mind? The *you* is confrontational: its intent is to infinitely diversify the outcome, rather than generalize. The pronoun is not a collective "You" which might lead to an editorial "We" or an anonymous "one"; rather, it postulates the grueling initiative of the First Person Singular: I—I, for one; You, for another. The "but" is similarly part of the grammar of confrontation: its intent, like the water spider's, is to go against the current, to "butt" its way *upstream* against the gravity of prevailing clichés and preconceptions. It prepares one for a rhetoric of contradistinction: "How do you know *but*" that something wholly *Other*, something unthought of by the generalist and the amenable man in the street, is actually the truth: that all others have been "led to believe in a lie" and rest on the platitudes of the "*With*-Seer"? Confronted with a bird, may we say, after Descartes: "*I see* it, therefore *it is* and *I am*? Seeing *is* believing!" "How do you know?" *Is* seeing believing, or does my seeing depend on a prior predisposition of belief? Is the Bird a Power—an "immense World of Delight"—rather than a concept or an ocular blip? Can we assume that all things are totally equivalent to their impact on our five senses? What if we had only four, like the blind or the deaf, or six, as the mystical assume? Would we have to alter the datum accordingly and amend our audio-tactile report? Have we—"lied"?

With all these uncertainties in mind, Blake sends up his Bird, as Noah sent out his dove after the Deluge to reconnoiter a drowned world. Let us treat it as a scientific experiment rather than an Old Testament myth concerned with the genesis of the human condition. Toss up Blake's Bird, as Coleridge launched his serpent and his water spider—and what happens? According to some, our visual faculties will report a vibration, a disturbance of the soma, a darkening of rods and cones, a sensation—and we pay attention. An experience is on the way to happen and must be dealt with. Our kinesthetic memory "reports" a visceral *lift*; our reason and memory impose the abstractions of language that reduce the form to a formula fixed by the conventions of verbal utterance to encode the visual signal: we *specify*—"bird in flight"; or the more knowledgeable "migrating ducks flying in V's," Latinated to an ornithologist's table of absolutes. *We then move on—* as indeed we must—to other forms, disturbances, darkenings, unknowns, crowding in on us from the world of *things*.

Ortega y Gasset would say that ours is a "fate of unremitting disquietude . . . a gratuitous weariness . . . perpetually harassed by our environment and tensely attentive to it." We live as "prisoners of the world, surrounded by things that terrify us, by things that enchant us, obliged all our lives, inexorably, whether we will or no, to concern ourselves with them. . . . Each one of us is always in peril of not being the unique and untransferable *self* which he is. . . . The condition of man is essential uncertainty."[10]

Blake, however, would put the question differently and probe for the delusions of the "untransferable self": alone, at the cutting edge of the "Other," have we truly *seen* the bird at all, any more than Machado's neophytes have seen the egg or confronted its possibilities as a phenomenon? Have we done anything more than exchange a sensation for a verbal reflex, or a gestural trap, or a nomenclatural "lie"? For both Blake and Ortega y Gassett, the uncertainties are seminal; human reality is coming to crisis in a critical way; we are turning motion and mass into a stifling contrivance of approximations and intrusions. We are in mortal danger of employing language to *undercut* or curtail an extraordinary plenum—shall we call it "an immense World of Delight?"— that ready-made discourse can only subvert in the utterance.

More to the point, we have ignored the poet's transformations of the operative words: forgotten that Blake's bird is a *"cutter"* of "airy ways"; that to "cut" is to pierce, to penetrate, to incise, to initiate some act of launching the will and energy ("Energy is eternal Delight") into a counter-force whose blockage might otherwise imperil or immobilize the flier. "Air," for the poet, is not "thin" or amorphous, or "ethereal," but a "way" of order, a lane, or a confluence of organized traffic, an invisible mapping of pockets, currents, energies, a meteorological freeway of thermal activity. Caught in the act of its "wingèd" prerogative, a bird is as inexhaustible as a planet or a solar system or an egg or an atom. "He who bends to himself a Joy / Doth the wingèd life destroy / But he who kisses the Joy as it flies / Lives in Eternity's sunrise." "A robin redbreast in a cage / Puts all heaven in a rage." It is an "airy way" that springs into place in the world's unboundable vacancy the moment the cage door is opened. But if the Bird always *cuts*, while the senses always *shut*, the "immensity" of the world is at risk, and "Delight" itself is made forfeit. . . . We are "lying." . . .

xi

Kestrel (kes'tral) *n* A European falcon (*Falco tinnunculus*) resembling the American sparrow-hawk, noted for its hovering habits. A windhover.

—*Standard College Dictionary*

The Windhover:
to Christ our Lord

I caught this morning morning's minion, king-
    dom of daylight's dauphin, dapple-dawn-drawn Falcon, in his
      riding
    Of the rolling level underneath him steady air, and striding
High there, how he rung upon the rein of a wimpling wing
In his ecstasy! then off, off forth on swing,
    As a skate's heel sweeps smooth on a bow-bend: the hurl and
      gliding
    Rebuffed the big wind. My heart in hiding
Stirred for a bird,—the achieve of, the mastery of the thing!

Brute beauty and valour and act, oh air, pride, plume, here
    Buckle! AND the fire that breaks from thee then, a billion
Times told lovelier, more dangerous, O my chevalier!

    No wonder of it: sheer plod makes plough down sillion
Shine, and blue-bleak embers, ah, my dear,
    Fall, gall themselves, and gash goldvermilion.

—Gerard Manley Hopkins

Hopkins's Windhover

Here are two modes of apprehending the Bird: (*a*) the Bird in the cage of language, taking its appointed place in a concordance of definitions and communicative conveniences; and (*b*) the Bird at large, aggrandizing the World's "Immensity," with the cage of language open to the mind's uncertainties. Let us look at the second, as we have it from Hopkins, for the imaginative particulars of a poet's quest for the ungraspable "truths" of Christ's immanence in His Creation: as a psalmic incarnation of "Delight."

From the outset, we are stopped by the oddity of the initiating verb: *caught*; we remember Blake's word for turning *nomina* into *numina* ("He who *kisses* the Joy as it flies / Lives in Eternity's sunrise") and sense something identical in the two contexts. Both imply something nimble, evanescent, momentary, elusive, chancy—maybe, even lucky; something that might well have escaped the catcher's "kiss" has been seized by an act of timely dexterity, like the kissing of billiard balls. Something not specifically intended for the perceiver's gaze has been disclosed, as the mystical like to say, inadvertently, "in the twinkling of an eye," for a moment only, to the awed beholder. The mood is one of *recency*—recency in the seeing and recency in the writing: "*this morning*." For Hopkins, as for Blake, the "caught" perception is the living perception, the infallible perception, the perception that never "*lies*."

There follows an immediate aggrandizement of the bird: from "morning's minion"—which is Anglicized French for *mignon*, the formula for diminutive endearment—to the courtly grandeurs of "kingdom of daylight's *dauphin*," which is standard French for "heir apparent," in the princely sign of the Dolphin. At the same time one is struck by the thermodynamic precisions that "cut an airy way" for the bird's embodiment of its attributes, as kestrel. What was formerly a void is suddenly *mapped* by the diversification of its expressive verbs: by massive compounds of doubled or trebled adjectives and nouns (*dapple-dawn-drawn, bow-bend, blue-bleak, gold-vermilion*). The bird has his way with the world in the exertions characteristic of his species: he *rides, rolls, strides, rings on a rein, swings, sweeps, hurls, glides, rebuffs*, and changes his guises as he goes. He is *minion, prince, fish, falcon, race-horse, skate, a bent bow*; he is *beauty, valor, act, air, pride*, and *plume*, before he reaches his epitome as fire-figure whose radiance is at once cosmological and microcosmic as a quantum equation or a Heraclitean koan. His glow flashes equally off the blade of a plowshare in a furrow or the innermost spark of exploding coal revealing the combustible ligature that held the coal together, kindled its interior oils, and expended itself totally in the disintegrating ash.

In the end, it cannot escape our notice that the Bird has been literally "immensified" into the "World" Blake foretold: Energy has been turned into Delight; intensity into immensity. Enormity of belief has been epiphanized as enormity of vision, "a billion times lovelier, more dangerous," in a devotional equation for "Christ Our Lord." At the same time, the sonnet form itself has been similarly "immensified," magnified, hyperbolized in a collateral act of compositional mimesis. The old prosody of sonnet, as Hopkins confided to a dazed generation, has been "sprung"— sprung as the coils of a spring are said to be "sprung" when removed from the confinement of their armature. The metric of conventional prosodic procedure—five feet of iambic pentameter to the line, with only minor deviations—will no longer contain the breathing of the poet; yet the pentametric undersong of sonnet goes steadily on encapsulating its "hidden variables" in units of five, as surely as the shell encapsulated the egg of Antonio Machado.

xii

I assert for myself that I do not behold the outward creation and that to me it is hindrance and not action; it is as the dirt upon my feet, no part of me. "What," it will be questioned, "when the sun rises, do you not see a round disk of fire somewhat like a guinea?" Oh no, I see an innumerable company of the heavenly host crying, "Holy, holy, holy is the Lord God Almighty." I question not my corporeal or vegetable eye any more than I would question a window concerning a sight. I look through it, not with it.

—William Blake

Blake and the "Holy-Holy-Holy" Sun

Let us follow the hyperboles of Blake to a similar extreme. Let us open his perspective of seeing to its visionary zenith to test its unity as an imaginative directive for poets and readers; let us return to Blake's "Holy-holy-holy Sun." Perhaps the first thing to be said about such a passage is that it belongs to the literature of assertion, rather than predication or definition—the uninhibited declaration of convictions and commitments which in the speaker's view do not need to be induced by rational processes of argument or hypothetical scrutiny of assumptions, but by aggressive enactments of the perceiver's *presence*.

For Blake, it would appear, wholehearted *witness*, the intuitive disclosure of *being*, of *Da-Sein*, is enough. (Coleridge was to call it "the mind's self-experience in the act of thinking.") Truth cannot be universally enlisted from a pre-existent repertory of terminal ideas immovable and alike for all. It cannot appeal to an ecumenical council of philosophers and seekers whose job it is to determine for others all outcomes, in advance of our engagement with time and contingency. Truth may not be borrowed from knowers and tellers who have preceded us and already committed their intimations to history, or theology, or the fine arts and natural sciences, as "laws." It does not lie quiet in closed systems any more than it drowses in closed senses: "All *Act* is virtue."

Blake's posture is militantly antinomian; he will not yield to the "majesty" of either the law or its syllogistic abstractions. One can only "*assert for oneself*," and that is precisely what Blake does, with all the entirety and effrontery at his command. What he asserts is a premise of the authority—one is tempted to call it the sanctity—of *Action*, not the physicist's "quantum" of it, but the plenum of its Being. According to Blake, true knowledge requires nothing less than the total mobilization of its integrity—an act of individual initiative that "cuts the airy way," like his flying Bird, penetrates the "outward creation" that is mere "hindrance and not action," and seizes those "immense Worlds of Delight" that are the triumph of the imagining identity. For Blake, all action is inward, sacred, apocalyptical, volatile, individuated; all hindrance of action is profane and corrupt. "Everything that *lives*," he says in the conclusion of his "Song of Liberty," "is holy"; everything that lives only partially is suspect and delusory. He then goes on to attack the whole world of approximation with a pseudo-question in which the inflection of the scandalized pharisee—all those who live by least common denominators and formulas of epistemological hearsay—is unmistakable: "What," he mocks, "when the sun rises, do you not see a round disk of fire somewhat like a guinea?"

Any beginner in Blake could tell you that everything is wrong with that question. In the first place, it reverses the parable of the

Bird and the Airy Way by diminishing rather than aggrandizing the dynamics of vision. A whole cosmology of interplanetary gases, the sun itself, is *reduced* to a "disk" of fire; and, for Blake, *all* encirclements—globes, circles, disks, spheres—are a form of hindrance or closure. The principle of fire, as anyone should know, is *airy*, like the flight of the Bird, and not global: a "round disk of fire" betrays the hindrance, rather than the action, of fire. Moreover, knowledge, for Blake, is not concerned with the partial or approximate likeness of things to other things—mere cursory *resemblances*. All true metaphors are hyperboles—larger than life. They are concerned with *excess* ("The road of Excess leads to the Palace of Wisdom") of likeness of things to other things, unconditional similitudes that lead to the equations of metaphor: what is "*somewhat* like" simply will not serve. The epitome of belittlement is reached in the substitution of a "guinea"—the tradesman's stereotype of value, turning fire into metal, coin of the realm—and the aerial into the terrestrial. And certainly *that* will not do, for heavenly currency!

All this is made to pivot finally on another of Blake's climactic negations: the stentorian "Oh, no!", and the hyperbole rejected by the cautious questioner: "I see, etc., etc. . . ." It would be wrong, I think, to read this imprudent, or even impudent, counter-assertion without leaving room for the satirist's touch of planned absurdity. If we find ourselves shocked and incredulous, we are *meant* to be left so. We might even play the pharisee's advocate and ask, of nobody in particular, "Did Blake *really* see and hear the heavenly hosts every time he looked at the sun? Can we take his Holy-Holy-Holy-Sun seriously? Did he steal some of his thunder from the Book of Psalms? Is this any 'truer' than the gold guinea of the man in the street and the 'Idiot Questioner?'"

The clue for the connoisseur of Blake lies in the three iterations of the word *Holy*—which is Blake's equation for the cubing of energy, as $E = mc^2$ was for Einstein's squaring of it—and elevates Blake's Sun-God to his special zenith over the Heavenly Hosts. For if, in the poetics of Blake, only "everything that *lives* is *holy*," his vision of the rising sun is an equation for Life itself raised to the third power: "*holy, holy, holy!*" He has not only trebled the sanctity of Creation, but said out of *joy* what Job said out of anguish: "I know that my Redeemer *liveth!*"

xiii

Not the iron tongue, but its vibrations pass into the metal of the bell.

—Samuel Taylor Coleridge

The Bell and the Artichoke: Coleridge and Neruda

Of course, it is possible to put the matter more temperately. Instead of equating poetry with *ekstasis* and the metaphysics of disorientation, we can ponder Coleridge's warning that the "fundamental presumption THAT THERE EXIST THINGS WITHOUT US" is, essentially, nothing but a "prejudice." It originates, he points out in Chapter XII of the *Biographia Literaria*, "neither in grounds or arguments, and yet on the other hand, [it] remains proof against all attempts to remove it by grounds or arguments . . . ; on the one hand [it] lays claim to IMMEDIATE certainty as a position at once indemonstrable and irresistible, and yet on the other hand, inasmuch as it refers to something essentially different from ourselves, nay even in opposition to ourselves, leaves it inconceivable how it could possibly become part of our immediate consciousness; (in other words, how that which ex hypothesi is and continues to be extrinsic and alien to our being, should become a modification of our being), the philosopher therefore compels himself to treat this faith as nothing more than a prejudice, innate indeed and connatural, but still a prejudice."

Granted even that "Matter has no *Inward*," as Coleridge remarks in an earlier chapter (VIII); that, for all the metaphysical heroism of a Blake or Hopkins, "We remove one surface, but to meet with another. We can but divide a particle into particles; and each atom comprehends in itself the properties of the material universe. . . . Not the iron tongue," he concludes unforgettably, "but its vibrations, pass into the metal of the bell. . . ." Pablo Neruda was to strike the sum even more piquantly a century later when he remarked with characteristic oafishness: "The poet's heart is an interminable artichoke."

Apparently, it is all too easy to be diverted from the "physics" to the "metaphysics" of seeing, just as Aristotle, after having completed his study of the physical universe as such, found it necessary to move on into the blue with his *Metaphysics*—which is merely basic Greek for "the book that came after my book about Physics." It would appear that nothing is more likely to entice physicists *beyond* their realm of chosen reflection than the study of physics itself. Physics has a way of driving out physics; and nowhere has that truth become more quixotic in its aftermath than in the causeries of quantum mechanics. In the great tradition of his classical predecessor, Werner Heisenberg's *Physics and Philosophy* of 1958 is followed by his *Physics and Beyond* in 1971. The fact that the phantom of the Thing ("no*thing* . . . some*thing* . . . every*thing* . . .") enchants, engrosses, beckons *elsewhere*, and eventually compels poet and scientist alike to question what lies "beyond" is precisely where their "complementarity" (Niels Bohr's word) is likely to constitute the "modernism" of a new millennium, whose name is Anything.

Notes

1. The dynamics of negative "capacitation" are everywhere apparent in the canon of the celebrated Odes by which Keats is best known. No less than four of the seven words which launch the confrontational imperatives of his "Ode on Melancholy" bristle with a negative bravura: "*No . . . no . . . go not . . . neither.*" The "Ode to a Nightingale" pivots on the negative denial of its opening stanza: "'Tis *not* through envy of the happy lot," and pursues its nullities to their vanishing point in the visionary and the oneirical. Stanza 2 of the "Ode on a Grecian Urn" is no less implacable in its onslaught on deprival—from "*no*" to "*canst not*," to "*nor ever*," to "*never, never*," to "*do not*," "*cannot*," "*hast not*," etc., etc. The effect is a kind of physics of imaginative force like the field physics of quantum, in which negatives and positives, particles and waves, position and momentum, emission and absorption, combine to produce the special voltage characteristic of both Romantic prosody and electromagnetic inquiry in nineteenth-century science.

2. Jacob Bronowski, "Knowledge or Certainty," *The Ascent of Man* (Boston: Little, Brown, 1973), pp. 365, 334.

3. Heisenberg, *Physics and Beyond*, p. 210.

4. Compare: "In order to construct a theory, it is not enough to have a clear conception of the goal. One must also have a formal point of view which will sufficiently restrict the unlimited variety of possi-

bilities.... Some physicists, among them myself, ... do not accept the view that events in nature are analogous to a game of chance.... Newton would not listen to a wave theory of light, for such a theory was most unsuited for his theoretical foundation.... He was justified. ... In my opinion quantum theory does not seem capable to furnish an adequate foundation for physics: one becomes involved in contradictions if one tries to consider the theoretical quantum description as a *complete* description of the individual physical system or event.... The complications met up to now by the very ingenious attempts [to do so] are already terrifying ... etc. etc." Albert Einstein, *Ideas and Opinion* (New York: Crown Bonanza, 1954), pp. 234–35.

5. *Madness and Civilization: A History of Insanity in the Age of Reason*, trans. Richard Howard (New York: Vintage, 1973), pp. 11, 12.

6. To the professed affinities of poetry and science and the pursuit of their "pleasures," add quantum laureate Steven Weinberg's "Scientific explanation is a mode of behavior that gives us pleasure like love or art." *Dream of a Final Theory* (New York: Vintage, 1994), p. 26.

7. Heisenberg, *Physics and Beyond*, pp. 40, 41.

8. See *Quantum Theory and Measurement*, ed. John Archibald Wheeler and Woyciech Hubert Zurek (Princeton: Princeton University Press, 1983), p. 210.

9. Sir Arthur Eddington, in *Quantum Questions*, ed. Ken Wilber (Boston: New Science Library, 1985), p. 171.

10. *The Dehumanization of Art* (Garden, City, N.Y.: Doubleday Anchor, 1956), pp. 166, 175.

12

Sight: Second or Sudden—Versions of Witness

"... this want of witness in brute Nature ..."
—Gerard Manley Hopkins

i

All of a sudden we see a dog, a cab, a house, *for the first time.* We are overpowered by the unique, the crazy, the ridiculous, the beautiful features of each object. The next moment, habit, with its eraser, has rubbed out this vivid picture. We stroke the dog, hail the cab, and live in the house. We do not *see* them anymore. . . . This is the role that poetry performs. It *unveils,* in the fullest sense of the word. It reveals, naked, and lit by a light which arouses the mind from its torpor, all the surprising things by which we are surrounded, and which our senses registered mechanically. . . . *Take a commonplace, clean it, polish it, and light it* so that it produces the same effect with its youth and freshness and spontaneity as it did originally, and you will have done a poet's work.

—Jean Cocteau, *Rappel à l'ordre*

JEAN COCTEAU: A DOG, A CAB, A HOUSE

My concern is with the physics of seeing rather than the metaphysics of it—with the "forgèd feature" of a usable universe seen in its naïveté as a *fait accompli* rather than with the shadowy apparatus by which the philosopher-mathematician erects his contradictory theories of knowledge and esthetics.

What happens, in the "rehearsals of own / Of abrupt self,"

when a thing is adequately and creatively *seen*? What is the *ring*, or the "feel," of a real, right, seen thing in the *raw* state, before poetry as such has been called in to operate upon the data of vision? How does it divulge itself to the poet, in his "witness of brute Nature," as an earnest of his "knowing"? More to the point, if truth is a venture in inwardness, rather than a conspectus of sensory externals, *what* "penetrates" *what* as the poet peels his "interminable artichoke" to its pith or "withers into truth?" Must it always be Blake's "Holy-Holy-Holy-Sun" and "immense Worlds of Delight," rather than ordinary English sunrises and kestrels coasting the thermal currents at the bidding of a dictionary—or aren't there homelier distinctions to be made? If "The Fool sees not the same tree that the Wise Man sees" (Blake), what was it the wise man saw that the fool did not, and what was the tree-in-itself after the wise man and the fool turned their gaze elsewhere a moment later?

What is "suddenly" *there*? And what is the unretrievable remainder?

Here, one is grateful for the testimony of Jean Cocteau, in his essay on the "professional secrets" of a poet, for fixing our attention on quotidian realities rather than interstellar vacancy. The opening phrase in itself is especially welcome as a poor man's deflation of Blake's runic extravagances: "*All of a sudden we see*"—a dog, a cab, a house—if we see it pristinely, *suddenly*, without diminution, as though "for the first time," and appropriate all that we see in a single blow of the eye. Ordinarily, it is Cocteau's belief, we tend to use the objects of the physical world as nomenclatural signifiers on a *tabula plena* rather than as events in themselves—mnemonic devices, like the conventional symbols on a map or a highway, to identify habitual areas of psychic traffic. We *glance* at objects merely, to reassure ourselves that—yes!—they are in their accustomed places in a scenario of repetitions, and then move on, as though the multiplicity of each day's events were distraction enough for mortal man, and the prospect of facing a day *continually* new in all its elements—like Adam's first day of Naming—filled us with terror and anxiety. We seek economies of observation to lighten the infinite burden of choices and challenges, and to allow us to deal punctually with a limited and predictable world. We ask for fictions of habit and convenience, and "erase" them from a crowded blackboard thereafter; for species rather than particularities, for precedents rather than the untried, for constructs rather than improvisations. We look for purpose, permanence, pattern, fixities—and we look away from chance and change and chaos.

Cocteau, on the other hand, offers a more strenuous proposal. His emphasis everywhere is on *penetration, connection, contact*—the uninhibited appropriation of *wholes* in acts of unprecedented seizure. For Cocteau, content with the accessible and the ordinary—a dog, a cab, a house—*every* act of seeing should be a revelation in almost the biblical sense of the word: a *disclosure*, by virtue of which the observer, ordinarily separated from the thing to be observed, is for a moment—suddenly!—made inseparable from it.

The "suddenness," the *un*readiness, is "all."

ii

> Suddenly I saw the cold and rook-delighting heaven
> That seemed as though ice burned and was but the more ice,
> And thereupon imagination and heart were driven
> So wild that every casual thought of that and this
> Vanished, and left but memories that should be out of season
> With the hot blood of youth, of love crossed long ago,
> And I took the blame out of all sense and reason
> Until I cried and trembled and rocked to and fro
> Riddled with light.
>
> —W. B. Yeats, "The Cold Heaven"

"What They Looked Likest"

It should matter to readers of poetry that it is the poets themselves who have acknowledged a factor of "suddenness" as both the begetter of the poem's occasion and as their sense of moving from miscellaneity to entirety, from the periphery to the center. Gerard Manley Hopkins, for example, will record in his *Note-Books* during a lull of priestly routine: "That autumn my eye was *suddenly caught* by the scaping of the leaves that grow in alleys and avenues: *I noticed it first* in an elm and then in limes"—and then concentrate on the particulars of *"what they looked likest when they first caught my* eye," because that was "best of all." In the same way, one can assume that his eye was suddenly "caught" by the morning flight of the windhover and drawn into the "scaping" of "air, pride, plume" that "buckled" it to its zenith as a sign of the indwelling Christ. Emily Dickinson will remark tersely in the course of a letter: "I think you would like the Chestnut Tree I met in my walk. It *hit my notice suddenly*—and I thought the skies were in blossom." It is clear that the chestnut tree was a *"meeting"* (if not, indeed, a concussion!) rather than a bypasser's notation: that her eye was "hit" and "suddenly" *seen through*—just as the color red was *felt through* on another occasion when "A circus passed the house—still I feel the red in my mind though the drums are out."

Or Yeats, caught up in the afflatus of the compositional moment, will whirl toward the reader with the outcry:

> Suddenly I saw the cold and rook-delighting heaven
> That seemed as though ice burned and was but the more ice—

There is no doubt that the poem that follows pivots on the word *suddenly*—that the suddenness is the source of both its compositional momentum and the special lighting that is the unforeseeable reward of that *suddenness*. We have here a literal instance of "illumination"—of a *glare* as frigid, as objective, as apocalyptical as the First Day of Creation itself: a clairvoyance at once penetrating, hallucinative, Adamic, with the heightened excitements and rhythmic discharges that presumably attend all visionary experience—even to a glacial reversal of the image of the Burning Bush that "burned with fire and was not consumed." The lines offer an almost clinical description of the processes attendant upon a timeless tradition of startled and intensified perception: what Cocteau called an "unveiling in the fullest sense of the word," "a light which arouses the mind from its torpor." Blake's vision of the "airy way" is also there, as well as Hopkins's "immensification" of the windhover: all three converge on a heaven, a flying bird—a rook, a kestrel, an undifferentiated paradigm of its species—and an "immense World of Delight" that brings its gelid intensities to bear on the eye of the beholder, like light on the point of an icicle.

For all the homespun "commonplaces" of Cocteau and Emily Dickinson—the dog, the cab, the house, the circus, the drums—we are back with the Holy-Holy-Holy-Sun, the heavenly host, the Psalmist's consortium of angels, after all.

iii

(*a*) The simple, imaginative mind may have its rewards in the repetition of its own silent working coming continually on the spirit *with a fine suddenness.*

—John Keats to Benjamin Bailey, November 22, 1817

(*b*) I think poetry should *surprise by a fine excess* and not by singularity. . . . It should strike the reader as a wording of his own highest thoughts and appear almost a remembrance.

—John Keats to John Taylor, February 27, 1818

Keats: Surprise and Excess

Yet surely there must be a vernacular which holds the universe of earthbound particulars to its workaday function of validating the ordinary without diminishing its capacity to astonish and concenter—a mode of chthonic discourse which puts the matter without the vatic hyperboles of the rhapsodist, and carries with it the poet's commitment to a *medium*, rather than a mania.

I think no one has given more thought to the priorities of the "sudden" and its holistic disclosure of the actual than Keats in his unobtrusive exchanges with friends; and before we move on, some final instances may help to anchor the ordinary to the universal. For all his epistolary intimacies, Keats's letters to Bailey and Taylor do not always make easy reading, but their rigors repay close and plangent scrutiny. Apparently, it was Keats's belief that we must consider *mind*, *imagination,* and *spirit* as three discrete entities or attributes indispensable to the right reading of poetry—a triad of mounting complexities that ensure deepest access to the matrix of the poet's medium, before accomplishing their diffusion. Like all major Romantics, Keats begins with *mind*—primal or "simple" mind—which opens toward the *imagination* and is then appropriated by it. In Keats's view, there are risks involved in the addition of imagination to mind which make necessary certain compensating "rewards" or premiums; and the transformation of "mind" into "spirit" is precisely the return to which Keats attaches highest importance. For Keats, imagination, in its "simplest," or most basic, state is the spiritualization of mind. Precisely what one is to understand by "spirit," however, is one of the major mysteries of Romantic discourse—in poetry as it is in quantum mechanics—where the intended context is clearly an agnostic, rather than a devotional, one. What is in question is the ponderability, rather than the imponderability, of the world.

For Keats it is the frailties of the human perceiver that give poignancy and urgency to the imaginative transaction: the "rewards," however subliminal, are "*intermittent*" and "sudden," and have nothing in common with the "abounding, glittering jet" that was Yeats's image for creative abundance. By "suddenness" Keats would seem to have had in mind an aroused awareness or a fugitive sense of tension *un*anticipated by the lucky recipient, a shock of cognition—whether of nightingales or Elgin marbles—that was unprecedented, disjunct, unique, and that left the perceiver with only the aftertaste of his mortality rather than the pleasures of *re*-cognition. In the "high requiems" of Keats, it is melancholy, rather than "Delight," that shimmers between the "vision" and the "waking dream." Keats calls it a "*fine* suddenness," one supposes, to distinguish it from a gross or a cursory suddenness, as one calls certain arts "fine" to distinguish them from habitual operations of craft. The "fineness," one assumes, lies in the "spiritualisation" of the suddenness—an inner, valuational dimension which turns things and thinking subliminal.

However, when one restores the intervening phrase, "may have its rewards... in the *repetition* of *its own silent working* coming continually...," one is left with a striking contradiction, or negation: the rewards of imagination are *not* disjunct, or without precedent, after all. On the contrary, what is "suddenly" given the viewer is the mind's "*repetition* of *its own* silent working"—

the confirmation of something *already* immanent in the mind of the reader and known by it as a latent intuition—an antecedent datum thrown into new perspective by recognition. If "spirit" remains a mystery, at least one can say it is the custodian of "what is already *there*": a keeper of universals, premonitions, epitomes, "fair Attitudes" and archetypes, eternals.

Further light is shed on all these matters in the remaining passage from Keats's letter to Taylor dated three months later. Here, "suddenness" is present again in another of its magical guises—the factor of *surprise*—and "fineness" is given a new gloss by Keats himself, by the addition of "excess." It goes without saying that surprise postulates the unexpected—the dispensation that is unique rather than tautological, singular rather than recurrent. Yet Keats surprises us again by another negation: "I think," he says, "poetry should surprise by a fine excess and *not* by singularity." Again we have a paradoxical synthesis of the atavistic and the *déjà-vu*, the immediate and the antecedent, the spontaneous and the datum that is already given, or latent, or repeated. A "fine excess," for Keats, is not a superaddition or a superfluity. It is not expendable. Rather, it is the *repetition* of something already silently working in the mind as part of the reader's initiative—the "leaven in the lump" traditionally associated with spiritual power. It is this, says Keats, that should strike the reader as a "*wording* of his own highest *thoughts*" and appear "almost a remembrance. . . ." Poetry, in other words, is a remembering of what we already know, the previously unuttered *wording of our own thinking*, as well as the poet's "highest thoughts."

It is this that adds "immensity" to "Delight," puts "heavenly hosts" around the Londoner's sunrise and "brightness" around the lock of Milton's hair in the all but forgotten stanzas to the poet who was to haunt Keats's earliest vision of the Sun-God Himself:

> A lock of thy *bright* hair—
> *Sudden* it came,
> And *I was startled* when I *caught* thy name
> Coupled so *unaware*;
> Yet, at that moment, temperate was my blood,
> I thought I had beheld it from the flood.
>
> —John Keats, "Lines On Seeing a Lock of Milton's Hair"

iv

> Take a commonplace, clean it, polish it, and light it so that it produces the same effect with its youth and freshness and spontaneity, and you will have done a poet's work.
>
> —Jean Cocteau, *Rappel à l'ordre*

"A Clean, Well-Lighted Place"

One is drawn to re-examine the injunction that concludes Cocteau's little mandate to working poets for final clues to the special lighting that seems to accompany the "brightness" on the hair of Milton, the blossomy skies over the chestnut tree in Emily's walk, the red in her mind after the circus has passed. Though we have Cocteau's assurance that any "commonplace"—a dog, a cab, a house—will serve, there was something about the overlay of the "sudden," the "first," and the "spontaneous" that was always dilating our eyeballs and glazing our vision, like belladonna. Readers of Cocteau have come to expect a mix of the music hall and the Parnassian in his private legerdemain as artist-equilibrist; and it is clear that the light that accompanies his "commonplaces" is histrionic as well as subliminal. Like most of his contrivances, there is a catch to his special lighting, and a trapdoor underneath the catch—a *"machine infernale"* for eternizing epiphanies and incongruities, which lights up the switchboard of a showman caught in an act of transcendental vaudeville. "*Étonne-nous!*" was Gide's challenge to his sidewalk coterie at the Deux Magots—and the *frisson* of the "astonishing" has followed the sweep of Cocteau's derring-do on the high-wire of Carnival ever since.

But his parting directive deserves a chary last look before we move on to other considerations, if only because it confirms the earlier witness of a priest, a recluse, and a youthful talent whose tardy search for a vocation is touched with the precocity of genius. "Take a commonplace, clean it, polish it, and light it . . . , and you will have done a poet's work": in other words, let us have a "clean, well-lighted place"—a neighborhood bar out of a fable by Hemingway, if need be, an altar, the master-switch of a proscenium—and "a poet's work" of transfiguration may yet give us Yeats's holocaustal dream of "A Cold Heaven." We are left to wonder, nevertheless, whether the light enjoined by Cocteau is secular or apocalyptical—the light of common day, or the sign of a burning bush that beckons the prophet toward an enigma of numinous combustion or precipitation. Do they mark polarities of the ordinary and the sacramental, or are the two as inseparable as particle and wave in a physics of imaginative uncertainty? Some final instances are needed to put the question in a calculus for which there is no answerable differential.

v

> And as he journeyed, he came to Damascus: and suddenly there shined round about him a *light from heaven*: And he fell to the earth and heard a voice saying unto him, Saul, Saul, why persecuteth thou me? And he said, Who art thou, Lord? And the Lord said, I am Jesus whom thou persecutest: it is hard for thee to kick against the pricks.
>
> And he *trembling and astonished* said, Lord what wilt thou *have me do?* And the Lord said unto him. Arise, and go into the city, and it shall be told thee what thou must do. And the men who journeyed with him stood speechless, *hearing a voice but seeing no man.*
>
> And Saul arose from the earth; and when his eyes were opened, he saw no man, but they led him by the hand and brought him into Damascus.
>
> And he was there three days without sight and neither did eat nor drink.
>
> —Acts 9: 3–9

Three Displacements by Light: Sacred and Profane

If Yeats's "Cold Heaven" can be regarded as an instance of "revelation secularized as imagination," or "a god-story in the guise of a poetic artifact," the preceding and following passages from the New Testament offer a striking reversal of the same phenomenon: Imagination divinized as holy revelation. In the case of Saint

Paul's vision of the risen Christ on the road to Damascus, we have a *conversion by light*, with all the Yeatsian apparatus of a heavenly dazzle, a "sudden" sunburst of unexpected disclosures, voices in a solitary landscape, reproaches, memories, outcries, the demoralization of "sense and reason," fear, trembling, astonishment, and a heart driven wild "as every casual thought of that and this vanishes." Like Blake, Paul is aware that imagination, or the gift of *seeing through* the visible, demands *language,* and that language postulates *action*; while "the men who journeyed with him stood *speechless,*" Paul *asks the question* of all artists overpowered by the disclosure of what is "suddenly *there,*" awaiting the acknowledgment of the perceiver: "Lord, what wilt thou have me *do?*" Like Blake's imagining man, Paul bows to the need for a creative outcome: "All Act is Virtue," says Blake—the imagined thing must be transformed into the enacted thing. And certainly the story of Saint Paul after his conversion is the extraordinary saga of a man of *action and language* who "imagined" the whole of the Catholic way for all Christians to come, in an epic that makes Ulysses look like a midsummer yachtsman taking the dawdler's way home.

> And after six days Jesus taketh Peter, James, and John his brother, and bringeth them up into a high mountain apart,
>
> And was transfigured before them: His face *did shine as the sun* and his raiment was *white as the light,* And behold there appeared unto them Moses and Elias as talking with him.
>
> Then answered Peter and said unto Jesus, Lord, it is good for us to be here: if thou wilt, *let us make here three tabernacles*, one for thee, and one for Moses, and one for Elias.
>
> While he yet spake, behold a *bright cloud overshadowed them*, and behold a voice out of the cloud which said, This is my beloved Son in whom *I am well pleased*: hear ye him.
>
> And when the disciples heard it, they *fell on their faces* and were *sore afraid*
>
> And when they had lifted up their eyes, they *saw no man, save Jesus only.*
>
> —Matthew 17:1–8

Here, the Christian imagination achieves the artist's miracle of turning the "suddenly seen thing" into a "magical" synthesis of Past, Present, and Future. We have again a "transfiguration by light," with a familiar imagery of "high places," a sunburst with an accompanying pageant of clouds, an exchange of language, great fear and trembling, and the curious addition of a building of "tabernacles." The atavistic theme, calling for a merging of "tradition and the individual talent," or the simultaneity of two times, is raised to its third power, in the imagined coexistence of Moses, regarded by Jews as the proto-prophet of his people, with a latter-day prophet, Elijah, and four contemporary figures who enter the Hebrew story some 900 years later. Jesus not only appears in his traditional guise as—literally—the *Light of the World*, but in his imaginative guise as the Pleasure Principle, or the *Delight of the World*: "This is my son, in whom I am *well pleased.*" The three "tabernacles," one supposes, symbolize the artist's need for ceremonious preparation and ritual forms—his belief that a momentous disclosure ought to be accompanied by its perpetuation in a *medium*—some visible artifact—an act of writing, a graven image, an altarstone, a temple, a wayside "tabernacle," all of which are modes of symbolic, as well as mnemonic, action. The fact that all three disciples thereafter "saw no man, save Jesus only," shows the single-minded attentiveness of the artist to his function. The disciples, counting themselves fortunate, are *concentrating* on the wonder of their good fortune. Their posture is "artistic" rather than forensic: the "self-annihilation" of the craftsman who has exchanged all that was *ego* for what Yeats was to designate as his "anti-self."

> Heaven is not like flying or swimming
> but has something to do with *blackness and a strong glare*
> and when it gets dark he will *remember something
> strongly worded to say* on the subject.
>
> —Elizabeth Bishop, *Seascape*

Finally, the lighting in a seascape by Elizabeth Bishop . . . What one notes very particularly is the *glare*—the "strong glare" over the blackness, a specifically meteorological glare that is nonetheless hypnotic or hallucinogenic, in the sense that it induces another "displacement by light"—an excess of light that narrows the pupil and fixes the gaze like a hypnotist's crystal. The condition is trance-like: there is flying and swimming and an airy mix of blackness and dazzle that not only jars the memory, but prepares the perceiver for *eventual language*: "When it gets dark he will remember *something / strongly worded* to say on the subject." Strong glare, to the poet-perceiver, portends strong language rather than a surrender to "habit, with its eraser." It is also significant that the words come *after* the "strong glare" has subsided into darkness—because, one supposes, for the poised pen of the poet, the darkness has *ink* in it, just as the glare has something of the *blank page* awaiting the imprimatur of the pen. In a word, all is in readiness for the imminent *"poem"*—indeed, the very poem we are now engaged in reading: that concussion of the pen's point on the papery void that produced the page-frights of Mallarmé; or the stage-frights of Cocteau, suddenly finding himself framed by a brilliantly lighted proscenium, with the whole of a switchboard concentering its circle for the star-turns of an aerialist, asking himself the question of all unrehearsed neophytes: "But what am I to do with my *hands*?"

vi

Look!
From a glass pitcher she serves
Clear water to the white chickens.

—William Carlos Williams

William Carlos Williams: The Glass Pitcher and the Nightingales

It would appear that the "mind aroused" from its "torpor" is not only "overpowering," but overpowered. It is likely to fall on its knees and *magnify* its object, just as the Saint and the Psalmist fall on their knees to "magnify their Lord" because the "hills do skip like rams" and the sun is "ready like a strong man to run a race." Awe, astonishment, and immensity creep in; and in the light of that immensity we know "something strongly worded" will follow when the enlargement and the illumination recede. Needless to say, if we open up all the heavens, like Yeats, and put the Lord of all the heavens on a cloud on the right hand of power, like Saint Paul and the disciples, we must expect the grandiose scale.

We cosmologize. We epiphanize. The "glare" or the Big Bang of the astrophysicist is at hand: the "rough beast" "slouches toward Bethlehem to be born."

That is *not*, however, the best way to hold fast to a "*commonplace*" or induce a temperate examination of the tangible and material world of *things*. Quantum mechanics teaches us to distinguish between the macrocosmic and the molecular modes of physical inquiry: one does not apply the human eye to the optics of the Palomar telescope and prepare for the biochemical minutiae of the microscope or the serenities of the windowpane. I should therefore like to return to the simplest possible measure—away from the "blackness and a strong glare" which Elizabeth Bishop insists *has heaven in it*, to the least eventful moment in the long day of a poet, a physician, and a taxpayer of Paterson, New Jersey: William Carlos Williams.

At first reading, the lines from Williams might seem thoroughly uneventful, low-keyed, expendable—a defective haiku, the connoisseur might hazard, of sixteen, rather than the traditional seventeen, syllables favored by the Japanese. Nothing warrants the special vigilance elicited by the exclamatory "Look!" in line 1, though the word points to a context that *should* produce a marvel. The poem has no "secrets"—yet the poet cries "Look!" as the magician cries "Lo and behold!" But what follows is a barnyard ritual of filling a chicken's watering pan and produces no prestidigitative egg. Why, then, this urgent pointing to a commonplace, *as though* it were a marvel, in the poop and banality of a chicken coop?

Actually, the lines do not stand alone as a text-in-itself, but constitute the fifth stanza of an implacably opaque and coarse-grained overlay of disparate contexts whose precise center is irrecoverable, but whose title specifies a "Brilliant Sad Sun" as its chosen subject. Cutting four ways, it ricochets from a Jersey luncheonette where "spaghetti [is] a speciality," and "oysters and clams" portend the last R-months of winter when shellfish are still a seasonal favorite. There follows a twofold invocation: to the Spring sun, viewed as a "huge appetite," and to a preoccupied spectator ceremoniously addressed as "Madam"; then the pitcher-bearer, summoned out of Mayaguez, it would seem, only to "croak" a raucous "*Bon Jor!*" to her mistress's houseguests and balance an "emptying dangle" of glassware; then back to "Madam" (for whose solace "Patti on her first concert tour / sang in your house in Mayaguez")—still nursing a melancholy that leaves the reader to ponder both the contradictions of the poet's title and his insistence on its incrementing paradoxes.

To all intents and purposes, then, Mr. Williams's poem has no compositional outcome but a broken sentence for the reader to contemplate, as construer of an unfathomable enterprise:

Brilliant Sad Sun

Lee's
Lunch

Spaghetti Oysters
a Specialty Clams

and raw Winter's done
to a turn—Restaurant: Spring!
Ah, Madam, what good are your thoughts

romantic but true
beside this gayety of the sun
and that huge appetite?

Look!
from a glass pitcher she serves
clear water to the white chickens

What are your memories
beside that purity?
The empty pitcher dangling

from her grip
her coarse voice croaks
Bon jor!

And Patti, on her first concert tour
sang at your house in Mayaguez and
your brother was there

What beauty
beside your sadness—and
what sorrow

All that stands firm, to fix its true context and polarize its conflicting disjunctions and dilemmas in the special lighting of the "brilliant sad sun," is the "haiku" of the pitcher-bearer, midway in a larger piece hurtling toward failure. It is precisely at this point, however, that the illuminations multiply rapidly: Why is the pitcher *glass*, the water *clear*, the chickens *white*? Is it customary to replenish a barnyard chicken pan from a transparent vessel that illumines the water within, as at a formal dinner party, catches the iridescence and ritual abundance of its pouring, and puts a blaze on the sunny morning? Why *whiten* the chickens ("Alas, a dirty bird!" Gertrude Stein was to observe in one of her "Tender Buttons") here, as in Williams's famous "Wheelbarrow" haiku? Why choose the word "serve," rather than the non-devotional "pour," in a service for chickens? Why should this not be read as an encoded transfiguration scene whose purpose it is to metamorphize the morning chores of a kitchen drudge into the rites of Hebe, cupbearer to Apollo—

> The god of life, and poetry, and light,
> The sun, in human limbs arrayed . . . (Byron)?

"Take a commonplace, clean it, light it": Cocteau's light-principle is again at work, organizing the transparencies—the glass, the water, the whiteness—with a jeweler's precision, carving the ordinary into a mathematic of optical angles, like a diamond-breaker's gem.

> My shoes as I lean
> unlacing them
> stand out upon
> flat worsted flowers.
> Nimbly the shadows
> of my fingers play
> unlacing
> over shoes and flowers.
>
> —William Carlos Williams,
>   "The Nightingales"

There is little likelihood, I submit, that we can turn the shoes of William Carlos Williams, or the nightly chore of unlacing them before going to bed in Paterson, New Jersey, into a Holy-Holy-Holy-Sun or an Immense World of Delight, or a rook-delighting heaven. Here, at last, we might have an epitome of the commonplace, the "anti-poetic," the banal. Yet—why should a poet's shoes "stand out" *now*, suddenly, for the first time, and become an object of celebration? Why does Williams suddenly see an habitual action as though it were a revelation?

For one thing, I should say it has something to do with an angle of vision, an unexpected displacement of habit, an accident of unprecedented propinquity that render the familiar a little monstrous and whimsical. The poet *"leans"*—and thereby alters his habitual perspective—bringing his eye nearer to its object than was previously customary or necessary. Who has not experienced the sense of estrangement brought about by some disorienting enlargement of minutiae—either a blade of grass seen, on a sunny day as we lie on our elbow and belly on a lawn, just a fraction of a inch from our eyeball; or some object generally held within reading distance, at arm's length from our eyes—suddenly brought close enough to make us wince or flinch at the violence of the confrontation? It was probably just such a moment that made the child in Whitman's poem bring a "leaf of grass" to the poet and baffle him with a question that taxed all his powers of analogy and definition: "A child said, What is grass? fetching it to me with full hands." Whitman's discomfiture is immediately apparent from his multiple answer: "I guess it must be the flag of my disposition, out of hopeful green stuff woven, / or I guess it is the handkerchief of the Lord / Or I guess it is a uniform hieroglyphic . . . / And now it seems to me like the beautiful uncut hair of graves. . . ." In the same way, Williams for a moment suddenly sees his shoes, and his fingers unlacing them, as Gulliver might have viewed the giantesses of Brobdingnab as he sits astride one of their nipples.

But there is also some "displacement-by-light," not, perhaps, as explosive and ominous as the ice-burst in Yeats's poem, but nonetheless present. It would be wrong to bypass the special lighting of Williams's "Nightingales." What angle of vision would make the "flat worsted flowers" on a Jersey rag rug "stand out," delineate the texture and patterns in the worsted's weave, cast longer shadows of fingers and laces over the shoes and flowers—all "as if for the first time"? Has the nightly perspective been altered because, for one reason or another, the lamp has been removed from its customary position *overhead*, which would deliver all things to "habit, with its eraser"? If so, *where* has it been placed?

For a moment, all seems "lit by a light which removes the mind from its torpor." We have, instead, the theatrical backlighting and the unnaturally prolonged shadows of surrealist art, the kind of floor-level distortions one remembers, for example, in Dalí or di Chirico. We get not only perspective by backlighting but also what Kenneth Burke has called "perspective by incongruity." We catch a moment of *relaxed undoing*, when the mind and the shoelaces are equally disengaged, and an ordinary action can strike home in its maximum purity, as a moment of pure *pleasure*.

We are back with the Pleasure Principle. This is a poem about *happiness*, like the poem about "my wife's pom-poms" or "On Gay Wallpaper," rather than "nightingales" or bedtime disrobing; and Mrs. Williams is doubtless angling her mirror in similar deshabille on the opposite side of the throw-rug. It may be this that accounts for the poet's whimsical awareness of his own *coziness*, when he can speak in the language of Whitman's "child," in "my secret mind / out of pure happiness" (*The Thinker*), from the privacy of a connubial game. The fantasy and the fingers are equally "nimble"; and there is a recognizably delighted "play" with the revealed incongruities of flowers, fingers, and shoes. The juxtaposition is as odd as Lewis Carroll's play with "ships and shoes and sealing-wax and cabbages and kings." The immediacies of being alive at an unguarded moment of time touch an intimate moment of piquancy: and "we are overpowered by the unique, the crazy, the ridiculous, the beautiful features of each object."

But why choose to give his poem the title of "The Nightingales" and—again!—add a bird to his riddle, as Yeats added a rook and Hopkins a windhover to theirs? In Keats's celebrated ode bearing a similar title, the nightingale is present in every stanza, along with the attributes traditionally associated with its species: its song, which Romantic poets have made legendary throughout the centuries; its natural habitat, which is British rather than American; its violent mythology of rape and mutilation, which persists to Eliot's *Wasteland*; its aura of sensuous arousal.

The answer, I think, lies in the "fingerplay" that the poet promised us would be "nimble" (as Jack's dauntless leap over the candlestick?). There is a hint of the child's game with shadows, backlighting, crossed wrists, and clasped thumbs—a mood at once ironical and wanton when the play of the mind and the fingers are one, and the gesture of a prankster's "nightingales" strikes home as a willfully infantile vagary. The smile of the erotic flickers for a moment through the feckless naïvetés of the context, together with the curve of its latent "jocundity," as in da Vinci. Obviously, the stereotype of this child's game is not enough to gratify the withheld humors of a mythology long linked with the nightingale. Indeed, the "flat worsted flowers" of a New Jersey interior have metamorphosed into a meadow by Botticelli, and Mr. Williams's little shadow play has turned into a satyr play.

13

Hopkins Observing: "Rehearsals"

These things, these things were here, and but the beholder
 Wanting; which two when they once meet,
The heart rears wings bold and bolder
 And hurls for him, O half hurls earth for him off under his feet.

—Gerald Manley Hopkins

i

"THESE THINGS, THESE THINGS WERE HERE, AND BUT THE
 BEHOLDER WANTING"

Apparently, there is no royal road to the "found world" of the actual. In the promissory realm of the "beholdable," the presence of things waits for the eye of the beholder to validate its reality in acts of palpable possession. Time and again we are forced back to that bleakest of categorical beginnings for a viable premise: Coleridge's assumption that "All knowledge rests on the coincidence of a Subject and an Object"—that nothing can be known at all, or that consciousness has nothing to enlist its sensuous potential until a thing to be perceived and an agent to perceive it have been united in a "realizing act of intuition." Found worlds, it would appear, are never really "given" the fortunate finder: they are either *taken*, or overtaken, in acts of solitary initiative, as invasions rather than gratuities. We always have to deal with two enigmatic variables: the "sentient knowing Mind,"[1] the identity aware of itself and interested in itself, directing its avidity and its curiosity on all things not itself; and the datum of finite existence—*faits* of the physical universe awaiting their transformation into "facts" of the mind, or feats of the imagination, upon which the subject exercises his consciousness.

The riddles of William Blake, the epigrams of Keats, the oracles and entertainments of Cocteau, Machado, Stevens, William Butler Yeats, and others are useful only insofar as they draw us away from prosodic considerations as the *cause* of the poems they incarnate, and focus attention on the observer and the thing observed as the true protagonists of the drama of imaginative initiative. On the other hand, the hazards of that drama have also been the subject of the poet's habitual concern. According to Wordsworth, "the world is too much with us":

> Getting and spending we lay waste our powers:
> Little we see in Nature that is ours.

Between the disuse and the misuse of the world, we have exchanged a participatory trust for a free fall of searches and seizures. What compels us to *imagine*, rather than to *know*, it may be, is the premise that the whole of the usable world lies in a state of perpetual incompletion—what Hopkins called "brute Nature" apart from all private witness—outside the individual perceiver, awaiting the act of human appropriation to make it "real." The most the observer can hope for is an extrapolation of attributes and manifestations that render the unutterable utterable—a lexicon for conferring spoken and written reality on our intimations of the "given." What is *really* "out there" may not even be a "prejudice," as Coleridge supposed, but an alphabet and abacus for our presumptive humanity.

Even Einstein, that magus of the finite—who, according to Schilpp, in 1949 still protested against the "uncertainties" of his quantal contemporaries: "You believe in a dice-playing God and I in perfect laws in the world of things existing as real objects"[2]—was compelled to concede that:

> The real is in no way immediately given to us. . . . The most elementary concept in everyday thought belonging to the sphere of the "real" is the concept of continually existing objects like the table in my room. The table, as such, however, is not given to me. . . . In my opinion it is of the greatest importance to be

conscious of the fact that such a concept, like all other concepts, is a speculative-constructive kind. Otherwise, we cannot do justice to those concepts of physics which claim to describe a reality, and one is in danger of being misled by the illusion that the "real" of our daily experiences "exists really" and that certain concepts of physics are "mere ideas" separated from the "real" by an unbridgeable gulf.

For further light on these matters, we can hardly do better than to draw on the example of the poets themselves—notably, Gerard Manley Hopkin, whose *Note-Books* give us direct access to the "rehearsals" of a dedicated—and predatory—sensibility, as well as a stunning nomenclature for dealing with its processes.

ii

Aug. 10—I was looking at high waves. The breakers always are parallel to the coast and shape themselves to it except where the curve is sharp however the wind blows. They are rolled out by the shallowing shore just as a piece of putty between the palms whatever its shape runs into a long roll. The slant ruck or crease one sees in them shows the way of the wind. The regularity of the barrels surprised and charmed the eye; the edge behind the comb or crest was as smooth and bright as glass. It may be noticed to be green behind and silver white in front: the silver marks where the air begins, the pure white is foam, the green/ solid water. Then looked at to the right or left they are scrolled over like mouldboards or feathers or jibsails seen by the edge. It is pretty to see the hollow of the barrel disappearing as the white comb on each side runs along the wave gaining ground till the two meet at a pitch and crush and overlap each other

About all the turns of the scaping from the break and flooding of the wave to its run out again I have not yet satisfied myself. The shores are swimming and the eyes have before them a region of milky surf but it is hard for them to unpack the huddling and gnarl of the water and law out the shape and the sequence of the running: I catch however the looped or forked wisp made by every big pebble the backwater runs over—if it were clear and smooth there would be a network from their overlapping, such as can in fact be seen on smooth sand after the tide is out—; then I saw it run browner, the foam dwindling and twitched into long

chains of suds, while the strength of the backdraught shrugged the
stones together and clocked them one against another

Hopkins Observing:
Looking at High Waves; Water Coming
Through a Lock

Though Hopkins's water studies in many ways call to mind the
more onerous reflections of da Vinci on the behavior of waves
written 400 years before, the privacy and brio of Hopkins's assault on his watery objective force us to acknowledge the special
priorities of the *seen*. Leonardo, probing for the physics of water—for a kind of hydrodynamics of marine causality to assist his
transcriptions into paint and canvas—is relentlessly dispassionate:

> When the wave has been driven on the shore by the force of the
> wind, it forms a mound by putting its upper part at the bottom
> and turns back on this until it reaches the spot where it is beaten
> back anew by the succeeding wave which comes from below and
> turns it over on its back, and so overthrows the mound and beats
> it back again on the aforesaid shore, and so continues time after
> time, turning now to the shore with its upper movement and now
> with its lower fleeing away from it etc. etc.[3]

Though Hopkins's focus is also on the undular dynamics of water and the heights to which it may attain, his appropriation of all
that *taxes* and *pleases* in the behavior of the coastal assault of
"high waves" gives a curious simultaneity to the purely consecu-
tive thrust of things. What dazzles—or dazes—is the ping-pong
of his readiness to alter his stance to the unforeseeable onrush of
attributes. The search for shapes in a metamorphic chaos,[4] the
extrapolation of forms from fluidity and the construing of the
forces that impart contour to watery momentum, are para-
mount.

Hence, the dizzying incrementation of directional lunges, the
emphasis on what is "parallel to the coast" or "shape[d] . . . to
it," the "rolls," the "rucks," the "creases," the "regularity of the
barrels," the "combs," the "crests," "scrolls," "mouldboards"
(one reaches for a dictionary), "feathers," "jibsails," "hollows,"

"long chains of suds." On the other hand, there is an anticipation of imminent cause for palpable effects—of an invisible continuum moving the visible, leaving its sensuous mark on the ricochet of attributes, "fetching forth" the idiosyncratic liquidity of water and showing "the way of the wind." In the special parlance of Hopkins, it is the "scaping" of the scene (in the painter's sense of the word) that gives the passage its quality of insatiable vigilance—the fixed determination to "law out the shapes and sequences of the running" with unpremeditated clues of color, transparency, weight, momentum, mass, deflection, that "surprise and charm the eye."

What distinguishes Hopkins's approach from Leonardo's is the *participatory* aspect of his seizure on his shifting objective—the unstinting deployment of his senses in disjunct and idiosyncratic volleys of unsorted particulars, without any foreseeable resolution. His priorities throughout are on immediacies: on process, rather than the terminal coalescence of things. For all his latent concern for causes, "unpacking" of the transient and inchoate—the ultimate "runnings" of the "sequences" which are the single-minded preoccupation of da Vinci—Hopkins is content to register his "pleasures" and "dissatisfactions" without any hint of exasperation or diminished avidity. He fixes on the improvisations of the "caught"—wisps, pebbles, twitchings, backdraughts, "swimmings," "dwindlings"—and forces them to the foreground of his indiscriminate pre-emption. *All* is equally present, plausible, ominous, crucial. Yet, he is ready, if need be, to reduce the whole of a stormy perspective to the tactile naïvetés of "a piece of putty [rolled] between the palms" or the *mot juste* of a passing backdraught "*shrugging*" the stones together with a beachcomber's insouciance and "*clocking*" (in which sense of the word?) the skeins of its aftermath with a sempstress's needle.

> Note on water coming through a lock.
> There are openings near the bottom of the gates (which allow the water to pass through at all times, I suppose.) Suppose three, as there often are. The water strikes through these with great force and extends itself into three fans. The direction of the water is a little oblique from the horizontal, but the great force with which it runs keeps it almost uncurved except at the edges. The end of these fans is not seen for they strike them under a mass of yellow-

ish boiling foam which runs down between the fans, and meeting covers the whole space of the lock-entrance. Being heaped up in globes and bosses and round masses the fans disappear under it. This turpid mass smooths itself as the distance increases from the lock. But the current is strong and if the basin into which it runs has curving banks it strikes them and the confusion of the already folded and doubled lines of foam is worse confounded.

Here, Hopkins chooses a situation in which force, in the bulk, as it were, is channelized, constrained, contoured, and modified by some natural obtruction; the whole volume of water is limited by a *lock* to bring it to crisis and render it expressive. At first he enlists *suppositions* ("the gate which allows the water to pass through at all times, I suppose. Suppose three"). He then moves on to *precedents* and rational foreknowledge: "as there often are." Thereafter, however, he submits to the total impact of the water: the shock of *force* on *containment*, or, as the physicists would say, of emission on absorption, and the resultant scaping, or shaping, of the water into "fans" or spectra. He then searches for clues of *direction*—obliquity, horizontality, curves—and *position*: water that goes *under* or *over*, or adjusts to "the whole space of the lock"—its entrances, basins, banks, etc., etc. Then follow the sensuous metaphors and hyperboles suggesting the likeness of water to other things: "globes," "bosses"; textural details of smoothness, "turpidness," "folds," "lines"; and, finally, the abandonment of all priorities, the luxurious surrender to "confusion worse confounded"—the breaking-point in which observation yields to the overabundance and accidentality of nature—"brute Nature," as Hopkins never doubted it to be, that confounds all "witness"—where the *viewer* is no longer the *construer*, and the surrender to pleasure is total.

iii

I have been watching clouds this spring and evaporation, for instance over our Lenten chocolate. It seems as if the heat by *aestus*, throes/ one after another threw films of vapour off as boiling water throws off steam under film of water, that is bubbles. One query then is whether these films contain gas or no. The film seems to be set with tiny bubbles which give it a grey and grained look. By throes perhaps which represent the moments at which the evener stress of the heat has overcome the resistance of the surface or of the whole liquid. It would be reasonable then to consider the films as the shell of gas-bubbles and the grain on them as a network of bubbles condensed by the air as the gas rises.—Candle smoke goes by just the same laws, the visible film being here of unconsumed substance, not hollow bubbles The throes can be perceived/ like the thrills of a candle in the socket: this is precisely to *reech*, whence *reek*. They may by a breath of air be laid again and then shew like grey wisps on the surface—which shews their part-solidity. They seem to be drawn off the chocolate as you might take up a napkin between your fingers that covered something, not so much from here or there as from the whole surface at one reech, so that the film is perceived at the edge and makes in fact a collar or ring just within the wall all round the cup; it then draws together in a cowl like a candleflame but not regularly or without a break: the question is why. Perhaps in perfect stillness it would not but the air breathing it aside entangles it with itself. The film seems to rise not quite simultaneously but to peel off as if you were tearing cloth; then giving an end forward like the corner of a handkerchief and beginning to coil it makes a long wavy hose you may sometimes look down, as a ribbon or a carpenter's shaving may be made to do. Higher running into frets and silvering in the sun with the endless coiling, the soft bound of the general motion and yet the side lurches sliding into some particular pitch it makes a baffling and charming sight. . . .

What you look hard at seems to look hard at you, hence the true and the false instress of nature.

Hopkins Observing: Evaporation, Precipitation, Crystallization

Moving away to the median and opposite pole of liquidity, we have Hopkins's extraordinary meditation on—of all things!—his cup of Lenten hot chocolate. Theologically speaking, we find liquid in its paradisal state of nubilation and evaporation, as he elsewhere compiles "little Stonehenges," or infernos of ice like Dante, or purgatorios of the thawed state in which "the ice broke up in just these pieces" in small comedies of disclosure.

Here, the leap from clouds to steaming chocolate, from the universal cosmos to a cup, is both uninhibited and absurdist. To water as such, Hopkins adds the further condition of a certain density, viscousness, weightiness, nebulosity: that is, he is concerned with showing the liquid in a state of stress and condensation. His inspiration is this, precisely: that for a "lawing out of the shapes" one need go no further than one's cup of Lenten chocolate, as Newton thought one need go no further than a falling apple to law out the secret doxology of gravity.

The permutations of energy, as Hopkins summons them up, are at once Protean and fanciful: we see water as vapor, steam, bubbles, gases, films, throes, shells, grains, thrills, wisps, collars, rings, hoses, ribbons, shavings, frets, coils, etc., etc. We note, also, the physicist's addition of *gas* ("air") to solidity or viscosity and sheer volume, as in the breaking wave—which acts almost like the addition of spirit to matter or a vacuum to the combustibility of an electron. The imagery enlisted for the task furnishes Hopkins, here, as always, with a kind of special nomenclature, like the nomenclature of the exact sciences, for dealing denotatively, rather than connotatively, with a unique and immediate instance of perception: the "throes," the "shells," the "grains," the "thrills," the "collars," the "hoses," the "shavings," the "frets," the "coils," are part of a technician's discourse for a "naming of the parts"—a species of imaginative engineering.

Yet the effect as a whole, *read aloud*, is *meditative* rather than nomenclatural—a kind of soliloquy as quizzical and shrewd as the set-piece from *Hamlet* on the being or non-being of all that remains "nobler in the mind." He moves back and forth, between the rim of the cup and the realm of the nebular, with not a moment's flinching at the incongruity of things. As always in Hopkins, there is no assumption that the kingdom of water must be kept distinct from the kingdom of metal or fabric or wood, that the mixing of metaphors debauches the integrity of the object observed.

"*Inscape*," in other words—Hopkins's words—leads the poet to the secret kinship of apparently unlike things, regardless of kingdom, as the least common denominator of all. He *ransacks* the visible, for the highest possible factor of the indwelling Creator, Who may incarnate Himself in a piece of potsherd or a carpenter's shaving—or a cup of Lenten chocolate—and epiphanize what a physicist might call its "hidden variables." The stressing of essences thus invites an unsettling coexistence of "bafflement" and "charm": candle smoke, eyebrow, egg-white are all made one in the service of private oddities and precisions. We are again in the world of the Walrus's ode to disorientation in *Alice in Wonderland*. Brought together, they mutually stare one down, without scruple or inhibition, while "what you look hard at seems to look hard at you."

> The winter was long and hard. I made many observations on freezing. For instance the crystal in mud.—Hailstones are shaped like the cut of diamond called brilliants.—I found one morning the ground in one corner of the garden full of small pieces of potsherd from which there rose up (and not dropped off) long icicles carried on in some way each like a forepitch of the shape of the piece of potsherd it grew on, like a tooth to its root for instance, and most of them bended over and curled like so many tusks or horns or/ best of all and what they looked likest when they first caught my eye/ the first soft root-spurs thrown out from a sprouting chestnut. This bending of the icicle seemed so far as I could see not merely a resultant, where the smaller spars of which it was made were still straight, but to have flushed them too.—The same day and others the garden mould very crisp and meshed over with a lace-work of needles leaving (they seemed) three-cornered openings: it looked greyish and like a coat of gum on wood. Also the smaller crumbs and clods were lifted fairly up from the ground on upright ice-pillars, whether they had dropped these from themselves or drawn them from the soil: it was like a little Stonehenge—Looking down into the thick ice of our pond I found the imprisoned air-bubbles nothing at random but starting from centres and in particular one most beautifully regular white brush of them, each spur of it a curving string of beaded and diminishing bubbles—The pond, I suppose from over pressure when it was less firm, was mapped with a puzzle of very slight cleft branched with little sprigs: the pieces were odd-shaped and sized—though a square angular scaping could be just made out in the outline but the cracks ran deep down through the ice markedly in planes and always the planes of the cleft on the surface. They remained and in the end the ice broke up in just these pieces.

Here, Hopkins pursues the metamorphoses of liquidity to its ultimate reversal in crystallization. His approach is characteristically avid: he probes *under* the icicle, the spur, the tusk, the filament, for the object to which it adheres, for clues to the shapes and forces that impart their own conformation to hardening matter and take direction and thrust from the processes that precede it.

The human artifact—a fragment of pottery—as it were, bears witness to the morphology of its incrementation: the icicle takes its shape from the potsherd it envelops, as an effect carries the secret of its cause, or an armature supports the weight of the clay and the continuing intent of the sculptor.

And it is a *sculpting* of the hardening water that Hopkins emphasizes as the source of its "scaping": the "forepitch of the shape of the piece of potsherd it grew on" that launched the dynamics of the freezing point. Here, his refinement of causality is almost obsessional in its quest for precision. The icicle, we are to undertand, "*rose up*" and "not *dropped off*" (as it might appear to the cursory bystander), each one "like a forepitch of the shape" it "grew on"; it then "bended over and curled," summoning up the energies that, working latently at first, disclosed their whole character and became "likest" themselves in the epiphanies of the root-hairs of the chestnut.

This, however, leaves Hopkins, like Yeats at the "Second Coming" of Bethlehem, still peering, probing, curious—"unsatisfied" with the "turbulence" of the compounding manifestation. He goes on to search for "resultants"—for change and enlargement that "flush" an object, lift it "fairly up from the ground," leaving one to wonder whether it had been *dropped* onto the soil from above or *drawn* into it from below. He peers into the ice for its *bubbles, centers, beads, brushes,* vestiges of *pressure, firmness,* clefts, slippages, planes, "*mapping out,*" as always, what he frankly admits to be a "*puzzle*" rather than a solution, as Thoreau did on Walden Pond,[5] and finally discovers that union of tensions and torsions that not only joined to consolidate the evanescent form, but foretell precisely how that form will relinquish the sum of its parts, held in precarious balance, when the thawing begins. In this sense, like the quark hunters of quantum in our own day, he touches the fault lines of a new reading of the modern, which opens the way from a physics of causality to a physics of imminence.

iv

Sunrise at Chagford. There was a remarkable fan of clouds traced in fine horizontals, which afterwards lost their levels, some becoming oblique. Below appearing bright streaks which crowded up one after another. A white mist in the churchyard, trees ghostly in it.

Sunset here also. Over the nearest ridge of Dartmoor. Sky orange, trail of Bronze-lit clouds, stars and streaks of brilliant electrum underneath, but not for this, but effect of dark intensified foreground. Long rounded ridge of Dartmoor deep purple, then trees on the descending hill, and a field with an angle so that the upper level was lighter green, the lower darker, then a purplish great brown field, then the manufactory with grey white timbers (it is built of wood) and grey shingle roofs.

Grey sky at Hampstead lately. Clouds showing beautiful and rare curves like curds, comparable to barrows, arranged of course in parallels.

Rain railing off something.

The butterfly perching in a cindery dusty road and pinching his scarlet valves. Or wagging, one might say. And also valved eyes.

Mallowy red of sunset and sunrise clouds.

Hopkins Observing: Celestial Mechanics

The effect here is especially interesting for its exploratory air of reconnoitering, as a muralist might rummage for the most suitable thickness of charcoal, slash the initiatory strokes and pigments on the soaking plaster, before the incisive moment of ongoing engagement. However, the talk is already very *painterly*: in the poet's concern for the structuring—or engineering—of space in terms of its tensions; the architectonic interaction of planes, horizontals, foregrounds, angles, levels, curves, parallels, characteristic of Hopkins, the intercommunication of stresses, etc., etc. One notes again the distinctions of near and far, the upper, the level, the "underneath." There follows the addition of light and dark, the indications of contrasts and intensities of color: sky, orange; clouds, "Bronze-lit," with streaks of "brilliant electrum"; ridges, purple; lighter and darker greens; purplish brown fields; grey white timbers, grey shingle, grey sky; the "mallowy" red of sunset and sunrise clouds—the vivid overlay of a palette on the charcoal of the confining lines, with the drawing visible underneath the scored plaster and paint.

In the midst of the soaking brush strokes, one asks: "But what is 'electrum?'" (surely a word to be reckoned with!)—and finds that the word is metallurgical and biochemical, as well as pigmental. In English, *electrum* applies to "native gold containing a large percentage of silver" (*Standard College Dictionary*)—and, at once, the landscape of Hopkins's Dartmoor flashes with gold leaf, like a medieval altarpiece. *Elektron* in Greek means *amber*: it was the rubbing of amber resins with cat's fur that, according to Steven Weinberg,[6] provided eighteenth-century physicists like Du Fay and Stephen Gray with their earliest clues to the phenomenon of electrical conduction. From *electrum*, to *electrons*, to the modern priorities of electromagnetic physics, with its emphasis on the micro-world of quantum, is a leap of cross-association that is bound to bemuse readers of Hopkins today as much as a similar caveat that Coleridge's "foremost concern was with electricity and magnetism . . . particularly the no-man's-land between electricity and chemistry" startled Romantic fundamentalists in 1971.[7] While there is no reason for imputing comparable predilections to Hopkins, along with the usual "spiritual exercises" required of priestly incumbents to the Society of Jesus, his insistence on the "streak of brilliant electrum" is uncannily apposite for the interplay of "resinous and vitreous electricity" that led to the electromagnetic mysteries of Faraday (1791–1867) and Maxwell (1831–1879). What impresses most in Hopkins is the mix of subliminal approximations that mingles specificities of color and light with a float of verbal and spatial uncertainties that carry him to the threshold of the physical sciences, like Coleridge,[8] in his search for particularity.

Time and again, one gets an echo from the language of "Water Coming Through a Lock" of a strategy for governing the ungovernable: in Hopkins's fondness for "fans" as the expressive enlargement of a perspective, whether it be water, or clouds, or peacocks; in *directional* clues of the oblique, the horizontal, the crowding and clouding of *masses*, the "losing" of levels and forces. In the end, the full rendering of both sunrise and sunset eludes him—just as he expected!—and he yields to the poet's pleasure of the *mot juste*: the bravura of "rain *railing off* something," the piquancy of the *pinching* or the *wagging* of butterfly wings, the baroquerie of spotting wings with "valved eyes," the correct artist's mix for the mealiness of sunset-red—yes, "mallowy" is the only word that will serve!

Feb. 23—A lunar halo: I looked at it from the upstairs library window. It was a grave grained sky, the strands rising a little from the left to right. The halo was not quite round, for in the first place it was a little pulled and drawn below, by the refraction of the lower air perhaps, but what is more it fell in on the nether left hand side to rhyme the moon itself, which was not quite at full. I could not but strongly feel in my fancy the odd instress of this, the moon leaning on her side, as if fallen back, in the cheerful light floor within the ring, after with magical rightness and success tracing round her the ring the steady copy of her own outline. But this sober grey darkness and pale light was happily broken through by the orange pealing of Mitton bells

Here again, Hopkins is at his familiar task of bounding the unboundable, laying on his charcoals with a mixture of maximum attack and minimal pressure—great traceries of the ineffable. At times, all seems like the merest webbing or sketching for a later assault on the architectonics of light. His stance is commonplace enough—a window of the upstairs library; but thereafter the effect is like someone writing on the zenith with infra-red ink, measuring the spaces with radioactive protractors. The language is at once "magical" and textural—a *weightless* language, as is proper for moon-walkers—full of pulls and oddities, strong feelings, weird stresses, imbalances, grainy cross-hatchings. On the other hand, we have an almost *sculptural* set-piece, drained of all color, like a frieze for the Parthenon, in which gods and goddesses assume their mythological functions—pagan rather than Hebraic—as spatial principles and guardians of cosmic gravity: "a grave grained sky," as Hopkins puts it, "the strands rising a little from the left to right."

We note the exact concern with *directions*, again—what is left and right, what is "pulled down and drawn below," "refraction of the lower air," tugs at the "nether left hand side . . . as if fallen back . . . within the ring." From the center of things we note a tactile sense of electromagnetic torsions, balances, *imperfections*, of things—the nether, the upper. The whole combines in a theater of forces, powers, magnitudes: a cosmological tableau, with the moon, like Diana herself, in the guise of an enormous lounging goddess "leaning on her side, as if fallen back." The darkness is "sober grey"; the light, "pale"; sound alone is felt as "orange"—bell sounds, a stained glass flashing out of nowhere. The "scientific rightness" of the passage finally defers to the "magical rightness" of things, a subliminal stationing, or posing, or draping of the forces in which elements are literally said to "rhyme" with other elements, and the draftsman's hand is seen tracing, ringing, copying, outlining a subjective impression of "gravity" in its physical and metaphysical sense: cheerfulness, steadiness, sobriety.

> Sept. 24—First saw the Northern Lights. My eye was caught by beams of light and dark very like the crown of horny rays the sun makes behind a cloud. At first I thought of silvery cloud until I saw that these were more luminous and did not dim the clearness of the stars in the Bear. They rose slightly radiating thrown out from the earthline. Then I saw soft pulses of light one after another rise and pass upwards arched in shape but waveringly and with the arch broken. They seemed to float, not following the warp of the sphere as falling stars look to do but free though concentrical with it. This busy working of nature wholly independent of the earth and seeming to go on in a strain of time not reckoned by our reckoning of days and years but simpler and as if correcting with and appealing to the world by being preoccupied with and appealing to and dated to the day of judgment was like a new witness to God and filled me with delightful fear

Here, the visual changes are as subtle and ambiguous as Nature can contrive—as anyone who has tried to pin down the *aurora borealis* in a winter sky and trace the pulsations with his eyeballs in a field of electrical forces is well aware. There can be no hope of an encompassing answer, no leisure for the separation of one visual signal from another in the delicate convulsions of the northern horizon. But the familiar painterly and architectonic guidelines—the distinction between firsts and seconds, the luminous and the dim, the sequences of the spasms, the beams, the arches, the earthlines—what is warped, falling, or concentrical or floating—are still at work "scaping" the unscapable, and finally reaching toward Deity, as Adam reaches for the hand of God in Michelangelo's Creation panel. Hopkins fills the ceiling of space, as it were, like a Vatican chapel, with constructs and intensities of areas and visual energies. The attempt to catch (with the *eye*, says Hopkins!) *the whole of a suddenness*, the subtle structuring of space itself, recalls Sir Joshua Reynolds's definition of the "sublime" in the *Discourses*, as that which "impresses the mind at once with one great idea—it is a single blow." Failing that—and what can the unaided eye do but fail?—Hopkins concludes, as he so often concluded the final sestet of his sonnets, by cramming his forms with a whole *theology* and metaphysics of sacerdotal vision. The final sentence is as complex and abstract as sophisticated Jesuitism can make it: with a doctrinal groping that surrenders the visual to the visionary, the savagery of the seen for the pieties of the Seer:

> This busy working of nature wholly independent of the earth and seeming to go on *in a strain of time* not reckoned by our reckoning of days and years but simpler and *as if correcting the preoccupation of the world* by being preoccupied with and appealing to and *dated to the day of judgment*, was like a *new witness to God and filled me with delightful fear*

If Blake had his Holy-Holy-Holy-Suns, Hopkins had his Holy-Holy-Holy-Auroras.

v

> One day when the bluebells were in bloom I wrote the following. I do not think I have ever seen anything more beautiful than the bluebell I have been looking at. I know the beauty of our Lord by it. It[s inscape] is [mixed of] strength and grace, like an ash[tree]. The head is strongly drawn over [backwards] and arched down like a cutwater [drawing itself back from the line of the keel]. The lines of the bells strike and overlie this, rayed but not symmetrically, some lie parallel. They look steely against [the] paper, the shades lying between the bells and behind the cockled petal-ends and nursing up the precision of their distinctness, the petal-ends themselves being delicately lit. Then there is the straightness of the trumpets in the bells softened by the slight entasis and [by] the square splay of the mouth. One bell, the lowest, some way detached and carried on a longer footstalk, touched out with the tips of the petals an oval / not like the rest in a plane perpendicular to the axis of the bell but a little atilt, and so with [the] square-in-rounding turns of the petals . . . There is a little drawing of this detached bell. It looks square-cut in the original

Hopkins Observing: The Bafflements of the Bluebell

At this point, I should like again to recoil from the twofold entanglements of cosmic and transcendental discourse, and return to the well-lighted "commonplaces" of Cocteau. Let me conclude with Hopkins's pursuit of the bluebell, or common cowslip, or wood hyacinth, or harebell, certainly the least flamboyant of English flora—unspectacular, ordinary, accessible as the squill or the field violet, which requires no metaphysical preparation like, say, lunar halos, crepuscular clouds, or Northern Lights in order to be put into their modest botanical places—yet regarded by Hopkins, to the very end, as unencompassable, requiring a crisis of identity in order to be seen in their true character as one of Deity's most enigmatic vegetables.

That Hopkins should make the bluebell a test of character and employ it as a prime example of "instress" (or "character," or "sake," or "self") leading directly to the doorstep of "the beauty of our Lord" is one of those paradoxes that turn Hopkins's *Note-Books* into a Book of Revelation, in which Perception as such is seen as a fifth horseman of the Jesuit's Apocalypse. Up to now we have been pursuing Hopkins's cue that "motion multiplies inscape" (which is also the cue of the modern physicist's pursuit of the infinitesimal)—even in his renderings of ice—that it is *action*, or the "behavior" of things, that "fetches out" their character or "throws out an Earthline" behind the evanescence of their mathematics. However, there are equally characteristic moments when Hopkins attempted to read objects *at rest*, as quantum physicists have probed for a "ground state" of the atom; and his bluebells show him at his habitual task of "fetching out" the inscape of things in a confined or arrested world of planted things.

In the above passage, the bluebells have apparently been removed from the planted state of initial fixities and thrown on a sheet of paper; one supposes it is white. What he gives us is what psychologists have called a *gestalt*—a functional configuration or synthesis of separate elements of sensuous seeing that create a syndrome of manifestations: the bluebell *drawn backwards*, *arched* down, their lines *striking* or *overlying*, *rayed*, *asymmetrical*, *parallel*, *nursing up* the precision of their *distinctness*, *straightness*, *detached*, *carried on*, *touched out with an oval*, *planed perpendicularly to an axis*, *atilt* or *squared with rounding turns*, or architecturally viewed as an "*entasis*," or the swelling in the shaft of a column. We have, in short, not a description, but a collage of torsions, tensions, directional, positional, tactile, kinesthetic: a composition by stresses. Or the piece as a whole can be viewed as a kind of dartboard at which a barrage of sensory shafts are hurled like missiles, all moving so fast that one can see only the shudder of the feathered end after the point has struck: a veritable arsenal of minuscule calculations turning *data* into *quanta*, with its characteristic leaps from one field of force to another.

In short, there is really no "stillness" at all, or rest for the object: for Hopkins, "still lives"—or *nature morte*—in art, as in quantum mechanics, are a contradiction in terms. "Inscape" here equals emission, kinesis, dynamics: a kind of total convergence of the style and impact of the flower upon the viewer, to the point where it becomes a single expressive entity and can be encompassed in its holistic simplicity by the reader as a matrix of reality. We generally say of odd, eccentric, and distinctive people: "What a *character!*"—and no one sensed the oddity of his stances more objectively than Hopkins.

> No doubt my poetry errs on the side of oddness. I hope in time to have a more balanced, Miltonic style. But as air, melody, is what strikes me most of all in music and design and painting, so design, pattern, or what I am in the habit of calling "inscape" is what I above all aim at in poetry. Now it is the virtue of design, or pattern, or inscape, to be distinctive and it is the vice of distinction to be queer. This vice I cannot have escaped.

But Hopkins had a host of other words for the "inscape by which I know the beauty of our Lord," and conceded its "dangers": *wit, genius, character*, "the handsome heart":

> I think then no one can admire beauty of the body more than I do, and it is of course a comfort to find beauty in a friend or a friend in beauty. But this kind of beauty is dangerous. And more beautiful than the beauty of the mind is beauty of character, the "handsome heart." . . . The soul may have no further beauty than that which is seen in the mind . . . and there may be genius uninformed by character.

Elsewhere he calls it "the eye and ace of the whole," "What they looked likest" when "first they met my eye," or their "sake," as in his letter to the poet Robert Bridges:

Sake is a word I find it convenient to use: I did not know when I did so first that it is common in German, in the form *sach*. It is the *sake* of "for the sake of", forsake, namesake, keepsake. I mean by it the being a thing has outside itself, as a voice by its echo, a face by its reflection, a body by its shadow, a man by his name, fame, or memory, *and also* that in the thing by virtue of which especially it has this being abroad, and that is something distinctive, marked, specifically or individually speaking, as for a voice an echo, clearness, for a reflected image, light, brightness; for a shadowcasting body, bulk, for a man of genius, great achievements, amiability, and so on. . . .

There is an even swifter rendering of the bluebell in another passage in which the "deeper instress" is said to "*float*" upon the mind in the kind of "notable glare" we have already examined in a number of key passages from other poets dealing with the "sudden" disclosure of wholes and entireties:

> May 11. Bluebells in Hodder wood, all hanging their heads one way. I caught as well as I could while my companions talked the Greek rightness of their beauty, the lovely/ what people call/ 'gracious' bidding one to another or all one way, the level or stage or shire of colour they make hanging in the air a foot above the grass, and *a notable glare the eye may abstract* and sever from the blue colour/ of *light beating up* from so many glassy heads, which like water is good to *float their deeper instress in upon* the mind.

And, of course, there are any number of passing allusions to instress as seeing-by-syndromes in a variety of unexpected contexts familiar to the reader of Hopkins's correspondence. I should like to conclude, however, with the really dizzying rendering of bluebells on May 11, "in the little wood between the College and the highroad."

> This day and May 11 the bluebells in the little wood between the College and the highroad and in one of the Hurst Green cloughs. In the little wood/ opposite the light/they stood in blackish spreads or *sheddings like the spots on a snake*. The heads are then like thongs and solemn in grain and grape-colour. But in the clough/ through the light/ they came in falls of sky-colour washing the brows and slacks of the ground with vein-blue, thickening at the double, vertical themselves, and the young grass and brake fern combed vertical, but the brake struck the upright of all this with

light winged transomes. It was a lovely sight.—The bluebells in your hand *baffle you with their inscape*, made to every sense: if you draw your fingers through them they are lodged and struggle/ with a shock of wet heads; the long stalks rub and click and flatten to a fan on one another like your fingers themselves would when you passed the palms hard across one another, making a brittle rub and jostle like the noise of a hurdle strained by leaning against; then there is the faint honey smell and in the mouth the sweet gum when you bite them. But this is easy, it is *the eye they baffle*. They give one a fancy of panpipes and of some wind instrument with stops—a trombone perhaps. The overhung necks—for growing they are a little more than a staff with a simple crook, but in water, where they stiffen, they take stronger turns, in the head like sheephooks or, when more waved throughout, like the waves riding through a whip that is being smacked—what with these overhung necks and what with the crisped ruffled bells dropping mostly on one side and the gloss these have at their footstalks they have an air of the knights at chess. Then the knot or 'knoop' of buds, some shut, some just gaping, which makes the pencil of the whole spike, should be noticed: the inscape of the flower most finely carried out in the siding of the axes, each striking a greater and greater slant, is finished in these clustered buds, which, for the most part are not straightened but rise to the end like a tongue and this and their tapering and a little flattening they have make them *look like the heads of snakes*

Finally, another extraordinary instance of "inscape-by-bafflement"! Here, the word "bafflement" (which should be regarded as another nomenclatural term in Hopkins's search for a technical vocabulary) must be read, not as an exasperated confusion, or a blur, or a thwarted determination to dominate an intellectual outcome, but as a happy embarrassment of riches—an ensemble of multiple choices and intensities: the coexistence of pleasing alternatives which "charm" and "law out the shapes," without a need to arrive at solutions by a process of studious elimination. Hopkins, it would appear, *can have them all*, as physicists lay claim to a "spectrum" for the quantum states of the atom in their reading of its magnitudes: and altogether they constitute what Keats must have meant when he called poetry a "fine excess."

Here, the bluebells, like the wave that was rolled through the palm of the hand like a piece of putty, are drawn through the fingers to enhance the *bafflement* of the viewer and call forth a further dimension of exertion and initiative: in the same way, one supposes, that he forced the water "through a lock" to determine the hydrodynamics of its movement. We should also note that the passage begins and ends with a *snake*—not the Edenic imagery of a Fall through the guile and malevolence of a Tempter, but as a joyous acknowledgment of the character and being of the *serpentine*, like Coleridge's serpent. The bluebells are first seen in "blackish spreads or sheddings like the spots on a snake," and last seen to taper and flatten "like the heads of snakes"; the snake is pre-Hebraic, Egyptian, primogenital: a totem of the chthonic knowledge of the world's body incarnate in the bluebell.

Thereafter, the "bafflement" multiplies incongruities in transsensual abandonment, as though it were the source of the faculty of *knowing* itself. There are grape colors, sky colors, vein blues, "transomes" (?), a shock of wet heads, hurdles, honey-smells, panpipes, trombones, hoods, crooks, whips, bells, knights on a chessboard, pencils, spikes, axes, tongues—all set down in unabashed exuberance. The oddity of the language is equally apparent and uninhibited: *spreads, cloughs, brows, slacks, grounds, uprights*, etc., etc.; visual, spatial, daemonic, and architectonic sensations of rigidity, turgor, fluidity, density, resiliency. The bluebell is physicalized in the pressure of fingers on the palms, animalized as snake, vegetalized as grape, passed through a spectrum of colors and then a whole gauntlet of the senses: touch, sound, smell, taste, sight, and purely whimsical byplays of pleasure like the panpipes, the knights at chess, and the flicker of snakes' tongues.

One reels at the speed and specificity of the "bafflements," trying to hold on to the bluebell itself in the volleys of unpredictable similitudes, flinching at the nearness of all its attributes, yet engrossed in the simultaneity of its manifestations—*handling* the flower in all its permutations: biting, rubbing, jostling, leaning, flickering, sensuously and sexually alert, while the flower—the more *unknowable* for its plurality—flashes intimations of its species.

That is the posture to which the "observing Hopkins" should be held, to the very end—the uncertainties which prepare Creation for the indwelling of its Creator and render Him indispensable to its adoration.

vi

Hopkins Observing: A Trial Balance

Such has not been the practice of specialists in Hopkins, however; they have had a way of closing the "sprung" world of Hopkins in a regimen for seeing defined by a special nomenclature that renders it more tractable than either his *Note-Books* or his canon of uneasy masterpieces warrant. The "saking," the "selving," the "stalling," the "stressing," the "stacking," the "scaping," the "pitching," perhaps, stabilize the "perturbations" of the "observing Hopkins" more than should be; the mercury still dances untidily in the calibrated columns after the readings of his interpreters. Disequilibrium haunts both the composition and the prosody of Hopkins in a way that seems never to have touched the quick of comparable talents like Donne, to whom the "trepidations of the spheres" were a similar source of metaphorical by-play in the epoch of Tycho Brahe, Kepler, and Galileo. For John Donne, writing in 1611, the

> New philosophy calls all in doubt
> The Element of fire is quite put out;
> The Sunne is lost, and th'earth, and no man's wit
> Can well direct him where to look for it.

But the "uncertainties" that "wrench and wring" the visionary life of Hopkins are not the uncertainties of Donne's "Anatomy of the World," and originate in the special excrucation of sensuous particulars that "hurl for him, O half hurl earth for him, off under his feet" and "direct him where to look for it." What makes the *Note-Books* indispensable is their insistence on the oddities and excesses of the "realizing acts of intuition" by which *things* move toward the poetic artifact itself—the shock of "poetry in its raw state," which, as Cocteau had occasion to remind us, should always induce a "*nausée*" of uncertainty in the viewer, upon language.

We need, finally, to speak of certain recurrent practices and idiosyncracies of the "observing Hopkins," who confided his intuitions to the "trial balance" of his *Note-Books*. Chief among them, of course, is the scintillating omnipresence of *minutiae*—what Blake called the "minute particulars of mankind"—which function like a calculus of infinitesimal variations. It is the eye for what is "counter, original, spare, strange" that *keeps the poet looking* and leads his eye *out* of the formula for the species to its unique instance. What puts the "dapple" on things is a "pie-ing" (*pi*-ing) (π-ing) of the universe that renders it "fickle, freckled," "brinded," "stippled," "plotted and pieced" like a clown's motley. *Particle* physics has recently given the esthetician's word for it—"*particulars*"—a fourth dimension of relevancy which equates it with the mathematician's search for the molecular exactitudes of quantum. Yet the exactitudes of Hopkins's *Note-Books* are no mere "schedule of pointer readings," like Eddington's atoms: they characteristically appeal to objects and elements *outside* themselves to identify what still remains to be known in the determinations of the "known." The fractal accumulation of precisions—often carried beyond the fifth decimal place of metaphor—only serves to underscore what continues to elude the knower. The *Note-Books* teem with buried analogies, images, cross-associations, disparate similitudes, sensory evasions, and equivocations. Staring into his Lenten chocolate, Hopkins sees "candle smoke," "the thrills of a candle," "napkins," "handkerchiefs," which crowd the field with uncertainties at the same time as they arouse contradictory delusions of "specificity" which turn particulars into enigmas.

Uncertainty increases with his constant movement from the substance of a thing into its essence—not, however, through a process of increasing abstraction, but through an unexpected *acceleration and bombardment of its substances*. Nothing is more characteristic of Hopkins than his fondness for *trains*, series, sequences, syndromes of objective notations covering the whole field of the object in flying volleys and taking pressure with their incrementation like the coils of a spring. We get depth and essence because the eye is literally *driven* into the substance by fusillades of penetrating *sensory*, rather than *conceptual*, blows. It should come as no surprise that Hopkins, inured to a Jesuit's "custody of the *eyes*"[9] that forced the novice's gaze downward into his boot soles, demurely "looking at neither persons or objects around him," should eventually fasten, with a pagan avidity, on the revelations of the incarnate Christ in a counterdisciplinary search for the substantive "glories" of His Creation. In effect, the *Note-Books* constitute a double-entried magnificat of alternate penances and celebrations, starvations, daemonic excesses, that call to mind the physicist's bombardment of the micro-world for nuclear intimations of the Given: it is as though the observing Hopkins is himself at once cloud chamber, super-accelerator, cyclotron, photomultiplier, beam-splitter, electromagnetic polarizer.

To put it another way: the intensity of Hopkins's absorption in what he sees brings him just as close to the condition of "science" as it does to "poetry" and "theology"; his engrossment in the *haecceitas* of things—the means by which a thing becomes and behaves like itself—leads him to the objective processes of observation we associate with the "scientific method." Looking into his Lenten chocolate, Hopkins observes: "It seems as if the heat by *aestus*, throes/ one after another threw films of vapour off as boiling water throws off steam under films of water, that is bubbles. *One query then is whether these films contain gas or no."* Here, the boiling of the water not only imitates the "poetics" of Machado's egg; it also anticipates the physicist's quest for the thermodynamics of liquid states and the heliocentric search for the gases of cosmological bodies.

It is hardly surprising to learn that Hopkins was actually a contributor to an avowedly "scientific" journal like *Nature* and that his descriptions of sunsets for the sun-watchers of Krakatoa and Sumatra in the aftermath of volcanic explosions half a planet away repeat the identical eccentricities of both his *Note-Books* and his poems:

> A bright sunset lines the clouds so that their brims look like gold, brass, bronze, or steel. It *fetches out* those dazzling flecks and spangles which people call *fishscales*. It gives to a *mackerel or dappled cloudwrack* the appearance of *quilted crimson silk* or a *ploughed field glazed with crimson ice.*
>
> On the 4th it appeared brown, like a *strong light behind tortoiseshell* or *Derbyshire alabaster*. It has been well compared to the color of *incandescent iron*. Sometimes it appears like a mixture of chalk with sand and muddy earth. The pigments for it would be ochre and red.
>
> It had a silvery or steely look, with the soft, radiating streamers and little colour; its shape was mainly *elliptical*, the slightly *longer axis* being *vertical*; the *size about 20°* from the sun each way. . . .

> After sunset the horizon was, by 4:20, lined a long way by a *glowing tawny light*, not very pure in colour and distinctly *textured in hummock bodies* like a *shoal of dolphins*, or in what are called *gadroons*, or as *the Japanese conventionally represented waves*.

All teems with the adjectival savageries we have already noted in the *Note-Books* of "Hopkins Observing": "fluted," "brindled," "reefed," "puckered," "frowning," "dappled," "mallow," as though painted from the one palette. Even in the purgatorial years of "Carrion Comfort" and the "Terrible Sonnets," we learn from R. B. Martin,[10] a "popular account of Light and Ether," and a paper on "Statistics and Free Will"—still classic concerns of quantum physicists seeking to mediate their options as mathematicians of Uncertainty—were among the projects with which a debilitated Hopkins sought to supplement his devotional obligations as Jesuit at large.

At the same time, his entries reflect a marked preference for the *object in motion*, which has been the *sine qua non* of experimental physicists from Newton to Schrödinger and Planck. His fondness for phenomena of passage, flux, meander—for the transitory detail apparent in its unique character only for a moment and thereafter transformed into another fugitive exactitude discernible in its true character for a moment in turn—is well known to all. He seeks out the natural forms that live by change, evanescence, instantaneity: cloud shapes, water shapes, sunsets, atmospheric overlays of texture and light; his is a universe that whirls almost visibly on its axis, agitated by winds, colors, vapors, tremors, and conflagrations, as in the paradoxes of Heraclitus.

Why the transitory, the short-lived, the metamorphic? Because here the challenge of vision is most graphic, the stress, richest; because the *stopped* thing, the life *stilled* into itself, untouched by the random and combustible, no longer flashes out evidence of its character. For Hopkins, it would seem, only the *done* thing is the expressive thing; only by reproducing in ourselves the momentum of the world can we bring ourselves to the pitch by which the forces of things are made visible in their true character. Only the *becoming* thing—mimetic, dramatistic, histrionic—in the barbaric parlance of Hopkins—will "flame out, like shining from shook foil." A thunderbolt-watcher and a pyrophile, like Heraclitus, Hopkins is literally concerned with the unforeseeable lightning flash over the stilled landscape, and with the distinction between one lightning flash and the next—with nuances of combustion rather than the painter's tableau of a "Storm Over Toledo":

> The lightning seemed to me white like a flash from a looking-glass, but Mr. Lentaigne in the afternoon noticed it rose-coloured and lilac. I noticed two kinds of flash but I am not sure that sometimes there were not the two together from different points of the same cloud or starting from the same point different ways—one a straight stroke, broad like a stroke with chalk and liquid, as if the blade of an oar just stripped open a ribbon scar in smooth water and it caught the light; the other narrow and wire-like, like the splitting of a rock and danced down-along in a thousand jags. I noticed this too, that there was a perceptible interval between the blaze and the first inset of the flash and its score in the sky and that that seemed to be first of all laid in a bright confusion and then uttered by a tongue of brightness (what is strange) running up from the ground to the cloud, not the other way

Finally, there is the curious sense of the viewer *alone* with the object, with nothing but his own identity and ingenuity to interpret it—a "naked-handed" encounter with phenomena caught in the act of manifesting their quiddities. If the separation of Subject and Object is in some ways a *sad* one—a pathos of isolation confronting the "brutality" of Nature—it is also militant, assertive, imaginative; that is, it is the source of a specifically human *point of view*. No one has made more of the solitary options of the Subject than Hopkins himself:

> I find myself both as man and as myself something most determined and distinctive, at pitch, more distinctive and higher pitched than anything else I see: I find myself with my pleasures and pains, my powers and my experiences, my deserts and guilt, my shame and sense of beauty, my dangers, hopes, fears, and all my fate, more important to myself than anything I see. And when I ask where does all this throng and stack of being, so rich, so distinctive, so important, come from/ nothing I see can answer me. . . . [S]earching nature I taste *self* but at one tankard, that of my own being. The development, refinement, condensation of nothing shews any sign of being able to match this to me or give me another taste of it, a taste even resembling it. . . . Part of this world of objects, this object-world, is also part of the very self in

question, as in man's case his own body, which each man not only feels *in* and acts *with*, but also feels and acts *upon*. . . . Within a certain bounding line all will be self, outside of it nothing; with it self begins from one side and ends from the other. I look through my eye and the window and the air; the eye is my eye and of me and me, the windowpane is my windowpane but not of me nor me

Matching his *Note-Books* to the canon of the Collected Poems, one concludes that *particularity of vision* (the *certainty* that one has seen precisely the oddities one has seen, and the determination to communicate the exact nuance at its most expressive moment of disclosure) also leads to *particularity of language, rhythm, imagery*—in short, to the modality of poetry itself, and to the idiom inseparable from the observer's identity. It is as though the privacy of the exactly inflected particular *stumbles* upon the condition of "poetry" without ever having really intended it. "Sudden" sight furnishes the poet with the irreversible datum of the imaginative occasion at its most decisive moment of disclosure; "second" sight identifies it as the means by which the whole experience of seeing was "brought to pitch," "instressed"—the identifying mark of the inwardness of the poet brought to bear on the externals of "brute Nature:"

> one light *raft* of beech which the wind *footed and strained on*
>
> a *pash* of *soap-sud-coloured gummy bimbeams rowing* over the leaves
>
> *ragged shoots* and *bushes* of water like a *mass of thongs of bramble*
>
> *water-sprigs* that *lace* and *dance* and *jockey* in the air
>
> *Cups* of the eyes, gathering back the lightly *hinged* eyelids. *Bows* of the eyelids. *Pencil* of eyelashes. *Juices* of the eyeball. Eyelids like *leaves, petals, caps, tufted hats, handkerchiefs, sleeves, gloves,* water like *bubbles in a quill*

Here, it would appear that spontaneity and cunning, the expendable and the indispensable nuance, infallibility and uncertainty, join in a paroxysm of simultaneity and become one and the same thing. The seminal insight for poets, as Coleridge was to discover for his own time, is that the whole ontology of their medium—its linguistics, its metrics, its analogical charge—flows out of some prior exertion of looking, knowing, naming which is "passional" and *preverbal*, and is, as often as not, "poetic" by "chance":

> [T]he origin of metre . . . I would trace to the balance in the mind effected by that spontaneous effort which strives *to hold in check the workings of passion.* . . . As *every passion has its proper pulse,* so will it likewise have its characteristic modes of expression.
>
> —*Biographia Literaria*, Chapter XVIII

In 1817, Coleridge was ready to state the premise chemically:

> [W]hatever else is combined with *metre* must, though it be not itself *essentially poetic,* have nevertheless some property in common with poetry, as an intermedium of affinity, a sort of (if I dare borrow a well-known phrase from technical chemistry) *mordaunt* between it and the superadded metre.
>
> —*Biographia Literaria*, Chapter XVIII

Doubtless, Coleridge's metaphor of a "mordaunt" for the bonding of phenomena with the "superadded metres" of poetry is a dividend of his lifelong association with the public discourses of Sir Humphry Davy (1778–1829),[11] whom he called the "first chemist of his age," in an era that was yet to produce the field physics and electrons of Thomson and Faraday and Maxwell. Recast into the parlance of our own century, the analogy might be transposed from chemistry to physics by a shift of vernacular. For experimental physicists today, we are told, the search for "phenomena" *precedes* the postulate that the phenomenon is already a datum immutably written into the cosmos, awaiting the mediation of the searcher. For J. H. Wheeler,[12] as for Cratylus the Heraclitean,[13] "No elementary phenomenon is a phenomenon until it is a registered [observed] phenomenon," and "what we call reality [is] an elaborate papier-maché construction of imagination and theory fitted between a few iron posts of observation." Nothing is *a priori* or *quod erat demonstrandum* in the pairing of things with the names for things: in the mechanics of quantum and the auguries of Heraclitus, both the "particulars" of Hopkins's world and Blake's vision of Jerusalem are *particles,* parcels, atomic packets of quanta encapsulating the world's energy, before they become lexical wave-lengths in the cloud chambers of the poet. The *words* are "counter, original, spare, strange," because the *data* to be identified originate in a special act of seeing which is *noetic* before it is poetic. All that is most idiosyncratic in the observer—his sensibility, his processes of association, analogy, memory, initiative—the whole machinery of instrumentality, combine with all that is most idiosyncratic in the thing to be observed, as its "mordaunt" or fixative; and what is fixed are not meanings and things, but the compositional integrity, of the *poem*. It is poetry first and essentially, not by the accident of its bonding with prosody, but because the poet has forced it to yield him the "corrosive" particular that is at once true for himself and innate to the object *as he saw it*, and then "fixed" its "affinities" on the platens of his medium without compromise or extenuation.

Notes

1. I. A. Richards, *Coleridge on Imagination* (New York: Harcourt, Brace, 1935), p. 51.
2. *Quantum Theory and Measurement*, ed. Wheeler and Zurek, p. vi.
3. *Selections from the Notebooks of Leonardo da Vinci*, ed. Irma A. Richter (London: Oxford University Press, 1953), pp. 23, 24.
4. According to Benoit B. Mandelbröt, whose concerns today are also with the "unpredictable irregularities of natural phenomena" and the "geometry of turbulence," the "study of circles and waves begs the physicist to 'take the measure of the universe.'" His province, in an age of computerized graphics, is with a "mathematical study of irregular continua" (*The Fractal Geometry of Nature* [New York: Freeman, 1982]) and confirms the preoccupations of earlier wavewatchers like Hopkins and Leonardo da Vinci in their search for "metamorphic" pattern and "chaos."
5. "The ice itself is the object of most interest, though you must improve the earliest opportunity to study it. If you examine it closely the morning after it freezes, you find the greater part of the bubbles, which at first appeared to be within it, are against its under surface, and that more are continually rising from the bottom; while the ice is as yet comparatively solid and dark, that is, you see the water through it. These bubbles are from an eightieth to an eighth of an inch in diameter, very clear and beautiful, and you see your face reflected in them through the ice. . . . But as the last two days had been very warm, like an Indian summer, the ice was not now transparent, showing the dark green color of the water, and the bottom, but opaque and whitish or gray, and though twice as thick was hardly stronger than before, for

the air bubbles had greatly expanded under this heat and run together, and lost their regularity; they were no longer one directly over another, but often like silvery coins poured from a bag, one overlapping another, or in thin flakes as if occupying slight cleavages. The beauty of the ice was gone, and it was too late to study the bottom." Henry David Thoreau, "House-Warming," *Walden*.

6. *The Discovery of Subatomic Particles* (New York: Freeman, 1982).

7. Owen Barfield, *What Coleridge Thought* (Middletown, Conn.: Wesleyan University Press, 1971), pp. 37ff.

8. For Coleridge's reflections on the "attraction and repulsion of light bodies rubbed by amber" and their bearing on the "phaenomena of electricity," see Volume I of his essays from "The Friend" as edited by Barbara E. Rooke (Princeton: Princeton University Press, 1964).

9. R. B. Martin, *Gerard Manley Hopkins: A Very Private Life* (New York: HarperCollins, 1991), p. 394.

10. Ibid., p. 394.

11. "Coleridge went to hear him 'to increase his stock of metaphors.'" "Davy, Sir Humphry," *Encyclopaedia Brittanica*, vol. 7.

12. "Law Without Law," *Quantum Theory and Measurement*, ed. Wheeler and Zurek, pp. 183–210.

13. SOCRATES: "The moment that the observer approaches, [things] become other, and of another nature, so that you cannot get any further in knowing their nature or state, for you cannot know that which has no state."

CRATYLUS: "True."

SOCRATES: ". . . If the very nature of knowledge changes, at the time when the change occurs there will be no knowledge; and if the transition is always going on, there will always be no knowledge, and, according to your view, there will be no one to know and nothing to be known. . . . Whether there is this eternal nature in things, or whether the truth is what Heraclitus and his followers and many others say, is a question hard to determine. . . . All things leak like a pot. . . ." Plato, *Cratylus*.

"It will always be possible to show how science is atomic, not to be grasped and held together, 'scopeless,' without metaphysics: this alone gives meaning to laws and sequences and causes and developments—things which stand in a position so peculiar that we can neither say of them they hold in nature whether the mind sees them or not again or that they are found by the mind because it first put them there. . . . The new school of metaphysics will probably encounter this atomism of personality with some shape of the Platonic Idea." G. M. Hopkins, *The Probable Future of Metaphysics*.

14
Hopkins Transforming: "It Changed Beautiful Changes"

Nature, the things we move about among and use, are provisional and perishable; but as long as we are here, they are our possession and our friendship, sharers in our trouble and gladness, just as they have been the confidants of our ancestors. Therefore, not only must all that is there not be corrupted or degraded, but just because of that very provisionality they share with us, all these appearances and things should be comprehended by us in a most fervent understanding, and *transformed*. Transformed? Yes, for our task is to stamp this provisional, perishing earth into *ourselves*, so painfully and passionately, that its being may arise again, "invisibly" in us. WE ARE THE BEES OF THE INVISIBLE. . . . We are the last perhaps to have still known such things. On us rests the responsibility of preserving, not merely their memory (that would be little and unreliable), but their human and laral worth. The earth has no other refuge except to become invisible: IN US, who, through one part of our nature, have a share in the Invisible.

—R. M. Rilke, Letter, November 13, 1925

i

Pied Beauty

Glory be to God for dappled things—
    For skies of couple-colour as a brinded cow;
        For rose-moles all in stipple upon trout that swim;
Fresh-firecoal chestnut-falls; finches' wings;
    Landscape plotted and pieced—fold, fallow, and plough;
        And all trades, their gear and tackle and trim.

All things counter, original, spare, strange;
   Whatever is fickle, frecklèd (who knows how?)
    With swift, slow; sweet, sour; adazzle, dim;
He fathers-forth whose beauty is past change:

                  Praise him.

Hopkins Transforming: The Observer as Celebrant

Fundamentally, the poem is a meditation on—or a celebration of—the theme unobtrusively written into Hopkins's glimpse into his cup of Lenten chocolate at a boil, as others might look into the crater of Vesuvius: "It changed beautiful changes." The theme is Ovidian as well as Franciscan, metamorphic as well as doxological: it celebrates divinity as the genius of change who delights in the diverse and the protean—in the "beauty" that is parti-colored, "couple-coloured," "pieced," "folded"—"*plotted*" as a landscape that bears the harrower's imprint, and the scheme of the planter's intent is visibly and designedly "plotted." Hopkins's unhusbandly adjective for agricultural and cosmological change is, however, unexpectedly jocular, Anglo-Saxon, archaic: "*pied*"; one wonders at its levity in the context of a priestly *magnificat*. The word survives today in only three of its retrospective guises, all of which require the glosses of the lexicographer: as the typesetter's word for a jumbled and disorderly font; as the suffix for the bird notorious for its hoarding of collectibles—the common *magpie*; and as the pastry-man's noun for the variety of postprandial delicacies "baked in a *pie*." The echo of a nursery rhyme where the best of the two elements, the pie and the bird, join in the hyperbole of "four and twenty blackbirds / Baked in a pie" and "set before a king" should not be overlooked. Though the drollery has no explicit bearing on the worshipful context of Hopkins's poem, the lexical oddity is by no means irrelevant to the transformations it accomplishes. It suggests that the transformative zeal of the poet is linguistic, as well as sacramental; that, for all the clerical ardor of his avowals, the true subject of his poem is its *language*, rather than its doctrinal thrust, and that the search for "transformations" should be semiotic as well as devotional. The child's fable and the elations of the priest are inseparable aspects of a single "spiritual exercise": Hopkins's cosmos is haunted by the "glory of God" and the Pied Piper of Hamlin—that mountebank singer in the clown's motley whom legend celebrates as the virtuoso of magical endangerment who opens and closes mountains and charms the rats from their cheeses. At the opposite end of the reader's memory lurks yet another intrusion, which is Euclidean rather than sacerdotal in character: the geometer's symbol for the transmutation of *number*—"π," the sixteenth letter of the Greek alphabet used to designate the ratio of the circumference of a circle to its fourth decimal place of diameters, in the measurement of magnitudes.

It is fair to ask whether there is any need to pursue such distractions to their conclusion in the "coalescence" of a poet's intent. Certainly, Hopkins shows no concern for their priorities: on the contrary, he throws other multiples into the "dapple" of unresolved ambiguities. For example, there is the archaism of "brinded" to jog the infantile memory of the reader. In the antiquities of Mother Goose, the dictionary reminds us, what is "brinded" or "brindled" is "tawny or grayish with irregular spots and associated with the *bovine*": there is also an earlier reverberation of the tradesman's "*brand*" as a manifest of ownership, and his practice of diversifying the implements with which Hopkins concludes his stanza a few lines later: "All *trades*, their gear and tackle and trim."

In the midst of these workaday matters that jostle the lexical oddities there is also a curious emphasis upon the paraphernalia of physical labor in their most elementary guises: on the *tool* as an extension of an object's resistance and a subject's force—all the proletarian hardware that particularize directed creative energy and accomplish the work of the world: the plow of the farmer, the cobbler's awl, the carpenter's plane, level, hammer, T-square—the "gear and tackle and trim" of those skilled to employ them. All partake of the "dapple" on things and bear diligent witness to the dispensations of a benevolent Creator. All have their effect upon the *language* of the poet as artisan-priest. If Hopkins "always knew in [his] heart Walt Whitman's mind to be more like [his] own than any other man's living," it is at least in part because Whitman "heard America singing" *at its work*, and Hopkins, the whole cosmos.[1]

A further aspect of the universal "*pie*-ing" of things is written into the opening sestet that carries the poet from the colors that "couple" in the air, to the earthbound markings of the cow, to the water-world of the trout, to the fire-world of the "chestnut-fall"—and back again into the "descending blue" of the hurrying atmosphere. The search is for the unchanging will that works behind all things that are "counter, original, spare, strange"—the principle of the Divine Mover *in repose*, as it were, behind all the phenomena of variety and multiplicity—"whatever is fickle, frecklèd—who knows how?" Sonally, the motif recurs as a dapple of *sounds*—the "couple-colouring" of a heavily compounded and hyphenated discourse: *apple–couple–stipple–fickle–freckle–dazzle*; and *couple–colour–rose-moles–fresh-firecoal–chestnut-fall–fathers-forth*. Philosophically, the "dapple" of things moves steadily forward toward a severer reduction of multiplicity to *twoness*—the diminution of pluralism to duality, with an emphasis on oppositional contrasts: *swift–slow, sweet–sour, adazzle–dim*. The minimal twoness of things, one supposes, is there so that the moral life of choice may be seen underneath the sensuous life, even though the sensuous matrix of the poem persists to the last and betrays the essential paganism of the would-be ascetic. It remains for a later poem, "Spelt from Sibyl's Leaves," to turn the total composition *ethical* and wind all on "two packs"; "two spools": black–white, *right–wrong*" for the conclusive summation of the poet-as-Sibyl.

So we get, in place of an ethos, or a "pathos," a lexical rather than a sacramental weighing of the total context: we are left to wrestle with the *verbal* transformations of a poet's artifact rather than the warnings of a moral world we must "beware of." The result is a quandary of contexts, subtexts, and Ur-texts for which there is no synoptic resolution, whose coexistence is a critical aspect of their "meaning." We have a fourfold series of adjectives that fixes the reader's attention on a disjunctive implosion of meanings whose import must be pondered *by the reader* with no expectation of a univocal outcome. *Later*, all may be "spelt" out of the "leaves" by a "sibyl"; but for the present the words must be set down as a differential equation for which there is no sovereign mathematic:

"*Counter*" = *contra*; contrary; possibly an *encounter*, with the suggestion of a conflict or a confrontation; a computation or tally; a surface for the exchange of commodities and fees; a computer of numbers.

"Original" = pristine; unique; never before encountered. Or (to throw the weight on the first, rather than the second, syllable) "*o*rigin-al," primordial—as it was "in the Beginning / Before it cloyed, before it clouded"; a clergyman's word, with the suggestion of latent or eventual Sin.

"Spare" = minimal, lean; non-essential, superfluous; that which is only and totally and without addition, *itself,* with the clergyman's suggestion of mercy in it, or an act of Grace. The witty will remember that Hopkins ended his "Leaden Echo" with five reiterations of "*despair*" and began his "Golden Echo" with the lexical reversal: "*Spare!*"

"Strange" = odd, never before encountered; all that is not oneself or lies outside oneself, with the suggestion of mystery in it; alien. Remember that the Greek word for stranger, outsider, alien is βάρβαρος: "Barbarian"; and the first line of Hopkins's companion-piece to the essential providence of things—"Hurrahing in Harvest"—gives a pagan's homage to a year's end "*barbarous* in beauty."

ii

Hurrahing in Harvest

Summer ends now; now, barbarous in beauty the stooks rise
Around; up above, what wind-walks, what lovely behavior
Of silk-sack clouds! has wilder wilful-wavier
Meal-drift moulded ever and melted across skies?

I walk, I lift up, I lift up heart, eyes,
Down all that glory in the heavens to glean our Saviour;
And eyes, heart, what looks, what lips yet gave you a
Rapturous love's greeting of realer, of rounder replies?

And the azurous hung hills are his world-wielding shoulder
Majestic—as a stallion stalwart, very-violet-sweet.
These things, these things were here and but the beholder

Wanting; which two when they once meet,
The heart rears wings bold and bolder
And hurls for him, O half hurls earth for him off under
   his feet.

Hopkins Transforming: The Observer as Artificer

Here, in a single sonnet, we have exemplified, celebrated, epitomized, the full cycle of "pitched observation"—the poet alone with his poem, moving away from the spontaneities of his *Note-Books* to the rigors of his medium. The preliminaries and the aftermath of the observer's encounter with his world, the substitution of composition for improvisation, of language for sensuous avidity, are set forth in the guise of a landscape-piece concerned with seasonal change and a pietist's thanksgiving for the fruits of autumn. It is initially significant that the season is not specifically addressed in either its positive guise as "autumn" or its pejorative and vernacular guise as a "Fall," but as a time of "harvest"—the "gleaning of our Saviour." The prose approximations of the notetaker and journalist (which I have already called "pre-poetic" in the sense that the poet is still engaged in the onlooker's labor of "observation") are still recognizable as a kind of patois in the polished block of the sonnet—all those stuttering immediacies of "wind-walks, "silk-sack clouds" like "meal-drift moulded ever and melted across skies," the hills "stallion stalwart," "very-violet-sweet" that characterize Hopkins's "journalese." The purely *theoretical* induction of his subject, however, the memoranda of an observer caught in the act of a meditative discipline, has been accomplished; what remains to be internalized is the "theoretical" *object* of the world's abundance: "these things, these things were here and but the beholder wanting." What follows is a movement away from "theory" to *practice*, with its insistence on the energetic appropriation of the "object," as verb after verb batters its way into the metrical matrix of an accelerated prosody with a pugilist's tactical agility: "I walk, I lift up, I lift up heart, eyes. . . ."

Since the speaker is a Jesuit priest, the cause given for the poet's onslaught is a devotional one: four words are enough to convey it to the reader: "to glean our Saviour." The effect, however, is almost raucously secular: a "rapturous greeting of realer, of rounder replies." Above all, for the reader of poetry concerned with the ontology of a transformative opportunity, what is perhaps most important of all is the undeviating insistence upon *objects*—"these things, these things"—which, once united with the observer and his medium, "hurl earth for him, O half hurl earth for him off under his feet."

The title—"Hurrahing in Harvest"—is characteristic of a poet who permits nothing to inhibit the instantaneous marshaling of his language in behlf of his sensuous predations. Its distinctly secular boisterousness (or boyishness)—the schoolboy's "hurrah!" in lieu of the priestly "Hosannah!"—carries with it the humors of an unpremeditated outburst. No less disarming is the anonymity of the poet's initial stroke: "Summer ends now"—a pedestrian statement delivered with the flat of the poet's quill. Actually, the words comprise three notes of a dominant theme for subsequent argumentation, ornamentation, elaboration: the dead center of a baroque invention on seasons ("summer"), conclusions ("ends"), and sensuous immediacies ("now") whose extravagance is straightway absorbed into the "barbarity" of the actual occasion. But: "Why the savagery and the haste?" one asks with a little dismay. Why "barbarous"? For the Attic Greek, what is "barbaric" was always primordial, unpruned, violent, estranging, uncivilized. We are plunged again into the universe of the "dapple," the "couple-coloured," the "pied," where all is "counter, original, spare, strange"—with a difference, however! Here, notations on the behavior of unruly phenomena are *pared to the frame* of the sonnet, even though their linguistic "wildness" is retained in the compounds that seem directly transcribed from the pages of his journals: "wind-walks," "silk-sack," "wilful-wavier" (to rhyme almost comically with "gave you a" and "Saviour").

Action moves toward action and begets action: the result is a *"meeting"* in Emily Dickinson's sense of the word, like the contact of two tinders. Elements hurtle toward each other, move upward and downward, walking, lifting, gleaning, greeting, replying. The savagery of the incarnate God is unmasked in its pagan animality, half Atlas, half centaur, with a "world-wielding shoulder" bent to the weight of the planet "as a stallion stalwart," and the thunderous pressure of verbal compounds charging the sonnet form like the chamber of a shell. At the same time, the landscape takes on a theological reciprocity like the order of a church service in which Creation responds to the priestly intermediary in an antiphony of "realer, of rounder *replies*," and is elevated like a wafer in the ritual chant of a litany. Subject and object, the beholder and the beheld, join in a kind of liturgical explosion—or Hallelujah chorus—with a velocity that sweeps on even after the union is accomplished. The ground is literally "pulled out from under," the invisible motion of the earth is made visible, as the observer tumbles onto its whirling surfaces like a ball onto the double circuit of a roulette wheel.

iii

Spelt from Sibyl's Leaves

Earnest, earthless, equal, attuneable, vaulty, voluminous . . . stupendous
Evening strains to be time's vast, womb-of-all, home-of-all, hearse-of-all night,
Her fond yellow hornlight wound to the west, her wild hollow hoarlight hung to the height
Waste; her earliest stars, earlstars, stars principal, overbend us,
Fire-featuring heaven. For earth her being has unbound, her dapple is at an end, as-
Tray or aswarm, all throughther, in throngs; self in self steeped and pashed—quite
Disremembering, dismembering all now. Heart, you round me right
With: Our evening is over us; our night whelms, whelms, and will end us
Only the beak-leaved boughs dragonish damask the tool-smooth, bleak light; black,
Ever so black on it. Our tale, O our oracle! Let life, waned, ah let life wind
Off her once skeined stained veined variety upon, all on two spools; part, pen, pack
Now her all in two flocks, two folds—black, white; right, wrong; reckon but, reck but, mind
But these two; ware of a world where but these two tell, each off the other; of a rack

Where, selfwrung, selfstrung, sheathe- and shelterless, thoughts
against thoughts in groans grind.

Hopkins Transforming: The Observer as Victim

The first matter to be considered is the linguistics of a title that holds the attention suspended between the apparent and the latent meanings, as between two magnets. What is apparent in the meaning is the ceremonious "spelling" of an enigma—a fateful pronouncement in the guise of a riddle, such as those traditionally assigned to sphinxes, seers, witches, magi, and "sibyls" that at one and the same time mask and disclose the will of the gods or the destiny of heroes. The "leaves" of the sibyl, like the tea leaves of the gypsy, constitute a kind of heraldry of the future, in which apparent accident and latent intention join to prefigure the secret necessity of things. To the eye, they appear as an unpremeditated arrangement of oak leaves, animal entrails, knucklebones, what you will—the inkblot of the Rorschach—whose pattern carries all the terror and attractiveness of chance. To the skilled binder of spells, however, they represent the manifest will of creation in the process of overtaking its intention—both the geometry and the symbolism of the unalterable.

Manifestly, then, "spelt from Sibyl's leaves," promises a reading of the Prophetess's "leaves"—with the strong implication that the answers will not be "spelled out" for us in the ordinary sense of the word, but "spelled *in*." That is to say, the poem aims at the binding of a spell rather than the dispelling of a riddle. The answers, like the riddle itself, will be recondite, delphic, and multiple: they will tantalize even while they divulge. Thus, the "spelling" is at once a lettering and an incantation; and the "leaves" are at once the pages of the sibylline books and the "beak-leaved boughs dragonish" of an afterglow that prefigure the landscape, a moment before they dissolve into it.

The second factor to be noted is that the poem, or "oracle," is, in effect, the configuration of *four* "leaves"—four phases in the joining of the meanings. The first phase "laws out" the imagery of evening and instresses a landscape, to the point at which the poet can live in it with his complete being. It inscapes the processes of one evening in the life of the poet—which may be any evening or the most fated evening in the life of the poet—and brings him to a pitch of unexamined terror. The poet makes no effort to shield himself from the vastness and the majesty of the scene he is contemplating, and discovers, when he has crossed over into the second quatrain of the octave, that he has crossed the invisible line between the "stupendous" and the sinister. At that point (line 5) contemplation moves in to humanize a scene that threatens to "dismember" the identity of the observer, who has passed into his object with a terrifying entirety. The poet begins to set bounds to an experience that might otherwise leave the "self in self steeped and pashed quite," without memory or character.

There follows a third phase, or "leaf," which voices the direct cry of the heart—an outcry wrung from the eighth line, in which the despair and fascination of the poet equally declare themselves: "Our evening is over us; our night whelms, whelms and will end us!" It is an immediate cry that knows nothing but its own superstitious terror. The naturally "dappled" world is suddenly a darkened world, a haunted world, filled with the *numina* that have always struck at the unprotected psyche with all the force of their savagery: "Only the *beak-leaved* boughs *dragonish* damask the tool-smooth, bleak light; black / Ever so black on it." There follows the fourth "leaf," or phase, on which the sibyl has inscribed her vision of the Last Day itself—an enchanted directive in the guise of a warning, an explanation, and a fated necessity.

So much for the *magical* order of a sonnet that, after all, not only is a *sonnet*, in spite of the overall "springing" of the rhythms, but is, in Hopkins's words, "the longest sonnet ever made and no doubt the longest in the making." From the very outset we are swept into the *substance* of the poet's thought by an act of compositional audacity that, for sheer verbal stress and the poet's insistence on the total penetration of the occasion, is almost unmatched in the history of English lyricism. It is a rising crescendo of *seven* adjectives in a series that not only drive the attention outward and upward like a rolling breaker, but crash on the uneasy attentiveness with an almost physical sense of assault and saturation: "Earnest, earthless, equal, attuneable, vaulty, voluminous . . . stupendous / Evening."

What is the force of these words in this sequence for this duration? Why, when the total onslaught of individually weighted words has spent itself on the noun that awaits it in the following line, like surf on a reef, do we feel that something has been *missed* and the Evening has *not* given up its secret? Metaphorically, we could say that it is because the word denied the poet—the preempted word marked by suspension points between "voluminous" and "stupendous"—is still in the keeping of the sibyl and can never be "spelled out of the leaves."

Linguistically, however, we have a better answer for our sense of loss, desperation, ineffectual violence. In the first place, for all the rising inflection of the sequence, there is no discoverable order of the *meanings* to guide our thinking to a similar effect of climax. Though the curve of the *sounds* strikes our ear with a sense of sonal inevitability, the *thought* is actually unstructured and unresolved, and each of the participating words presents us with a semantic dilemma. The abstractness of the language, moreover, makes it difficult for the reader to appeal to the senses for another *ordre du coeur* to structure our feelings and induce a comparable sense of contextual inevitability. What, then, are we to make of these words? Another "differential equation for which there is no sovereign mathematic," like Hopkins's series of four in "Pied Beauty"?

"*Earnest*" = Here, the word really relates to the subject, rather than the object observed. The evening is "earnest" because the occasion which it has created for the poet is somber, critical, baffling, unyielding, and requires the total vigilance of the watcher. Looking "earnestly" into the evening, the evening looks back "earnestly" at the poet: "whatever you look hard at seems to look hard at you." The poet demands an "earnest" of their confrontation.

"*Earthless*" = Here, the real bafflement of the poet is apparent in a curious sense of *placelessness,* an eerie suspension half in the world and half out of it. What shall we do with this word as an attribute of the evening? Read it as "unearthly," or project it directly into its implied opposition: airy, spacy, insubstantial—something "not of this earth"?

"*Equal*" = Here, the abstraction of the poet—and perhaps a hint of the resolution he seeks—is most apparent. In what sense is the evening "equal"? In the sense that darkness equalizes all colors, expunges all distinctions, erases all outlines, "equalizes" the infinite differentiation of Being with the blind uniformity of Non-Being? Is the effect of the word to remind us that "evening" in the literal sense of the word, involves the "*even-*ing" out, the leveling down, the flattening away of unlikeness? If so, is the word a threatening one or a reassuring one? Is it the "equalizing" factor of evening that accounts for the gravity and anxiety of the poet's mood? We have our answer in the second quatrain of the octave: "For earth her being has unbound; her dapple is at an end, as /Tray or aswarm, all throughter, in throngs; self in self steeped and pashed—quite / Disremembering, dismembering all now."

"*Attuneable*" = Here again, the word is unexpected and unexpectedly laborious. Doubtless, it flows out of the context of the word that precedes it as a musical equivalence for "equality"; "attuneable": that which submits itself to an ordering of sounds; that which may be pitched to the order of the scale. The senses are touched, for a moment, by a sonal image of harmony; but the next moment the mind takes it up as a concept that serves the moral framework of the poem. "Attuneability" has something to do with conformity, obedience, decorum, submission to a larger order of the universe disclosed to us in the final phase of the poem: "Let life, waned, ah, let life wind / Off her once skeined, stained, veined variety upon, all on two spools. . . ." The tone of warning and command in the oracular answer is plain; and the implication is equally inescapable: conform or perish! To be "attuneable" is to defer to the moral imperative of things.

The last three words may be taken in a series: "*vaulty, voluminous . . . stupendous*" since all three relate to scale and size and are, in fact, a progression from an idea of comprehensible dimension, to one of incomprehensible grandeur. The first word may be said to construe space architecturally, and "pitch" it upward: evening is "vaulty" as the curve of a Gothic arch is said to be "vaulty"—the word, in fact, is the priest's word for structuring space as a cathedral. Here, the height is both containable and worshipful. Similarly, "voluminous" has both the word "luminous" in it—that "wild hollow hoarlight hung to the height"—and the word "volume," which can refer concretely to the sibylline book from which the poem as a whole "spells out" one leaf, or more probably and abstractly to the physicist's concept of unmeasured mass. In the latter sense, the word then leads us out of the world of light, into the world of bulk, without the containing outline of a "vault."

At this point, all structured thought breaks down completely in the three points of suspension—dot-dot-dot—leading to—what?—a desperate last word after an ungratified silence: the word "stupendous." In general terms, "stupendous" is one of those portmanteau words carrying with it the maximum extension of all one has *ceased* to think about systematically; it is the word that makes finally clear to us that the poet's linguistic crescendo has *gotten him nowhere*. It does not curve down on the opposite apex of the arch "like a vault"; it is simply whelmed in unlimited space and allowed to disappear like an exhalation. The word registers, then, at the opposite end of an ambitious series, in its primary meaning of *stupefying*: to be struck, stunned, or amazed for want of an appropriate hyperbole. As such, it furnishes our first measure of the terror to which the evening has brought the poet and indicates the need for the remainder of the poem to press for a magical answer.

So much for the opening crescendo, which might be compared to seven tones of a musical scale awaiting the eighth and culminating note which never comes. As such, it reminds one of Wordsworth on "Mutability":

> From low to high doth dissolution climb.
> And sink from high to low, along a scale
> Of awful notes, whose concord shall not fail. . . .

The poet then proceeds to apply the "stupendous" scale to his evocation of the evening: Evening "*strains to be* time's vast, womb-of-all, home-of-all, hearse-of-all night." The instress of the stupendous is revealed in the emphasis on *process*—the process of *becoming*, by which *evening* "strains to be" *night*; on the other hand, "strain" also has in it the poet's and the musician's word for melody, measure, the phrase. It is followed by another series, this time heavily hyphenated: a triad that analogizes the process of evening-into-night in terms of human progressions: the womb, the home, the hearse. Here, all is made to resonate against the pathos of human mortality, moving, as the poem as a whole moves, from light to dark, from white to black, with the warning: "reckon but, reck but, mind / But these two; ware of a world where but these two tell, each off the other." Meanwhile, the poet watches the transmutation of twilight into night-light, and the emergence of the first stars, "fire-featuring heaven."

The image should be a comforting one; it has order, degree, sequence, definition, illumination, and a promise of solicitous containment: the heaven, "fetched out," as Hopkins would say, with its "earlstars, stars-principal" and "overbending" the observer, seems like a solution of what before appeared merely "stupendous." However, the poet is compelled to return to all that he has suspended between the three points that separated "voluminous" from "stupendous" in line 1. Latent terror becomes manifest; and he fastens with despairing avidity on the spectacle of pure chaos: the unbinding of being, the straying and swarming of "dapple," "self in self steeped and pashed," "dismemberment." In this mood, the last of all shapes visible in the failing light appears to him as both an omen and a prophecy. They are the "leaves" of the sibyl: "beak-leaved" in their suggestion of the harpy, "dragonish" in their suggestion of the monstrous, yet fastidiously silhouetted with the magical calligraphy of the oracle, "tool-smooth," black, "ever so black on it."

We come then to the "telling of the tale," in direct response to the outcry of the poet. The words pour out in the cadences of the Sibyl herself—part charm, part hallucination, part admonition, with an almost audible sound of whirling bobbins, the crossing threads, the thickening textures of the Prophetess's "spools"—a heavy damask of warnings, assurances, stresses, and sounds. The "tale" under the skeins of incantation and the ominous rattling of spools is purgatorial in the most strenuous sense of the word. It is the same tale of spiritual desiccation explored to the last extremity of its "wretchedness" in the "gall" and "heartburn" of the watershed year (1885) that produced both "Carrion Comfort" and the panic sequence of "the terrible sonnets," along with Hopkins's valedictory reading of the Sibylline "leaves." Though the effect of the latter is concessive—"*Let* life, waned, ah let life wind / Off"—it ends as an admonition "spelling out" the purpose and the urgency of the unalterable: "reckon but, reck but, mind / But these two; ware of a world where but these two tell, each, off the other!" Between choice and necessity, the whole of the human condition, "selfwrung, selfstrung," is stretched as on a "rack" in the posture of crucifixion. The agony, it is clear, is moral and intellectual: a crisis of duality in which "*thoughts* against *thoughts* in groans grind," and the "body of a death" is at hand.

The doubleness or contrariety of things is not a favorable one for dialectics, however; the victimage is visceral in its immobilization of the thinker. Its effect is to traumatize all choice and wait upon grace—to ethicize existence by packing the senses on "two spools," in "two flocks, two folds"; to force a devotional criterion from the sensuous life of extension. For the movement from "black-and-white" to "right-and-wrong" is precisely a movement from the empirical to the ethical life, from the sheer proliferation of *things* to the "still point" at which the drama of opposition forces the single-minded commitment of the observer, and all future change is forfeit. Here, all "dapple" is "at an end," being is bound and unbound, self is "dismembered," and the spirit ascends the frame of the universe like a cross or a rack in the last initiative of the chooser. The tableau is a harsh one; but it has for its model the example of Christ Himself, and for its spiritual meaning Paul's psychology of grace and his pre-emption of all purely secular change:

> I know that in me (that is, in my flesh) dwelleth no good thing; for to will is present with me; but how to perform that which is good, I find not. . . . For the good that I would, I do not: but the evil which I would not, that I do. . . . O wretched man that I am! who shall deliver me from the body of this death?
> —Romans 7:18–20, 8:24

Here, both the poet's metamorphic passion for the fleeting, and the sinner's search for the Unchanging Will, meet, full circle, in a paroxysm that equates all being with the mystery of a Fatherhood fixed past all change, in a penitent's eschatology of the beautiful:

> Whatever is fickle, frecklèd (who knows how?)
> With swift, slow; sweet, sour; adazzle, dim;
> He *fathers-forth whose beauty is past change*:
>
> Praise him.

iv

That Nature is a Heraclitean Fire and of the Comfort of the Resurrection

Cloud-puffball, torn tufts, tossed pillows flaunt forth, then chevy on an air-
Built thoroughfare: heaven-roysterers, in gay-gangs, they throng; they glitter in marches.
Down roughcast, down dazzling whitewash, wherever an elm arches,
Shivelights and shadowtackle in long lashes lace, lance, and pair.
Delightfully the bright wind boisterous ropes, wrestles, beats earth bare
Of yestertempest's creases; in pool and rutpeel parches
Squandering ooze to squeezed dough, crust, dust; stanches, starches
Squadroned masks and manmarks treadmire toil there
Footfretted in it. Million-fueled, nature's bonfire burns on.
But quench her bonniest, dearest to her, her clearest-selved spark
Man, how fast his firedint, his mark on mind, is gone!
Both are in an unfathomable, all is in an enormous dark
Drowned. O pity and indignation! Manshape, that shone
Sheer off, disseveral, a star, death blots black out; nor mark
    Is any of him at all so stark
But vastness blurs and time beats level. Enough! the Resurrection,
A heart's clarion! Away grief's grasping, joyless days, dejection.
    Across my foundering deck shone
A beacon, an eternal beam. Flesh fade, and mortal trash
Fall to the residuary worm; world's wildfire, leave but ash:
    In a flash, at a trumpet crash,
I am all at once what Christ is, since he was what I am, and
This Jack, joke, poor potsherd, patch, matchwood, immortal diamond,
Is immortal diamond.

HOPKINS TRANSFORMING: THE OBSERVER AS COMFORTER

Here, the title prepares us for a tutelary piece in the "essayistic" mode of Dryden or Pope—a "spiritual exercise" in which precepts rather than passions predominate, and the sedulous Loyolan mediates between the "natural" and the preternatural worlds in behalf of an edifying analogy: "That Nature Is a Heraclitean Fire and of the Comfort of the Resurrection." To all intents and purposes, Hopkins's concerns are pastoral, forensic, hermeneutical: a bonding of pagan with liturgical postulates, the physics of Heraclitus with the mystery of the Resurrection. The result should be a differential equation in which two aspects of the "natural" life—Christ's and Heraclitus's—are joined in a single consolatory premise for the spiritual "comfort" of the worshiper.

Poetry has precedents for this genre—"essays" on "criticism" and "man," in the prosody of an earlier century which preferred the pincer-movement of the couplet to the ellipses of the ode in its pursuit of the "heroic." One assumes that the procedure of Hopkins will be similarly gnomic, discursive, linear—in the "middle style" of investigative rhetoric that avoids subjective intrusions and measures its initiative with a certain dialectical composure. What one gets, however, is another bombardment from the natural world of phenomenological chaos, a hugger-mugger "roystering in gay-gangs" of seminal particulars that blind the senses with flying particles and keep them in dizzying collision: "cloud-puffball, torn tufts, tossed pillows," "shivelights and shadowtackle," "squandering ooze to squeezed dough, crust, dust," "squadroned masks and manmarks"—a fusillade that batters Heraclitean "aether" and is trampled to "treadmire" without regard for causes, sequences, or progressions.

The effect is equinoctial as well as seasonal: spring and autumn compete for the poet's context in a "whitewash" and "bright wind boisterous" that "ropes, wrestles, beats earth bare"; "chevy on an air-built thoroughfare" alternately "parches," "stanches," "starches" all that it unleashes, and detonates its rhythms in a serial offensive of expletives. Not until the ninth line of the rocketing prosody is there any mention of the Heraclitean firestorm promised by the title: only then does all that was airborne or "footfretted" turn into a "bonfire" of "firedints" and "sparks" in Hopkins's accustomed manner. A line later, however, the feathery excitations of the poet's onslaught are suddenly "levelled," "blotted," "darkened," "blurred," "drowned," "black[en]ed out," and Hopkins unexpectedly abandons the frenzy of his vigil as "unfathomable."

One wonders, with some discomfiture, *why?* Since "fire" is

the Ionian element designated as Hopkins's chosen subject, the absence of it in line after line of the unfolding "essay" leaves one with a feeling of blockage and misdirection. Somehow, the governing pretext for the poem has been swept away by a prosody that rebounds on itself like a failing kite in skittery entanglements and finally declares its subject "unfathomable:" there is a crumpling and disfigurement in which a whole field of forces and particulars is deflected by priestly scruples, and immobilized. The result is a compositional anomaly that casts a wide net of end-rhymes, with double knots of replication and sonal redundancies that drive the sound inward as well as outward, and assumes the unlikely profile of an Italian sonnet mounted on *two* concluding sestets. The preciosities are sesquipedalian in the extensional sense of a motet by Palestrina or a recitative by Monteverdi, and culminate with the bravura of a double coda that dares to rhyme "deck shone" with "Resurrection" and "I am and" with "di-am-ond." In the end it is the Jesuit keeper of the spindle who moves in to finally deflate the lurching prosody and tether the poet's initiative. Diamonds and matchwood replace Ionian fire; and despite an unforgettable finale, the conflagrations are banked and Hopkins's "essay" remains—*unwritten.*

What, it is fair to ask, might that "essay" have entailed, and what is the physicist's or metaphysicist's understanding of a "Heraclitean Fire" today? Presocratic expertise has long wrestled with the arcana of the Heraclitean mode: as is well known, his notations take the form of conundrums or *koans* which still embroil interpreters in midrashic debate and require the intervention of a sibyl, who never comes. Commentators like Plato, Plutarch, Strabo, Pliny, Aristotle, and Theophrastus have pondered the mysteries of the "cuckoo-voiced Heraclitus, mob-reviling man of riddles" and "Dark Philosopher" of aethers and "burners." There are essays on Parmenides of Elea (another keeper of the Heraclitean flame) and "The Probable Future of Metaphysics" in Hopkins's *Note-Books* which bristle with further surprises and give unexpected modernity to his canon as a whole.

The pedantries of Heraclitean scholarship, however, are not in themselves germane to the strange lapses and lacunae of Hopkins's putative discourse on Fire. No one need pause, for example, to review the fourfold cosmogony of elements—earth, air, water, fire—and ask again whether for Heraclitus the domain of "aether" is subsumed in the domain of cosmological fire, as a threefold matrix or *logos* of creation.

What is important to Hopkins's poem is the human certainty or uncertainty of things, the vulnerability of the poet as he pursues his quest for the "comforts of the Resurrection" and collates a pagan creation-story with the premises of the Catholic way. The fact that Hopkins's creation myth is Heraclitean rather than Johannine—that Ionian fire displaces the "darknesses" of Genesis and the "lights" of Saint John to "witness" the Word—merits a word in its own right as an aspect of the abiding Platonism of Hopkins's theogony. Elsewhere, his whole canon crackles with fires in much the same way as the cosmos of Heraclitus blazes with aerial "kindlings," "lightnings," conflagrations: it is incendiary as well as apocalyptical. For Heraclitus, a "thunderbolt steers the totality of things";[2] and for Hopkins, the "grandeur of God . . . / Will flame out like shining from shook foil," "a billion times / told lovelier, more dangerous," with the violence of a quantal "Big Bang." His "gleanings of the Saviour" smolder with "fresh-firecoal chestnut-falls," "blue-bleak embers"; "brim in a flash full," "fire-featuring heaven"; "on an age-old anvil wince and sing"; "flash from flame to flame" in an "electrical horror" of shipwrecks, a "plumed purple of thunder." Nature is a hearthstone on which "kingfishers catch fire," "dragonflies draw flame," Tom Navvy "rips out rockfire," Felix the farrier "fettles for the great gray drayhorse his bright and battering sandal," "the world's wildfire leaves but ash," precisely as the Heraclitean Zeus is a keeper of thunderbolts and the fermentation of "aethers." In this sense, it can be said that Hopkins paganizes the Catholic way in a private mystique that unites Hellenistic epistemology with the orthodoxies of the Eucharist and provides the "comfort of the Resurrection" for petitioners of the Paraclete.

What surprises in the present sonnet is the fact that "fire" is the chosen element of Hopkins, as vicar of the Paraclete ministering to the "comforts of the Resurrection." Orthodox dogma, from the "altarfires" and Armageddon of Revelations to the holocausts of Dante's *Inferno*, typically reserve that element for the punitive finalities of the sinner and the irreversible anguish of the damned. According to Hopkins, "The lost are like this, and their scourge to be / As I am mine, their sweating selves; *but worse*." That he should couple "Heraclitean fire," however, with the eschatology of Resurrection is neither Loyolan nor canonical to the manuals of Jesuit piety. That fire is also no guarantor of personal "comfort" is also obvious from the confessional sonnets, justly called "terrible," which precede his poem, which grimly reject all "comfort" as "carrion," or suicidal, and cry from the red heats of "an age-old anvil": "Comforter, where, where is thy comforting?"

> I cast for comfort I can no more get
> By groping round my comfortless than blind
> Eyes in their dark can day, or thirst can find
> Thirst's all-in-all in all a world of wet.

For Hopkins the suppliant, there is no balm in either Heraclitus or the priest's exemplum of the Resurrection; just as for Hopkins the poet there was no "essay" on "nature as a Heraclitean fire" in the poem announcing the coexistence of the two as the avowed subject of the poet-priest. But in the quantum world of Heisenberg and Bohr, toward which Hopkins the Observer also beckons today, this union of opposites would be called a "complementary" one, and their inseparability would be viewed as a paradox encompassing the holistic reciprocity of things. In the opinion of experimental and theoretical physicists now seeking to "grasp one and the same event by two distinct modes of interpretation," both the "uncertainties" of Heisenberg and the "complementarity" of Niels Bohr are indispensable aspects of a new enablement serving the duality of particle and wave, position and momentum, emission and absorption. As Heisenberg goes on to explain: "The two modes are mutually exclusive, but they also complement each other; and it is only through their juxtaposition that the perceptual content of a phenomenon is fully brought out"[3] in the calculus of the quantal Observer.

Atomic theory has not lacked for Jesuits—like Roger Boscovich of Ragusa and the Collegium Romanum whose mathematical passion enjoyed the patronage of Louis XVI of France and the British Royal Society and remains "central to much modern speculation on the nature of matter."[4] There is no reason for assuming that the electromagnetic forays of Maxwell and Faraday, Hopkins's great contemporaries, were ever one of his avocational hobbies, despite his preoccupation with "ethers" and "statistics";[5] but we have Heisenberg's assurance that the metaphysics of Heraclitus is the Hellenistic precursor of the physics of quantal statisticians today. According to Heisenberg, "The views of modern physics are very close to those of Heraclitus, if one interprets his element fire as meaning energy. Energy is in fact *that which moves*; it may be called *the primary cause* of *all change, and energy can be transformed into matter or heat or light.* The strife between opposites in the philosophy of Heraclitus can be found in the strife between two different forms of energy."[6]

It remains to be noted, as epilogue to the "poetics of Uncertainty," that a comparable "strife between opposites," a nexus of "hidden variables" embracing all that is coexistent, contradictory, incompatible, but nonetheless volatile, comprises a quantum of linguistic and metaphorical charges that work the "changes" of the imaginative process for poets as well as physicists. If the "heats" and the "lights" of Hopkins, the would-be Comforter, are as "unfathomable" as the Heraclitean fires that promise a "resurrection," the physics of their transformation repeats a "complementary" magic that "causes all change" in the world of particles and waves, and constitutes a "poetics" for scientists of a changing dispensation.

The last word on visionary and linguistic Uncertainty must be left for Hopkins himself in his cautionary letter to a laureate who blew neither hot nor cold, dealing with both the Incarnation and the modernities served by poets and physicists in their pursuit of the Inconceivable:

> [Y]ou say something I want to remark on: 'Even such a doctrine as the Incarnation may be believed by people like yourself', as a mystery, till it is formulated, but as soon as it is it seems dragged down to the world of pros and cons, and '*as its mystery goes*, so does its hold on their minds'. . . . You do not mean by mystery what a Catholic does. You mean an interesting uncertainty: the uncertainty ceasing interest ceases also. This happens in some things; to you in religion. But a Catholic by mystery means an incomprehensible certainty: without certainty, without formulation there is no interest . . . ; the clearer the formulation the greater the interest. At bottom the source of interest is the same in both cases, in your mind and in ours; it is the unknown, the reserve of truth beyond what the mind reaches and still feels to be behind. . . . There are some solutions to, say, chess problems so

beautifully ingenious, some resolutions of suspensions so lovely in music that even the feeling of interest is keenest when they are known and over, and for some time survives the discovery. How must it then be when the very answer is the most tantalising statement of the problem and the truth you are to rest in the most pointed putting of the difficulty!⁷

Notes

1. Letter to Robert Bridges, October 18, 1882, in *The Letters of Gerard Manley Hopkins to Robert Bridges*, ed. Claude Colleer Abbott (Oxford: Oxford University Press, 1953), p. 155.

2. T. M. Robinson, *Fragments/Heraclitus: A Text and Translation* (Toronto: University of Toronto Press, 1987), Fragment 64.

3. *Physics and Philosophy: The Revolution in Modern Science* (New York: Harper & Row, 1958; repr. 1962), p. 71.

4. Robert H. March, *Physics for Poets* (New York: McGraw-Hill, 1970), p. 71.

5. "My little Paper on *Statistics and Free Will* obeyed the general law and did not appear. . . . But . . . I get into print in a way I would not. My father wrote a little book on Numbers [*The Cardinal Numbers*, by Manley Hopkins, published in 1887], the numbers one to ten, a sketchy thing, raising points of interest in a vast, an infinte subject: the *Saturday* lately had a paper on this book, making great game of it from end to end (of it and the article), including something I had contributed to it; however I was not named." Letter to Bridges, October 19, 1888, in *Letters*, ed. Abbott, p. 294.

6. *Physics and Philosophy*, p. 71.

7. Letter to Bridges, October 24, 1883, in *Letters*, ed. Abbott, pp. 186–87.

www.ingramcontent.com/pod-product-compliance
Lightning Source LLC
Chambersburg PA
CBHW051421290426
44109CB00016B/1383